David Bepler

Bepler's Handy Manual of Knowledge and Useful Information

David Bepler

Bepler's Handy Manual of Knowledge and Useful Information

ISBN/EAN: 9783337218980

Printed in Europe, USA, Canada, Australia, Japan

Cover: Foto ©Andreas Hilbeck / pixelio.de

More available books at **www.hansebooks.com**

BEPLER'S

Handy Manual of Knowledge

AND

Useful Information

BY

DAVID BEPLER

SAN FRANCISCO

THE BANCROFT COMPANY

1890

PREFACE

In issuing this volume the author aims to produce, in a clear and practical manner, a book of useful information for persons in all walks of life, and especially for those whose time is limited. Often when seeking such information as is here presented in a handy form valuable time is wasted looking through books, papers, etc. The public will at once see the advantage of having before them, arranged under proper heads and compiled from authentic sources with the strictest accuracy, data such as tables of weights, measures, etc., important events, and in fact a vast storehouse of general and practical information.

THE AUTHOR.

INDEX

Abbreviations, Dictionary of..98
Abbreviations used by Physicians in Prescriptions, Medical Books, etc........111
Active Volcano, the highest..18
Age and Mortality of Mankind..152
Age which Different Animals Attain..72
Alloys or Composition of Metals...161
American Proverbs and Maxims..87
Anchors a Vessel must Carry...160
Ancient Money, its value..198
Animal-power..75
Animals, size of..144
Anthracite Coal, the largest deposit..67
Antidotes and Treatments for Poisons..50
Area of the Principal Countries of the World..169
Area of Most Notable Park of the World..203
Area of the British Empire and Colonies...278
Area and Population of the Earth by Continents..140
Area of the States and Territories of the United States...............................216
Armories and Arsenals of the United States..215
Artificial Echo, the most remarkable known..257
Attorney-Generals of the United States..230
Average Percentage of Alcohol in Wines and Liquors....................................274
Average Annual Rainfall in the United States..293
Average Annual Temperature in the United States.......................................292
Average Weight of an American Man and Woman..25
Authors, their pen names..267
Bait for Different Kind of Game...144
Balloons, remarkable ascensions...162
Bank of England, facts about it...200
Banker's Table..166
Banks in the United States, a few facts about them....................................199
Banks of Europe, when established...199
Baseball Plates, distances..106
Battles of Revolutionary War..172
Bell, the largest in the world..19
Bells, weight of the largest..107
Belts, a few facts about them...77
Bible Facts and Figures...148
Bills of Exchange...166
Biographies of the Presidents of the United States....................................290
Birds and Beasts, how they are grouped..129
Birds, Life Period of...129

Index—*Continued*

Birds, Speed of..143
Boiler Iron, the thickness and pressure allowed by United States law........ 75
Bridges, notable ones of the world... 70
British Empire and Colonies...273
British House of Commons... 65
Broker's Technicalities..168
Builder's, Facts for.......................... 79
Business Law in Daily Use............ 162
Butter and Cheese, the amount obtainable from milk...............................206
California Game Law.......... 176
California Governors.......................... 282
California, Mechanics' Lien Law of......... 177
Californians, Facts for............ 175
Canals, the greatest in the world...129
Canning Fruits, Amount of Sugar required and time of Boiling....................295
Capitals of the Different States............................. 60
Capitals of the Principal Countries of the World..............................169
Capitol City (Washington, D. C.)..266
Carrying Capacity of a Freight Car..160
Cascades and Waterfalls, their elevation..133
Cataract, the greatest in the world.. 21
Cave, the largest in the world..256
Centennarians..106
Centennial Calendar...................... 295
Chemical Substances, their common names..................... 49
Chronological List of Noted Events of the World...............................187
Church, the largest in the world... 25
Clothes, what to do when they take fire............. 158
Coal, what a ton of it contains......................... 161
Colleges, the oldest in the United States.....................................210
Composition of the Human Body..156
Congress, what it costs per annum..126
Continental Congresses, when and where they met...................... 171
Countries, the three largest... 20
Countries of the World, their form of government, title of ruler and term
    of office 243
Countries of the World, their ruler's name, ruler's salary or civil list and
    prevailing religion...245
Currency of Different Commercial Nations.. 45
Dates of Dignities.. 91
Dates on which the American Republics Declared their Independence........239
Day of the Origin of their Names... 41
Decisive Battles of the World.. 69
Decorative Work Paste............................ 139
Degrees of Heat and Cold Required to Freeze, Melt, and Boil Different
    Substances...83, 85
Density of Population..150
Desert, the largest in the world.. 19
Diamond-Cutting House, the largest...106
Diamonds, French paste...150
Diamonds, the largest found.. 24

Index—*Continued*

Diamonds, Value of...106
Difference of Time between Washington and other Cities..................184
Distance Around the World in Traveling...141
Distance from New York City to Various Places.................................181
Distance from San Francisco to Various Places.................................180
Earth, Weight of..119
Electric Lights, the largest in the world.. 22
Elevation of Localities Above the Sea Level.....................................130
Emblematic Names of States of the United States............................. 42
Engineer's Duties About the Boiler... 73
English Money... 37
Epochs and Eras...269
Execution, the fashion in different countries....................................213
Expansion and Contraction of Railway Track by the Different Temperature..184
Expectation of Human Life...196
Exports of Different Countries..141
Extreme Heat in Various Countries...210
Fecundity of Birds..128
Fecundity of Fish..128
Fictitious Names of Cities of the United States................................. 43
Financial Crises...166
Fires, Notable Historical..196
First Steam-propelled Vessel that Crossed the Ocean.....................208
First United States Flag...206
Flower, the largest known...258
Food, the time required to digest it... 44
Formation of the Union (United States)...172
Fortification, the largest in the world...256
Fortress, the greatest in the world.. 24
French Dynasties and Sovereigns.. 65
Fresh Water, the largest body of it..256
Game Laws of California..176
General Councils..114
Generals Commanding the United States Army.................................270
Glossary of some California Names.. 25
God, the name in different languages..187
Gold, a few facts about it...200
Gold Leaf, thickness...152
Gold, the value of a ton of it... 80
Government of Foreign Countries..239
Government of the United States..174
Governors of California..282
Greatest Men of History, classified in groups................................... 17
Hanging Bell, the largest in the World..256
Harvest Dates of the World..204
Heart, facts about it..156
Heaviest Men Known...145
Height and Weight of Ladies...146
Height of Cascades and Waterfalls..133
Height of the Principal Monument, Towers and Pyramids...............107

Index—*Continued*

Number of Days it takes to travel to the Principal Cities of the World from
  San Francisco..183
Number of English Yards in Miles of Different Nations................................ 35
Number of Pounds to the Bushel.. 36
Number of Years Seeds Retain their Vitality...203
Oceans, Size of...139
Official Census of the United States...266
Oils, classified...160
Oil, the amount in seeds..208
Oldest Colleges in the United States...210
Oldest Newspaper in the World... 73
Origin of Orchard and Garden Fruits and Number of Varieties.............................207
Origin of the Names of the Days... 41
Origin of the Names of the Months... 41
Park, the most extensive in the world..257
Parks, their area..203
Patent Fees of Different Nations...197
Pen Names of Popular Writers...267
Percentage of Alcohol in Wines and Liquors...274
Periods of Gestation of Animals, Birds, etc..128
Philosophical Facts..283
Planet Earth, facts about it...140
Planets, distance from the sun...131
Planets, their size and number of moons they have......................................131
Planets, their velocity of speed...132
Planets, the length of their days..132
Planets, the time in which they revolve around the sun.................................132
Pleasure Park, the largest in the United States.. 24
Poison, Antidotes and Treatment for.. 50
Polish for Fine Hardwood...137
Popular and Electoral Votes for the Presidents of the United States....................286
Population, Area and Capitals of Different Countries....................................163
Population of Cities in the United States..260
Population of the British Empire and Colonies..278
Population of the Earth According to Race..140
Population of the Earth by Continents..140
Population of the largest Cities of the World..259
Population of the United States since 1776...266
Portraits on Bank Notes of the United States...251
Postage Rates..218
Postmasters-General of the United States...229
Presidents of the Continental Congresses...171
Presidents of the United States..223
Pulse in Health, The...157
Pyramids, their height...107
Pyramid, the largest in the World.. 19
Railroad, the highest in the United States... 23
Railway signal code.. 59
Rebellions in the United States..236
Relative Value and Weight of Wood..296
Religion that prevails in different Countries..245

Index—*Continued*

Rifles used in the Armies of different Nations.....................275
Rivers, the longest, their length.....................138
Rivers, the two longest in the World.....................23
Roman Money.....................37
Royalty, what it costs England.....................64
Rulers of England.....................61
Rulers of France.....................65
Rulers of Germany.....................116
Rulers of Prussia.....................118
Rulers of the principal Countries of the World.....................245
Rules for calculating the speed of Pulleys.....................76
Salaries of California State Officers.....................177
Salaries of State Governors.....................60
Salaries of the British Cabinet.....................64
Salaries of the United States Judges.....................128
Salaries of the United States Legislative Officers.....................127
Salaries of the United States Military and Naval Officers.....................197
Salaries of the United States Ministers to Foreign Countries.....................127
Salaries or Civil List of Rulers of different Countries.....................245
Salary of the President of the United States.....................126
Seas, size and length of.....................139
Seating Capacity of noted public buildings.....................254
Secretaries of Interior of the United States.....................231
Secretaries of Navy of the United States.....................228
Secretaries of State of the United States.....................225
Secretaries of Treasury of the United States.....................226
Secretaries of War of the United States.....................227
Seeds, the number of years they retain their vitality.....................203
Seven Dolours of the Virgin Mary.....................68
Seven in the Bible.....................68
Seven Sleepers.....................68
Seven Wise Men of Greece.....................68
Seven Wonders of the World.....................68
Shortest and longest verse in the Bible.....................145
Shrinkage of Casting.....................78
Silver, the value of a ton of it.....................80
Size of Animals.....................144
Size of Lakes.....................139
Size of Oceans.....................139
Size of Planets and the number of moons they have.....................131
Size of Seas.....................139
Smallest locomotive in the world.....................113
Smallest steam engine in the world.....................113
Small people or dwarfs.....................115
Smokestacks, the largest in the world.....................258
Sound, the distance it may be heard.....................91
Specific gravities of bodies.....................84
Speed of birds.....................143
Standard railroad time.....................182
Standard Silver Dollar, a brief history of it.....................269
Standard weight of United States Coins.....................35

Index—*Continued*

States and territories, their area, when admitted into the Union, when and where first settled..216
States and territories, their capitals, term of office, and salaries of governors 60
Stationary engines, the largest in the world.................................257
Statute of Limitation on debts, notes, etc., of the different States...........214
Statue, the largest in the world..................................20
Steam engine, the smallest in the world..........................113
Strength of belt leather......................................78
Strength of different materials...............................284
Strength of ice of various thicknesses..........................91
Suffrage, qualifications required in different States.................221
Suspension Bridge, the largest in the world........................19
Table of approximate numbers for measuring circles, spheres, cubes, etc ... 81
Tallest men known...146
Telegraph wire, the longest span in the world.....................257
Telescopes, the largest......................................258
Ten laws of health..156
Ten seven years of life......................................158
Term of Office of Ruler of different countries.....................243
Term of Office of State Governors 60
Theater, the largest in the world..............................24
Thickness of boiler iron and pressure allowed by the United States laws......75
Three largest countries in the world............................20
Time in which various planets revolve around the sun.................132
Time on shipboard, divided into three watches.......................59
Time required for digesting food...............................44
Title of Rulers of different countries..........................243
Towers, the height of the highest..............................107
Tower, the highest in the world...............................67
Treaties of the World ratified by different nations since 1140.........246
Treatment of various causes (medical)..........................153
Trees, the largest in the world................................24
Tunnels, the longest in the world.............................149
Tunnel, the longest in the world..............................257
Turf terms (dictionary)......................................119
Two longest rivers in the world...............................23
United States Custom duties...................................270
United States land offices...................................233
United States of Brazil......................................238
United States Squadron Stations..............................208
Universities, the largest in the world.........................295
University, the largest in the world...........................21
Useful Information (law).....................................164
Value of a bar of iron worked in various forms....................185
Value of a ton of Gold or Silver..............................80
Value of Ancient Money.......................................198
Value of Diamonds...106
Value of Foreign Coins in United States Money 167
Velocity of Bodies..71
Velocity of Speed of Planets.................................132
Ventilation..157

Index—*Continued*

Vice-Presidents of the United States................................223
Wall, the greatest in the world.................................. 22
Walnut Stain.. 137
Wars of the United States.,..................................222
Waterfalls and Cascades, their elevation........................133
Waterfall, the highest in the world.. 21
Wedding Anniversary..........................\................147
Weight and Height of Ladies...................................146
Weight of a Cubic Foot of Earth, Stones, Metals, etc............ 85
Weight of Various Breeds of Poultry.. 147
Weight of Liquids per Gallon.................................. 79
Weight of the Earth...119
Weight of Large Bells of the World............................107
Weight of United States Coins................................. 36
Weights and Measures:
    "   Ale or Beer Measure.. 32
    "   Apothecaries' Measure (liquid)............................. 31
    "   Apothecaries' Weight (dry)................................ 32
    "   Assayers' Weight..251
    "   Avoidupois Weight... 31
    "   California Lot Measure.....................................252
    "   Circular Measure.. 34
    "   Cloth Measure...252
    "   Common Measures and Weights Equivalent in Metric System........ 29
    "   Comparison of Measures of Capacity........................252
    "   Cubic Measure... 30
    "   Diamond Weight...251
    "   Drop Liquid Measure.......................................252
    "   Dry Measure....................... 33
    "   English Money... 37
    "   English Wine Measure...................................... 34
    "   Iron and Lead Weight......................................252
    "   Liquid or Wine Measure.................................... 32
    "   Long Measure.. 30
    "   Measure of Time... 34
    "   Metric System Dry Measure................................. 28
    "   Metric System Cubic Measure............................... 28
    "   Metric System Equivalents in Common Measure.... 30
    "   Metric System Liquid Measure.............................. 28
    "   Metric System Long Measure................................ 28
    "   Metric System Square Measure.............................. 29
    "   Metric System Weights..................................... 29
    "   Paper Measure...252
    "   Shipping Admeasurement.................................... 33
    "   Square Measure.. 31
    "   Surveyor's Long Measure................................... 34
    "   Surveyor's Square Measure................................. 34
    "   Table of Miscellaneous Weights............................ 35
    "   Troy Weight...251
    "   United States Money.......................................252
    "   Units (measure)...252
Weights and Measures used in Foreign Countries.................253
What a Horse can draw..291
What Congress Costs per Annum..................................126
What Housekeepers Should Remember..............................205
What Royalty Costs England..................................... 64
What there is in a ton of coal.................................161
What to do when the clothes take fire 158
When State elections are held..................................234
When the Legislatures of different States meet.................234
Where and when the Continental Congresses met..................171
Whirlpool, the most remarkable in the world................... 28
Wonders in America... 49
Words of Wisdom for the People................................. 55

TREASURY

OF

USEFUL INFORMATION

❋

Greatest Men of History, Classified in Groups

POETRY

Homer, Pindar, Æschylus, Sophocles, Euripides, Aristophanes, Menander, Luceritius, Virgil, Dante, Rabelais, Cervantes, Shakespeare, Milton, Scott, Moliere, Goethe, Burns, Longfellow.

ART

Architects, Sculptors, Painters and Musicians

Phidias, Praxiteles, Leonardo da Vinci, Raphael, Michael Angelo, Corregio, Titian, Rubens, Rembrandt, Bach, Handel, Mozart, Beethoven

RELIGION

Religious Founders, Reformers and Theologians

Oriental Religions—Confucius, Buddha, Mahomet. Christianity—St. Paul, St. Augustine, St. Bernard, St. Francis, Erasmus, Luther, Calvin, Loyola, Bossuet, Wesley.

PHILOSOPHY

Metaphysicians, Psychologists and Moralists

Pythagoras, Socrates, Plato, Aristotle, St. Thomas Aquinas, Bacon, Descartes, Spinoza, John Locke, Leibnitz, Berkeley, Hume, Kant.

HISTORY
Historians, Orators and Critics

Herodotus, Thucydides, Demosthenes, Cicero, Tacitus, Plutarch, Montaigne, Montesquieu, Voltaire, Diderot, Lessing, Gibbon.

SCIENCE
Mathematicians, Physicians and Naturalists

Hippocrates, Archimedes, Galen, Copernicus, Keppler, Galileo, Harvey, Newton, Linnæus, Lavoisier, Bichat, Cuvier.

INDUSTRY
Inventors, Discoverers, Philanthropists

Gutenburg, Columbus, Palissy, Franklin, Howard, Montgolfier, Arkwright, Watt, Stephenson, Edison.

POLITICS
Warriors and Statesmen

Pericles, Alexander the Great, Hannibal, Cæsar, Charlemagne, Alfred the Great, William the Conquerer, Charles V, William the Silent, Richelieu, Cromwell, Peter the Great, Frederick the Great, Washington, Jefferson, Nelson, Napoleon I, Wellington, Gladstone, Blaine, Lincoln, Bismark.

MARVELS OF NATURE AND ART
Highest Mountain in the World

The loftiest mountain is Mount Everest of the Himalaya Range, having an elevation of 29,002 feet above the sea level.

Highest Mountain Range in the World

The highest mountain range is the Himalayas, the mean elevation being 18,000 feet above the sea level.

Highest Active Volcano in the World

The highest volcano is Popocatepetl in Mexico. It is 17,784 feet above the sea level and it has a crater of over three miles in circumference and is 1,000 feet deep.

Largest Pyramid in the World

The largest pyramid is that of Cheops in Egypt, it is 456 feet hight its original height was 479 feet, its sides are 746 feet in length against 764, its original length. It originally contained 89,028,000 cubic feet of masonry, it now contains 82,111,000 cubic feet of masonry, its weight is estimated at 6,316,000 tons.

Largest Desert in the World

The largest desert is the Sahara, in Northern Africa, extending from the Atlantic Ocean on the west to the Valley of the Nile on the east, about 3,000 miles in length, and its average width is about 900 miles, its area 2,000,000 square miles.

Largest City of the World

The largest city is London, England, its population numbers 4,021,880 souls. New York, U. S., is fifth in size, its population being 1,550,000.

Largest Suspension Bridge in the World

The largest suspension bridge is the New York and Brooklyn. It was commenced in 1870 under the direction of civil engineer J. Roebling and was completed in 13 years. The size of New York caisson is 172 x 102 feet; size of Brooklyn caisson, 168 x 122 feet; timber and iron in caissons, 5,253 cubic yards; concrete in wellholes, chambers, etc., 5,669 cubic feet; weight of New York caisson, 7,000 tons; weight of concrete filling, 8,000 tons; New York tower contains 46,945 cubic yards masonry; Brooklyn tower contains 38,214 cubic yards masonry; length of river span, 1,595½ feet; length of each land span, 930 feet and 1,860 feet; length of Brooklyn approach, 971 feet; length of New York approach, 1,562½ feet; total length of bridge, 5,989 feet; width of bridge, 85 feet; number of cables, 4; diameter of each, 15¾ inches; height of tower above roadway, 159 feet; weight of each anchorage plate, 23 tons; height of bridge above high-water mark, 135 feet; and the bridge cost $15,000,000.

The Largest Bell in the World

The largest bell is the great bell of Moscow, Russia, at the foot of the Kremlin. Its circumference at the bottom is nearly 68 feet, and its height more than 21 feet. In its thickest part it is 23 inches, and its weight has been estimated to be 443,772 pounds. It has never been hung, and has probably been cast on the spot where it now stands. A piece of the bell is broken off. The fracture is supposed to have been occasioned by water having been thrown on it when heated by the building erected over it being on fire.

Largest Statue of the World

The largest statue is Bartholdi's Statue of Liberty in New York harbor. This colossal statue was given by the people of the republic of France to the people of the United States of America, as a monument of ancient friendship and as an expression of the sympathy of France in the centennial of American Independence. It rests upon Bedloe's island in New York harbor, and in the face of the great cities of New York, Brooklyn, Jersey City and Hoboken. The Government has promised to maintain it in perpetuity as a lighthouse and beacon. The statue is 150 feet in height and cost $250,000. For the purpose of transportation from France the statue was divided into 300 distinct parts. The pedestal, including the foundation, is 182¾ feet above low water. The pedestal proper is 62 feet square at the base, 41¾ feet square at the top, and is 117 feet to the base of the statue. The entire length is 309 feet above low water. On the face of the pedestal are bronze shields, which display the coats-of-arms of the different States and Territories. From base of figure to top of torch is 151 feet; from base of figure to top of diadem, 116 feet; from the heel to the top of the head, 111½ feet; length of index finger, 8 feet; circumference of the same at second joint, 4 feet 8 inches; the finger nail is 1.14x85 feet; height of head, 14½ feet; width of eye, 2 feet; length of nose, 3 feet 7 inches. The statue is provided with an electric light, which is visible 50 miles at sea.

The Largest Inland Sea in the World

The largest inland sea is the Caspian, lying between Europe and Asia. Its greatest length is 760 miles, its greatest breadth is 270 miles, and its area is 180,000 square miles. The Caspian Sea lies 84 feet below the sea level.

The Three Largest Countries of the World

The largest empire is that of Great Britain comprising 8,567,658 square miles, more than a sixth part of the land of the globe, and embracing under its rule nearly a sixth part of the population of the world.

The next largest is Russia, having 8,352,940 square miles.

The third largest is the United States of America, containing 3,581,243 square miles including Alaska, it ranks fourth in population with its 60,000,000 of people.

The Highest Natural Bridge in the World

The highest natural bridge in the world is in Rockbridge County, Virginia, U. S., it extends over Cedar Creek, it has an arch 200 feet in height, and the upper surface of the bridge is 240 feet above the stream.

The Most Remarkable Natural Bridge of the World

The most remarkable natural bridge is the Jisrel Hajar, which spans a gorge not far from the ruins of the Temple of Adonis, in the province of the Lebanon in Syria. It is a flat piece of limestone from 10 to 15 feet thick, perfectly arched on the under side. The gorge is about 150 feet across, and the bridge is about 100 feet from the bed of the torrent below.

The Largest University of the World

The largest University is Oxford University, at Oxford, England. It consists of 21 colleges and 5 halls. Oxford was a seat of learning as early as the time of Edward the Confessor; University College claims to have been founded by Alfred the Great.

Greatest Cataract in the World

The greatest cataract is the Niagara Falls, the Horseshoe Fall on the Canadian side has a perpendicular descent of 158 feet; the height of the American Fall is 167 feet. The Horshoe carries a larger volume of water than the American Fall, is about 600 yards wide and extends from the Canadian shore to Goat Island. Geologists are agreed that the cataract was once six miles nearer to Lake Ontario than at present.

Highest Waterfall in the World

The highest waterfall is the Yosemite of California. It is formed by the Yosemite Creek, which is an affluent of the Merced River. The average width of the stream in Summer is about 20 feet and its depth about 2 feet. From the edge of the cliff, from which the water plunges, to the bottom of the valley the vertical distance is about 2,550 feet, but the fall is not one perpendicular sheet of water.

Natural Echoes, the Most Remarkable in the World

The most remarkable natural echoes are those of Eagle's Nest on the banks of Lake Killarney, in Ireland, which repeats a bugle call until it seems to be sounded from a hundred instruments.

Largest Electric Lights on Earth

The largest electric light is at the Sydney Lighthouse, Australia, which has a power of 180,000 candle-power, and can be seen 50 miles. The second largest is at Paris in the Palais de l'Industrie, of 150,000 candle-power. The next is at Marseilles, France, of 40,000 candle-power. The fourth largest is at San Jose, California, U. S., of 24,000 candle-power, and sheds its light two miles.

The Highest Inhabited Place in the World

The highest inhabited place is the Port House of Ancomarca, on the Andes, in Peru, South America. It is 16,000 feet above the sea level.

Largest Passenger Locomotive in the World

The largest passenger locomotive was built by the Rhode Island Locomotive Works for the New York, Providence and Boston Railroad Company. The main driving wheels are 6 feet in diameter and set but 7 feet 6 inches apart. The cylinders are 18 inches in diameter, with two-foot stroke. The boiler is 54 inches in diameter at the smokestack, with a wagon top. It extends to the very end of the cab, and necessitates the elevation of the engineer's seat to a height far above the fire door. Three tons of coal are consumed before the locomotive will move, and she carries four tons of coal on her tender. The tank of the tender will hold 4,000 gallons of water. The total weight of the locomotive proper is 95,000 pounds. The weight on the driving wheels is 66,000 pounds. Everything about the locomotive is steel. There is not a particle of brass or bright work about her. She made a run of 62½ miles in 62½ minutes, pulling at the same time eight cars, four of which were Pullman cars.

Greatest Wall in the World

The greatest wall is the Chinese Wall, built by the first Emperor of the Tsin dynasty, about 221 B.C., as a protection against the Tartars on the North. It traverses the northern boundary of China, and is carried over the highest hills, through the deepest valleys, across rivers and every other natural obstacle. Its length is 1,250 miles, including a parapet of five feet; the total height is 20 feet, its thickness at the base 25 feet, and at the top 15 feet. Towers or bastions occur at intervals of about every 300 feet.

Highest Railroad in the United States

The highest railroad in the United States is the Denver and Rio Grande Railroad, at Marshall Pass, 10,855 feet above the sea level.

Most Remarkable Whirlpool in the World

The most remarkable whirlpool is the maelstorm off the northwest coast of Norway, Europe, and southwest of Moskenasol, the most southerly of the Lafoden Isles. It was once supposed to be unfathomable, but the depth has been shown not to exceed 20 fathoms. The whirlpool is navigable under ordinary circumstances, but when the wind is northwest it often attains great fury and becomes extremely dangerous. Under strong gales the maelstorm has been shown by official statistics to run at the rate of twenty-six miles an hour.

Two Longest Rivers of the World

The longest river is the Mississippi River, that is if we include the Missouri with it, its length, from its head-waters Lake Itasca, in the Rocky Mountains to its mouth, where it empties into the Gulf of Mexico, is 4,160 miles. The Amazon, of South America, is next. It rises in the Andes Mountains, about 60 miles from the Pacific Ocean, and flows including its windings, a distance of 4,000 miles to the Atlantic Ocean, into which it empties under the equator in Brazil. The average velocity of the current is 3 miles an hour. It is navigable for large ships 2,200 miles from its mouth. The area drained by the Amazon and its tributaries is estimated at 2,000,000 square miles. The Amazon enters the ocean through an estuary about 150 miles wide. So great is the volume and impetus of the river that its fresh water is carried unmixed into the sea about 200 miles.

Largest Library in the World

The largest library is the Bibliotheque National in Paris, France, founded by Louis XIV. It contains 1,400,000 volumes, 300,000 pamphlets, 175,000 manuscripts, 300,000 maps and charts, and 150,000 coins and medals. The collection of engravings exceed 1,300,000, contained in some 10,000 volumes. The portraits number about 100,000. The building which contains these treasures is situated on the Rue Richelieu, Paris, France.

Largest Pleasure Park in the United States

The largest pleasure park in the United States, and one of the largest in the world, is Fairmount Park, Philadelphia, which contains 2,745 acres.

Largest Diamonds Found

The largest diamond in the world (if indeed, it be a diamond), is the Braganza, which forms part of the Portugese crown jewels. It weighs 1,880 carats. However, not a little doubt exists of its being a diamond, as the Government has never allowed it to be tested. It was found in Brazil in 1741. The largest tested but uncut diamond is the Mattan, belonging to the Rajah of Mattan, in Borneo. It is of pure water, weighs 367 carats, and is of a pear shape, indented at the thick end. It was found about 1760 at Landak, in Borneo. It has been the cause of a sanguinary war. Before it was cut the Kohinoor, which is one of the English crown jewels, was the largest tested diamond. It then weighed 793 carats. When in the possession of Emperor Aurengebe it was reduced by unskillful cutting to 186 carats. During the Sikh mutiny it was captured by British troops and presented to Queen Victoria. It was recut, and now weighs 106 1-16 carats.

Largest Theater in the World

The largest theater is the new Opera House in Paris, France. It covers nearly three acres of ground. Its cubic mass is 4,287,000 feet, it cost 63,000,000 francs.

Largest Trees in the World

The biggest trees are the mammoth trees of California. One of the grove in Tulare County, according to measurement made by members of the State Geological Survey, was shown to be 276 feet high, 106 feet in circumference at base, and 76 feet at a point 12 feet above the ground. Some of the trees are 380 feet high and 35 feet in diameter. Some of the largest trees that have been felled indicate an age of from 2,000 to 2,500 years.

Greatest Fortress in the World

The greatest fortress from a strategical point of view is the famous stronghold of Gibraltar, belonging to Great Britain, situated upon the most southern point of land upon the coast of Southwestern Spain, Europe. It occupies a rocky peninsula jutting out into the sea about three miles long and three-quarters of a mile wide. One central rock rises to a height of 1,439 feet above the sea level. Its northern face is almost perpendicular, while its east side is full of tremendous precipices. On the south it terminates in what is called Europe point. The west side is less steep than the east, and between its base and the sea is a narrow, almost level span on which the town of Gibraltar is built. The fortress is considered impregnable to military assault. The regular garrison in time of peace numbers about 7,000 men.

Largest Church in the World

The largest church is the basilica of St. Peter's in Rome, Italy. Its dimensions are as follows: length of interior, 613 feet; breadth of the nave and aisles, 197¾ feet; height of the nave, 152 feet; length of the transepts, 446½ feet; diameter of the dome, including the walls, 195 feet, or nearly two feet more than that of the Pantheon; diameter of the interior, 139 feet; height from the pavement to the base of the lantern, 405 feet; to the summit of the cross outside, 448 feet. The whole of St. Peter's Cathedral in London, Eng., might stand within the shell of St. Peter's with room to spare.

Average Weight of an American Man and Woman

Average weight of an American man is 141½ pounds, and an American woman is 124½ pounds.

Glossary of some California Names

San is masculine for Saint or Holy, and Santa is feminine.
Alameda (al-a-ma'-da). Grove of elms.
Alcatraz (al-ka-traz'). Pelican or seafish.
Almaden (al-ma-dan'). the mine (Arabic).
Alvarado (al-va-ra'-do). The white road.
Alviso (al-ve'-so). The view.
Anaheim (a-na-hime'). Anna's home (German).
Amador (a-ma-dor'). The lover.
Benicia (ba-ne'-she-a). Corruption of Venicia.
Bodega (bo-da-ga). A vault.
Buena Vista (boo-a'-na vees'-ta). Good view.
Calaveras (kal-a-va'-ras). The true skull.
Chico (che'-co). Very small.
Cinch (sinch). To bind with a girth.

Contra Costa (con'-tra cos'-ta). Opposite coast.
Corral (cor-ral'). Yard inclosure.
Coyote (ky-o'-ta). A kind of wolf.
Dalles (dals). Stone spout for water. (French.)
Del Monte (del-mon'-ta). Of the mountain.
Del Norte (del-nort'-a). Of the north.
Eldorado (al-do-ra'-do). The golden.
Farallones (far-a-lo'-nas). Rocky islands in the sea.
Fresno (fras'-no). The Ash tree.
Laguna (la-goo'-na). A marsh or shallow lake.
Lobos (lo'-bos). Wolves.
Loma Prieta (lo-ma pre-a'-ta). Dark Mountain.
Los Angeles (los an'-ga-las). The Angels.
Los Gatos (los ga'-tos). The cats.
Marin (ma-ren'). Of the sea.
Mariposa (ma-ra-po'-sa). The butterfly.
Martinez (mar'-te'-naz). Name of a person.
Merced (mar-sad'). Mercy, pay or gift.
Modoc (mo'-doc). Strange or hostile Indians (Aztec).
Monte Diablo (mon'-ta de-a'-blo). Devil mountain.
Monterey (mon'-ta-ra'). The king's mountain.
Nevada (na-va'-da). Snowy.
Ojai (o-hi).
Oroville (o-ro-vel'). Gold town.
Pah Utes (pa'-utes). Utahs that live near water. (Indian.)
Pajaro (pa-ha-ro). The bird.
Paso Robles (pa'-so ro'-bels). Pass of Oaks.
Pescadero (pas-ca-da'-ro). The fish.
Petaluma (pet-a-loo'-ma). Low Hills. (Indian.)
Placer (pla' sar). Gold diggings, pleasure.
Plaza (pla' za). Square place or public space in a town.
Plumas (plu'- mas). Feathers.
Potrero (po-tra'-ro). Pasture ground.
Presidio (pra-se'-de-o). Garrison, fortress.
Rincon (ren-con'). Corner.
Rio Vista (re'-o ves'-ta). River view.
Sacramento (sa'-kra man'-to). Sacred mind.
Salinas (sa-le'-nas). Place of salt.
San Andreas (san and-ras'). St. Andrew
San Benito (sau ba-ne'-to). St. Benedict.
San Buenaventura (san boo-wan'-a-van-too'-ra). St. Goodfortune.
San Diego (san de-a'-go). St. James.

San Francisco (san fran-ses'-co). St. Francis.
San Joaquin (san wa-ken'), St. Joachim.
San Jose (san ho-za'). St. Joseph.
San Juan (san wan). St. John.
San Lorenzo (san lo-ran' zo). St. Lawrence.
San Luis Obispo (san lu-es o-bes'-po). St. Louis the Bishop.
San Mateo (san ma-ta'-o). St. Matthew.
San Pablo (san pa'-blo). St. Paul.
San Pedro (san pa'-dro). St. Peter.
San Rafael (san ra-fa'-al). St. Raphael.
Santa Clara (san-ta cla'-ra), St. Clara.
Santa Cruz (san-ta cruz'). Holy Cross.
Saratoga (sara-to-ga). Healing water in a rock. (Indian.)
Saucelito (sa'-sa-le-to). Little willow.
Shasta (shas'-ta). Stonehouse or cave. (Indian.)
Sierra (se-a' ra). Saw or mountain chain.
Solano (so-la'-no). The potato.
Sonoma (so-no'-ma'). Valley of the moon. (Indian.)
Sonora (so-no'-ra). Harmonious sound.
Tahoe (ta'-ho). The big or deep water. (Some say it means grass-
hopper. (Aztec.)
Tamalpais (ta-mal-pas'). Country of tomales eaters.
Temescal (tam-mas-cal'). Sweathouse. (Aztec.)
Tomales (to-ma-las). A kind of food.
Tulare (tu-la'-ra). The tule or rush. (Indian.)
Tule (tu-la). The rush or juncus plant. (Indian.)
Utah (u'-ta). Mountain dwellers. (Indian.)
Vacaville (va'-ca-vel). Cowtown.
Vara (va'-ra). A measure about 33½ inches.
Vallejo (va-la'-ho). Big Valley.
W alla Walla (wa'-la wa'-la). Away down (Indian.)
Yerba Buena (yer'-ba boo-a'-na). Good herb.
Yolo (yo'-lo). Region of rushes or tules (Aztec.)
Yosemite (yo-sem'-i-ta). Large grizzly bear (Indian.)
Yreka (yĕ-re'-ka). Cave mountain.
Yuba (yoo'-ba). From uvas, grapes.

WEIGHTS AND MEASURES

Metric System

Metric System of weights and measures permissible. By an Act of
Congress, approved in July, 1866, the use of the weights and measures
of the metric system is made permissible; and contracts are declared
not to be invalid because the weights and measures expressed or
referred to therein are weights and measures of that system.

Measures of Length

0.001 meter	equals	1 millimeter	equals	0.0394 inches
0.01 meter	"	1 centimeter	"	0.3937 inches
0.1 meter	"	1 decimeter	"	3.937 inches
1 meter	"	1 meter	"	39.37 inches
10 meters	"	1 dekameter	"	393.7 inches
100 meters	"	1 hectometer	"	$328_{\tfrac{1}{3}}$ feet
1,000 meters	"	1 kilometer	"	$3,280\tfrac{1}{3}$ feet
10,000 meters	"	1 myriameter	"	$\begin{cases} 32,808\tfrac{1}{3} \text{ feet} \\ 6.2137 \text{ miles} \end{cases}$

Measure of Volume—Cubic Measure

1 cubic centimeter	equals	1 milliliter	equals	0.001 liter
10 cubic centimeters	"	1 centiliter	"	0.01 liter
0.1 cubic decimeter	"	1 deciliter	"	0.1 liter
1 cubic decimeter	"	1 liter	"	1 liter
10 cubic decimeters	"	1 dekaliter	"	10 liters
0.1 cubic meter	"	1 hectoliter	"	100 liters
1 cubic meter	equals	1 kiloliter or stere	equals	1,000 liters

Dry Measure of Metric System

1 milliliter equals 0.061 cubic inch.
1 centiliter " 0.6102 cubic inch.
1 deciliter " 6.1022 cubic inches.
1 liter " 0.908 quart.
1 dekaliter " 9.08 quarts.
1 hectoliter " 2 bushels and 3.35 pecks.
1 kiloliter, or stere equals 1.308 cubic yards.

Liquid Measure of Metric System

1 milliliter equals 0.27 fluid drachm.
1 centiliter " 0.338 fluid ounce.
1 deciliter " 0.845 gill.
1 liter " 1.0567 quart.
1 dekaliter " 2.6417 gallons
1 hectoliter " 26.417 gallons
1 kiloliter, or stere equals 264.17 gallons

Weights of Metric System

1 cubic millimeter equals 1 milligramme equals 0.001 gramme.
10 cubic millimeters " 1 centigramme " 0.01 "
0.1 cubic centimeter " 1 decigramme " 0.1 "
1 cubic centimeter " 1 gramme " 1 "
10 cubic centimeters " 1 dekagramme " 10 grammes.
1 decaliter " 1 hectogramme " 100 "
1 liter equals 1 kilogramme or kilo equals 1,000 grammes.
10 liters " 1 myriagramme equals 10,000 grammes.
1 hectoliter equals 1 quintal equals 100,000 "
1 cubic meter " 1 millier or tonneau equals 1,000,000,000 grammes.

Measure of Surface or Square Measure

1 square meter equals 1 centare equals 1550 square inches
100 square meters " 1 are " 119.6 square yards
10,000 square meters " 1 hectare " 2.474 acres

Common Measures and Weights Equivalents in Metric System

1 inch equals 2.54 centimeters.
1 foot " .3048 meter.
1 yard " .9144 "
1 rod " 5.029 meters.
1 mile " 1.6093 kilometers.
1 square inch equals 6.452 square centimeters.
1 " foot " .0929 " meter.
1 " yard " .8361 " "
1 " rod " 25.29 " meters.
1 acre equals .4047 hectare.
1 square mile equals 259. hectares.
1 cubic inch " .1639 cubic centimeter.
1 " foot " .02832 " meter.
1 " yard " .7646 " "
1 cord equals 3.624 steres.
1 liquid quart equals .9465 liter.
1 gallon equals 3.786 liters.
1 dry quart equals 1.101 liters.
1 peck equals 8.811 liters.
1 bushel " 35.24 "

Metric System Equivalents in Common Measure

1 milligramme equals 0.0154 grain avoirdupois.
1 centigramme   "   0.1543   "   "
1 decigramme   "   1.5432   "   "
1 gramme   "   15.432   "   "
1 dekagramme   "   0.3527 ounce   "
1 hectogramme   "   3.5274 ounces   "
1 kilogramme or kilo equals 2.2046 lbs avoirdupois.
1 myriagramme equals 22.046 lbs avoirdupois.
1 quintal   "   220.46   "
1 millier or tonneau equals 2204.6 lbs avoirdupois.

STANDARD MEASURES AND WEIGHTS
Long Measure

48 hairbreadth equal 1 inch.
3 barleycorns equal 1 inch.
12 lines equal 1 inch.
12 inches equal 1 foot, ft.
3 feet equal 1 yard, yd.
5½ yds equal 1 rod, perch or pole.
40 rods or perches equal 1 furlong
8 furlongs equal 1 mile, m.
3 inches equal 1 palm
4 in. equal 1 hand (horse meas.)
9 inches equal 1 span.
240 yds. equal 1 cable's length.
6 feet equal 1 fathom.

3 miles equal 1 league.
60 naut. or geog. m. equal 1 deg.
69½ statue m. equal $\begin{cases} 1 \text{ equatorial} \\ \text{deg. nearly} \end{cases}$
18 inches equal 1 cubit.
21.8 inches equal 1 Bible cubit.
2½ feet equal 1 military pace.
3 feet equal 1 common pace.
3.28 feet equal 1 meter.
880 fathoms equal 1 mile.
1-60 of a degree equal 1 knot.
3 knots equal 1 marine league

Long measure is used in measuring distances, where length only is considered.

Cubic Measure

1728 cubic inches - - equal	1 cubic foot.
27 cubic feet	"	1 cubic yard.
40 feet of round or } 50 feet of hewn timber)	"	1 ton or load.
42 cubic feet	"	1 ton of shipping.
16 cubic feet	"	1 cord-foot.
8 cord-feet or} 128 cubic feet)	"	1 cord.
108 cubic feet	"	1 stack of wood.
24¾ cubic feet	"	1 perch of stone or masonary.

Cubic measure is used in measuring solid bodies, having length, breadth and thickness; as timber, stone, boxes of goods, the capacity of rooms, etc.

Square Measure

144 square inches equal	1 square foot.
9 square feet	"	1 square yard.
30¼ square yards	"	1 square rod.
40 square rods	"	1 rood.
4 roods		
160 square rods	} "	1 acre.
640 acres	"	1 square mile.

Square measure is used in measuring surface, as land, flooring, etc.

Avoirdupois Weight

16 drams -	equal	1 ounce, oz.
16 ounces	"	1 pound, lb.
28 lbs. (old)	"	1 quarter, qr.
4 quarters (old)		
100 lbs., pounds	} "	1 hundred-weight.
20 hundred-weight	"	1 ton.
100 pounds	"	1 cental.
175 troy pounds	"	144 avoirdupois.
1 troy pound	"	5,760 grains.
1 avoirdupois pound	"	7,000 grains.

Avoirdupois weight is used to weigh all coarse articles as hay, meat, fish, potash, groceries, flax, butter, cheese, etc., and metals except precious metals. Formerly, the usual custom was to allow 112 pounds for a hundred-weight and 28 pounds for a quarter, but this practice has very nearly passed away. The Custom-house still continues to use the old usage.

Apothecaries' Measure—Liquid

60 minims or drops, m. equal	1 fluid drachm.
8 fluid drachms	"	1 fluid ounce.
16 fluid ounces	"	1 pint (octarius).
8 pints	"	1 gallon (congius).

These Apothecaries' weights and measures are used by Apothecaries and Physicians in compounding medicines, but drugs and medicines are bought and sold by Avoirdupois weight.

Apothecaries' Weight—Dry

20 grains equal 1 scruple.
3 scruples " 1 dram.
8 drams " 1 ounce.
12 ounces " 1 pound.

Liquid or Wine Measure

4 gills - - - equal 1 pint, pt.
2 pints " 1 quart, qt.
4 quarts " 1 gallon, gal.
42 gallons " 1 tierce.
1½ tierce or 63 gallons " 1 hogshead, hhd.
84 gallons " 1 puncheon.
1½ puncheon or 126 gallons " 1 pipe.
2 pipes " 1 tun.
231 cubic inches " 1 gallon.
10 gallons " 1 anker
18 gallons " 1 runlet.
31½ gallons " 1 barrel.

This measure is used to measure water, wine, spirits, cider, oil, honey, etc. In London the gill is usually called a quartern.

Ale or Beer Measure

2 pints - equal 1 quart.
4 quarts " 1 gallon.
9 gallons " 1 firkin.
2 firkins " 1 kilderkin.
2 kilderkins " 1 barrel.
1½ barrels " 1 hogshead.
1⅓ hogsheads " 1 puncheon.
1½ puncheons " 1 butt.

Used to measure beer, ales, porter, etc. An ale gallon measures 282 cubic inches.

Dry Measure

2 pints	-	equal	1 quart, qt.
4 quarts	- -	"	1 gallon, gal.
2 gallons,	- -	"	1 peck, pk.
4 pecks	- - -	"	1 bushel, bu.
36 bushels	- - -	"	1 chaldron, ch.
4 bushels (in England)		"	1 coon.
2 coons	" "	"	1 quarter.
5 quarters	" "	"	1 wey.
2 weys	" "	"	1 last.

A gallon, dry measure, measures 268 4-5 cubic inches. Dry measure applies to all goods that are not liquid and are sold by measure, as corn, grain, fruit, salt, coal, etc.

Shipping Admeasurement

Register ton. For register tonnage or for measurement of the entire internal capacity of a vessel :

100 cubic feet equal 1 register ton

This number is arbitrarily assumed to facilitate computation.

Shipping ton. For the measurement of cargo :

40 cubic feet equal
- 1 U. S. shipping ton.
- 32.146 U. S. bushels.
- 31.16 Imperial bushels.

42 cubic feet equal
- 1 British shipping ton.
- 33.75 U. S. bushels.
- 32.749 Imperial bushels.

1 U.S. or Winchester bushel equals 2150.42 cubic inches

1 Imperial bushel equals 2218.192 cubic inches.

1   "   "   "   1.0315157 U. S. bushels.

1 English quarter equals
- 8¼ U. S. bushels (nearly).
- 8 Imperial bushels.
- 17,745.54 cubic inches.
- 10.2694 cubic feet.

350 cubic feet equal 1 keel

Surveyor's Square Measure

625 square links equal 1 square rod, sq. rd.
16 " rods " 1 " chain, sq. ch.
10 " chains " 1 acre, A
640 acres equal 1 square mile, sq. mi.
36 square miles or 6 miles square equal 1 township, tp.

Surveyors' Long Measure

7.92 inches equal 1 link.
25 links " 1 pole.
100 links " 1 chain.
10 chains " 1 furlong.
8 furlongs " 1 mile.

Used by surveyors, civil engineers, etc., in measuring distances.

Measure of Time

60 seconds, sec. equal 1 minute, min.
60 minutes equal 1 hour, hr.
24 hours " 1 day, dy.
7 days " 1 week, wk.
2 weeks " 1 fortnight.
4 " " 1 month, mo.
13 months 1 day 6 hr. equal 1 Julian year.
365 days 6 hours equal 1 Julian year.
366 days equal 1 leap year.
12 calendar months equal 1 year.

Used for computing time.

Circular Measure

60 seconds " equal 1 minute '.
60 minutes " 1 degree °.
30 degrees " 1 sign s.
90 degrees " 1 quadrant.
12 signs " a circle.
4 quadrants ⎫
360 degrees ⎭ equal a circumference of a circle.

Used in measuring latitude, longitude, etc.

English Wine Measure

18 U. S. gallons - equal 1 runlet.
25 English gallons ⎫ " 1 tierce.
42 U. S. gallons ⎭
7½ English gallons " 1 firkin of beer.
4 firkins " 1 barrel.
52¼ English gallons ⎫ " 1 hogshead.
63 U. S. gallons ⎭

Number of English or United States yards in Miles of Different Nations.

NAME	YARDS	NAME	YARDS
Arabian	2,148	Luthenian	9,784
Bohemian	10,187	Oldenburg	10,820
Brebant	6,082	Persian (paisang)	6,082
Burgundy	6,183	Polish (long)	8,101
Chinese (His)	682	Polish (short)	6,095
Dutch (Ure)	6,395	Portuguese (leguos)	6,760
Danish	8,244	Prussian	8,498
English (U. S.)	1,760	Roman (modern)	2,035
English (geographical)	2,025	Roman (ancient)	1,613
Flemish	6,869	Russian (verst)	1,167
German (geographical)	8,100	Saxon	9,905
Hamburg	8,244	Scotch	1,984
Hanover	11,559	Silesian	7,083
Hesse	10,547	Spanish (leguas)	4,630
Hungarian	9,113	Spanish (com.)	7,416
French (art leagues)	4,860	Swiss	9,166
French (marine)	6,075	Swedish	11,704
Legal League (2,000 toises)	4,263	Turkey	1,821
Irish	3,338	Tuscan	1,808
Italian	2,025	Vienna (post mile)	8,296

Table of Miscellaneous Weights

14 pounds equal 1 stone (horseman's weight).
56 pounds " 1 firkin of butter.
64 pounds " 1 firkin of soft soap.
112 pounds " 1 barrel of raisins.
256 pounds " 1 pack of soft soap.
196 pounds " 1 barrel of flour.
200 pounds " 1 barrel of beef, pork or fish.
280 pounds " 1 barrel of salt, New York.
22 stones (301 lbs), equal 1 sack of wool.
17 stones 2 lbs (240 lbs.), equal 1 pack of wool.
60 pounds equal 1 truss of hay (new).
50 pounds " 1 truss of hay (old).
40 pounds " 1 truss of straw.
400 pounds " 1 bale of cotton.

Number of Pounds to Bushel

Recognized by the Laws of the United States.

Wheat	60	Dried Peaches	33
Shelled corn	56	Dried Apples	24
Corn in Ear	70	Onions	57
Rye	56	Salt	50
Oats	32	Stone Coal	80
Barley	48	Malt	84
Irish Potatoes	60	Bran	30
Sweet Potatoes	50	Plastering Hair	88
White Beans	60	Turnips	57
Castro Beans	46	Unslacked Lime	80
Clover Seed	60	Corn Meal	50
Timothy Seed	45	Fine Salt	62
Flaxseed	56	Hungarian Grass-seed	48
Hempseed	44	Ground Peas	24
Peas	60	Onion Sets	14
Blue Grass Seed	14	Onion Tops	25
Buckwheat	52	Onion Bottoms	35

Coke..................46

Standard Weight of United States Coins

(GOLD.)

$20 equals 516 grains.
$10 " 258 grains.
$5 " 129 grains.
$3 " 77.4 grains.
$2.50 " 65.5 grains.
$1 " 25.8 grains.

(SILVER.)

1 dollar equals 412.5 grains.
50 cents " 192.9 grains.
25 cents " 96.45 grains.
20 cents " 77.16 grains.
10 cents " 38.58 grains.

English or Great Britain Currency

VALUE IN U. S. GOLD COIN

4 farthings qr.	equal	1 penny ct.	$0.02.
4 pence	"	1 groat	0.08.
12 pence	"	1 shilling s.	0.24.
2 shillings	"	1 florin fl.	0.48.
5 shillings	"	1 crown	1.21.
20 shillings	"	{ 1 sovereign or £ pound sterling.	$4.86.
21 shillings	"	1 guinea	5.10.

Roman Money

Roman money mentioned in the New Testament reduced to United States and English Standard.

	£.	s.	d.	far.	$	cents.
A Mite	0	0	0	0.75	0	.00343.
A Farthing (about)	0	0	0	1.50	0	.C0687.
A Penny or Denarius	0	0	7	2	0	13.75.
A Pound or Mina	3	2	0	0	13	75.

AMERICAN PROVERBS AND MAXIMS

A game is never won until its ended.
A fair exchange is no robbery.
A burnt child avoids the fire.
A shoemaker should stick to his last.
A bad oath is better broken than kept.
A stitch in time saves nine.
A short horse is soon curried.
A rolling stone gathers no moss.
A setting hen never grows fat.
A miss is as good as a mile.
A bird in hand is worth two in the bush.
A smooth sea never makes skilled mariners.
A rotten apple infects its companions.
A guilty conscience needs no accuser.
A drowning man catches at straws.
A new broom sweeps clean.

A fool for luck.
A penny saved is as good as a penny earned.
A dead Injun is a good Injun.
A fool and his money are soon parted.
A barking dog seldom bites.
A friend in need is a friend indeed.
A stream cannot rise higher than its fountain.
A quiet tongue makes a wise head.
An idle brain is the devil's workshop.
An honest man is the noblest work of God.
An honest confession is good for the soul.
An ounce of prevention is worth a pound of cure.
All is fish that comes to my net.
All is not gold that glitters.
All is well that ends well.
All is fair in love or war.
As many opinions as people.
As the cock crows the young one learns.
As the twig is bent the tree's inclined.
As you raise them so you have them (children).
As well be out of the world as out of the fashion.
Artists are born, not made.
Accidents will happen in the best of families.
Accidents are the result of carelessness.
Always kick the dog that's under.
An old fox is not easily caught.
A cheerful spirit sweetens toil.

Better wear out than rust out.
Better let well enough alone.
Better late than never.
Better the day, better the deed.
Better do it than wish it done.
Better have two cooks than one doctor.
Better be at the end of a feast than at the beginning of a fray.
Better to have the goodwill, even of a dog.
Better to have two strings for one bow.
Better still to have two beaux.
Be sure of a new friend before cutting an old one.
Be sure you are right, then go ahead.
Be sure your sin will find you out.
Be just, before you are generous.

Begin on the best and you'll always have the best.
Bygones have no right to be heard.
Blessings brighten as they take their flight.
Birds of a feather flock together.
Biters are sometimes bitten.
Be sure to know what you are talking about.
Beauty is only skin deep.
Beauty is a blossom.
Beauty unadorned, adorned the most.
Brevity is the soul of wit.
Birth is much, breeding more.
Brag is a good dog, holdfast a better.
Borrowed garments never fit well.
Bought wit is the best wit.
Bricks don't make a home nor binding a book.

Circumstances alter cases.
Creaking ships run a long while.
Competition is the life of trade.
Corporations have no souls.
Curses like chickens go home to roost.
Charity should begin at home.
Coming events cast their shadows before.
Confessing a fault half amends it.
Convince a man against his will, and he's of the same opinion still.
Can't get blood out of a turnip.
Cut your coat according to your cloth.
Charity covers a multitude of sins.

Discontent is a charming lap-dog.
Desperate diseases require desperate remedies.
Dropping water wears the rock.
Domestic infelicity is a thorn in the flesh.
Death loves a shining mark.
Dreams go by contraries.
Don't meet trouble half way.
Don't cook a hare before you catch it.
Don't throw money into a hopper.

Every stream findeth its own channel.
Every man is his own doctor.
Every man is supposed to know his own business best.
Every trade has its tricks.
Every dog has his day.

Hunger is good sauce.
He laughs best who laughs last.
Harder the storm the sooner over.

It is hard to teach an old dog new tricks.
It is easy to advise other folks.
It is a long lane that has no turning.
It takes all sorts of people to make a world.
It never rains but it pours.
It is truth that cuts.
It is an ill wind that blows nobody good.
It is bad luck to turn back.
It is good luck to turn back once.
It is a poor rule that wont work both ways.
It is easy to make straw men.
It is well to have the courage of one's convictions.
It takes two to make a bargain.

Jack of all trades, master of none.

Know which side your bread is buttered.

Least said soonest mended.
Learn to run yourself and be content.
Lazy folks take most pains.
Lose your due, get no thanks.
Live and learn.
Live and let live.
Let not zeal outrun discretion.
Let the devil have his due.
Little cares bring heavy griefs.
Little leaks sink great ships.
Little pitchers have big ears.
Little boats should keep near shore.
Little folks should be seen and not heard.
Listeners hear no good.

The Origin of the Names of the Months

January.—The Roman Janus presided over the beginning of everything; so the first month was named after him.

February.—The Roman festival Februs was held on the fifteenth day of this month, in honor of Lupercus.

March.—Named after the Roman's god of war—Mars.

April.—From the Latin, Aprilis, derived probably from asperire, to open, because spring-time generally commences and the buds burst open in this month.

May.—Latin, Maius, derived probably from Maia, a feminine divinity worshiped at Rome on the first day of this month.

June.—Juno, a Roman divinity worshiped as the Queen of Heaven.

July.—Julius, Julius Cæsar was born in this month.

August.—Named by the Roman Emperor, Augustus Cæsar, after himself, as he regarded it a lucky month, being the month in which he won several of his famous victories.

September.—Septem, the Latin for seven; September was the seventh month in the old Roman year.

October.—Octo, the Latin for eight, it was the eighth month in the old Roman year.

November.—Novem, the Latin for nine, it was the ninth month in the old Roman year.

December.—Decem, the Latin for ten, it being the tenth month in the old Roman year.

The Origin of the Names of the Days

Sunday.—It was so-called because it was anciently dedicated to the worship of the sun.

Monday.—Means literally, the day of the Moon.

Tuesday.—Was dedicated to Tuisco, the Mars of our Saxon Ancestors, the deity or god that presided over wars, combats, strife and litigation.

Wednesday.—It's so-called from Wodin or Odin, a deity or chief among ancient nations of Northern Europe.

Thursday.—It is named after Thor, the old Teutonic god of Thunder.

Friday.—Is named from Frea or Friga, a goddess of the old Saxon mythology.

Saturday.—Means simply Saturn's day, the name being derived from the deity of that name.

EMBLEMATIC NAMES OF STATES OF THE U. S.

STATE NAME	EMBLEMATIC NAME.
Arkansas	Bear State.
California	The Golden State.
Colorado	Centennial State.
Connecticut	Nutmeg or Freestone State.
Delaware	Diamond State.
Florida	Peninsular State.
Georgia	Empire State of the South.
Illinois	Prairie or Sucker State.
Indiana	Hoosier State.
Iowa	Hawkeye State.
Kansas	Garden of the West.
Kentucky	Corn Cracker State.
Louisiana	Creole State.
Maine	Pine Tree State.
Massachusetts	Old Bay State or Old Colony.
Michigan	Wolverine or Lake State.
Minnesota	Gopher State.
Mississippi	The Bayou State.
Missouri	The Pennsylvania of the West.
Nevada	Sage Hen State.
New Hampshire	Granite State.
New Jersey	Jersey Blue.
New York	Empire or Excelsior State.
North Carolina	Old North or Turpentine State.
Ohio	Buckeye State.
Oregon	Webfoot State.
Pennsylvania	Keystone State.
Rhode Island	Little Rhody.
South Carolina	Palmetto State.
Tennessee	Big Bend State.
Texas	Lone Star State.
Vermont	Green Mountain State.
Virginia	{ Old Dominion, Mother of States, or Mother of Presidents.
West Virginia	Pan Handle State.
Wisconsin	Badger State.

Fictitious Names of Cities of U. S.

City Name.	Fictitious Name.
Baltimore	Monumental City.
Boston	Hub of the Universe, Puritan City or City of Notions.
Brooklyn, N. Y.	City of Churches
Buffalo	Queen City of the Lakes
Chicago	Garden City
Cincinnati	Queen City
Cleveland	Forest City
Detroit	City of Straits
Hannibal, Mo.	Bluff City
Indianapolis	Railroad City
Keokuk, Ia.	Gate City
Louisville	Falls City
Lowell	City of Spindles
Nashville	City of Rocks
New Haven	City of Elms
New Orleans	Crescent City
New York	Empire City or Gotham
Philadelphia	Quaker City or City of Brotherly Love
Pittsburg	Smoky City or Iron City
Portland, Me	Forest City
Rochester	Flour City
Springfield, Ill.	Flower City
St. Louis	Mound City
Washington, D. C.	City of Magnificent Distances

National Flower of Different Nations

STATE	EMBLEM	STATE	EMBLEM
Athens	Violet	Italy	Lily
Canada	Sugar Maple	Prussia	Linden
Egypt	Lotus	Saxony	Mignonette
England	Roses	Scotland	Thistle
France	Fleur de Lis	Spain	Pomegranate
Germany	Cornflower	Wales	Leek
Ireland	Shamrock	......	......

TIME REQUIRED FOR DIGESTING FOOD

Name of Food	How Cooked	Hrs. Min.
Apples, sweet	Boiled	2.30
Apples, sweet, mellow	Raw	1.30
Apples, sour, hard	Raw	2.50
Barley	Boiled	2.00
Bass, striped	Broiled	3.00
Beans, Lima	Boiled	2.30
Beans, pod	Boiled	2.30
Beans and green corn	Boiled	3.45
Beef	Fried	4.00
Beefsteak	Broiled	3.00
Beef, fresh, lean, dry	Roasted	3.30
Beef, fresh, lean, raw	Roasted	3.00
Beef, salt	Boiled	2.45
Beets	Boiled	3.45
Bread, corn	Baked	3.15
Bread, wheat, fresh	Baked	1.30
Butter	Fresh	3.30
Cabbage	Raw	2 30
Cabbage, with vinegar	Raw	2.00
Cabbage	Boiled	4.30
Carrots	Boiled	3.15
Catfish	Fried	3.30
Cheese, old	Raw	3.30
Chicken	Fricasseed	2.45
Codfish, cured dry	Boiled	2.00
Custard	Baked	2.45
Duck, tame	Roasted	4.00
Duck, wild	Roasted	4.30
Eggs, fresh	Raw	2.00
Eggs, fresh	Scrambled	1.30
Eggs, fresh	Roasted	2.15
Eggs, fresh	Soft boiled	3.00
Eggs, fresh	Hard boiled	3.30
Eggs, fresh	Fried	3.30
Fowls, domestic	Roasted	4.00
Hash meat and vegetables	Warmed	2.30
Lamb, fresh	Broiled	2.30
Lamb	Boiled	2.30
Milk	Raw	2.15

Name of Food	How Cooked	Hrs. Min.
Milk - - -	Boiled - - -	2.00
Mutton - - -	Boiled - - -	3.00
Mutton - - -	Roasted - - -	3.15
Oysters, fresh -	Raw - - - -	2.55
Oysters, fresh - -	Roasted - - -	3.15
Oysters, fresh - -	Stewed - - -	3.30
Pigs' feet, soused - -	Boiled - - -	1.00
Pork, fat and lean - -	Roasted - - -	3.15
Pork, recently salted -	Stewed - - -	3.00
Pork, recently salted - -	Fried - - -	3.15
Potatoes, Irish - -	Baked - - -	2.30
Potatoes, Irish - -	Boiled - - - -	3.30
Rice - - -	Boiled - - -	1.00
Sago - - - -	Boiled - - - -	1.45
Salmon, salted -	Boiled - - -	4.00
Sausages, fresh - -	Broiled - - -	3.15
Soup, barley - -	Boiled - - -	1.30
Soup, bean - - -	Boiled - - -	3.30
Soup, chicken - -	Boiled - - -	3.00
Soup, mutton - - -	Boiled - - -	3.30
Soup, beef, vegetables -	Boiled - - -	4.00
Tripe, soused - -	Boiled - - -	1.00
Trout, salmon, fresh -	Boiled - - -	1.30
Turkey - - - -	Roasted - - -	2.30
Veal - - -	Boiled - - -	4.00
Veal - - - -	Fried - - -	4.30

CURRENCY OF DIFFERENT COMMERCIAL NATIONS

Argentine Confederation

100 centesimos equal -	1 dollar or patacon, equal $1.00
17 patacons equal - - - -	1 doubloon

Austria

100 kreutzers equal - -	1 florin, equal $0.47

British India

12 pies equal - - - - - 1 anna
16 anas " - - 1 rupee, equal $0.48
15 rupees " - - - - 1 mohur
Lac of rupees equal 100,000, equal - - £10,000
Crore of rupees equal 10,000,000 equal, - £1,000,000

Italy

100 centesimi equal - 1 lira, equal $0.193

Burmah

4 great riveh equal - - - 1 bais, equal $0.03
4 bais equal - - - - 1 math
4 math " - - - - 1 tical or kyat

Canada

Accounts are kept in dollars and cents; and also in pounds, shillings and pence. See United States and Great Britain.

Cape of Good Hope

(See Great Britain)

Chili

100 Centavos equal - - 1 peso (dollar), $0.96

Mexico

100 cents equal - - 1 dollar, equal $1.00

Norway

24 skillingen equal - - - 1 mark or ort
5 marks equal - - 1 species-daler, equal $1.07
100 ore equal - - - 1 krona, equal $0.25

Portugal

400 reis equal - - - - 1 cruzado
480 reis equal - - - 1 cruzado novo or pinto
1,000 reis equal - - - - - $1.08
4,500 reis equal - - 1 pound (English Coin)

Denmark

12 skillings equal	-	-	-	1 mark
6 mark equal	-	1 rigsbankdaler (rixdaler) $0.53		

Egypt

3 asper equal	-	-	-	1 para
40 para equal	-	-	-	1 piastre, equal $0.05

France

100 centimes equal	-	-	1 franc, equal $0.193
20 francs equal	-	-	1 napoleon or louis

Germany

10 pfennings equal	-	-	-	1 groschen
10 groschens equal	-	-	1 mark, equal $0.235	
30 groschens equal	-	-	-	1 thaler

Gibraltar

16 quartos equal	-	-	1 real
12 reals equal	-	-	1 dollar, equal $1.00
100 cents equal	-	-	1 dollar
10 decimas de real vellon equal	-	1 real de vellon	
20 real de vellon equal	-	1 dollar, equal $1.00	
100 reals de vellon equal	-	-	1 doblon

Greece

100 lepta equal	-	1 dracham, equal $0.193

Holland

100 cents equal	-	1 gulden or florin, equal $0.40

Russia

100 copecks equal	-	1 silver rouble, equal $0.72
10 roubles	-	equal 1 imperial
The paper rouble equal	-	$0.60 (about)

Siam

200 to 450 courties or bier equal	·	1 p'hainung
4 p'hainungs equal	- - -	1 fuang
2 fuangs equal	- - -	1 salung or miam
4 salungs equal	- - -	1 tical
4 ticals equal	- -	1 tamlung, equal $2.40

Spain

100 centimos equal   -   -   1 peseta, equal $0.19

Sweden

100 ore equal   -   -   1 rixdaler, equal $0.27

Turkey

40 paras equal -   -   -   -   1 piastre
100 piastres equal   1 medjidie or liro turca, equal $4.32

Belgium

100 centimes equal   -   -   1 franc, equal $0.193
20 francs equal   -   -   1 napoleon or louis

Brazil

400 reis equal	- - - -	1 cruzardo
480 reis "	- -	1 cruzardo novo, or pinto
1,000 reis "	- -	1 milreis, equal $0.55

Japan

10 mons or sepei equal	- - -	1 rin
10 rin equal	- - - -	1 sen
100 sens or tempos equal	-	1 yen, equal $1.00

China

10 cash equal	- - -	1 candareen (fun)
10 candareens equal	- - -	1 mace (tsien)
10 mace equal	- - -	1 tael (leang)

Among foreigners 1,000 cash (about) 1 dollar.

U. S. of Colombia

10 centavos equal   -   -   -   -   1 decimo
10 decimos equal   -   -   1 peso, equal $1.00

GREAT WONDERS IN AMERICA

Croton Aqueduct, in New York City.
City Park, Philadelphia, Penn., the largest public park in the world.
Lake Superior, the largest lake in the world.
Mammoth Cave, in Kentucky.
Niagara Falls, a sheet of water three-quarters of a mile in width with a fall of 175 feet.
Natural Bridge, over Cedar Creek, in Virginia.
New State Capitol, at Albany, New York.
New York and Brooklyn Bridge.
The Central Park in New York City.
Yellowstone National Park, in Wyoming Ter.
Washington Monument, Washington, D. C., 555 feet in height.
Yosemite Valley, California, 51 miles from Coulterville. A valley from 8 to 10 miles long, and about 1 mile wide. Has very steep slopes about 3,500 feet high; has a perpendicular precipice 3,089 feet high, a rock almost perpendicular, 3,270 feet high; and waterfalls from 700 to 1,000 feet high.

CHEMICAL SUBSTANCES—THEIR COMMON NAMES

Common Name	Chemical Name
Ammonia	Volatile Alkali
Aqua Fortis	Nitric Acid
Aqua Regia	Nitro-Muriatic Acid
Blue Vitriol	Sulphate of Copper
Cream of Tartar	Bitartrate Potassium
Calomel	Chloride of Mercury
Chalk	Carbonate Calcium
Caustic Potassa	Hydrate Potassium
Chloroform	Chloride of Gormyle
Common Salt	Chloride of Sodium
Copperas or Green Vitriol	Sulphate of Iron
Corrosive Sublimate	Bi-Chloride of Mercury
Diamond	Pure Carbon
Dry Alum	Sulphate Alluminum and Potassium
Epsom Salts	Sulphate of Magnesia
Ethiops Mineral	Black Sulphide of Mercury
Fire Damp	Light Carburetted Hydrogen
Galena	Sulphide of Lead
Glauber's Salt	Sulphate of Sodium

Chemical Substances—*Continued*

Common Name	Chemical Name
Glucose	Grape Sugar
Goulard Water	Basic Acetate of Lead
Hartshorn	Carbonate of Ammonia
Iron Pyrites	Bi-Sulphide Iron
Jeweler's Putty	Oxide of Tin
King's Yellow	Sulphide of Arsenic
Laughing Gas	Protoxide of Nitrogen
Lime	Oxide of Calcium
Lunar Caustic	Nitrate of Silver
Mosaic Gold	Bi-Sulphide of Tin
Muriate of Lime	Chloride of Calcium
Nitre of Saltpetre	Nitrate of Potash
Oil of Vitriol	Sulphuric Acid
Potash	Oxide of Potassium
Realgar	Sulphide of Arsenic
Red Lead	Oxide of Lead
Rust of Iron	Oxide of Iron
Salmoniac	Muriat of Ammonia
Salt of Tartar	Carbonate of Potassa
Saltpetre	Salt of Nitric Acid and Potash
Slacked Lime	Hydrate Calcium
Soda	Oxide of Sodium
Spirits of Hartshorn	Ammonia
Spirit of Salt	Hydro-Chloric or Muriatic Acid
Stucco or Plaster of Paris	Sulphate of Lime
Sugar of Lead	Acetate of Lead
Verdigris	Basic Acetate of Copper
Vermilion	Sulphide of Mercury
Vinegar	Acetic Acid (Diluted)
Water	Oxide of Hydrogen
White Precipitate	Ammoniated Mercury
White Vitriol	Sulphate of Zinc

Antidotes and Treatment for Poisons

Immediately on discovering that poison has been swallowed, send for a physician with all possible haste. Until his arrival, the treatment should either be with a view to removing the poison by an emetic or neutralizing its effects by an antidote.

Emetics

Ground mustard, a tablespoonful in a tumbler of warm water, is an emetic usually quickly procured. Give the patient one-fourth of it at once, and follow with a cup of warm water. Repeat the dose every minute or two until vomiting takes place. Give moderately warm water freely. Mustard has a special value in most cases where an emetic is needed, as it is also stimulating in its effects. Common salt is also used as an emetic, a teacup of water with as much salt as the water will dissolve, being given every few moments until vomiting occurs.

Tickling the throat with a feather, or with the finger, is a valuable aid to the action of an emetic. After vomiting takes place, the white of eggs in warm water, warm milk, gum arabic water, or flour and water, may be given to further cleanse the stomach and to soothe the irritated mucous membrane.

Antidotes

The following table gives the common poisons and suggestions as to the treatment for each poison, and together with the above, may be of assistance until the arrival of a physician.

Acids (mineral).—Chalk, magnesia (plaster off wall), solution of cooking soda, or saleratus; then barley water, linseed tea, or olive oil.

Aconite.—Emetics, stimulants external and internal.

Antimony.—Strong tea in large quantities.

Aqua Fortis.—Same as acid, mineral.

Arsenic.—Give milk in large quantities, or the white of eggs, or flour and water; follow with stimulants.

Argenti Nit.—Large teaspoonful of salt in cup of water, repeat in ten minutes; then give castor oil and linseed tea or barley water.

Bad Fish or Other Food.—Emetics; then a large dose of castor oil with some warm spice, mustard plaster to pit of stomach if necessary.

Bedbug Poison.—Same as corrosive sublimate.

Blue Vitriol.—Same as cupri sulph. and copper.

Cannabis Indica.—Hot Brandy and water, lemon juice, vegetable acids, vinegar. Allow patient to sleep, blister to nape of neck.

Cantharides.—Emetics, followed by barley water, flax-seed tea, or other soothing drinks.

Carbolic Acid.—Give flour and water, or glutinous drinks.

Antidotes—*Continued*

Caustic Potash.—Same as Potash.

Caustic Soda.—Same as Potash.

Chlorine Water.—Albumen (white of egg) milk, flour.

Chloroform.—Pour cold water over the head and face (get the head as low as possible), excite respiration, artificial galvanic battery.

Chloride of Tin.—Milk in large quantities with magnesia, chalk, or whiting in it; raw eggs beaten up with water or milk.

Chloral Hydrate.—Same as Chloroform.

Chloride of Zinc.—Milk with white of eggs in it. Large doses.

Cobalt.—Same as arsenic.

Carbonate of Soda.—Prompt emetic, soap or mucilaginous drinks.

Bi-Carbonate of Potassa.—Magnesia or soap, dissolved in water, every two minutes.

Colchicum.—Emetics, then barley water, linseed tea, etc. If stupor (coma) be present, give brandy, coffee, ammonia.

Conium.—Emetics, followed by stimulants externally and internally.

Copper.—Milk and white of eggs; large quantities; then strong tea. Don't give vinegar:

Copperas.—Emetics, and same as carbonate of soda.

Corrosive Sublimate.—White of eggs in a little water. Repeat dose at intervals of two or three minutes until patient vomits. Use milk or flour and water if you can't get eggs.

Croton Oil.—Emetics, then flaxseed tea, gum arabic water, slippery elm, etc.

Cupri Sulph.—Same as copper.

Cyanide of Potassium.—Same as prussic acid.

Digitalis.—Emetic, keep the patient lying down. Stimulants externally and internally.

Fowler's Solution.—Same as arsenic.

Haschisch.—Same as Cannabis Indica.

Hemlock.—Same as conium.

Henbane.—Same as hyoscyamus.

Hyoscyamus.—Emetics, lemon juice, stimulants, external and internal.

Hydrocyanic Acid.—Fresh air and artificial respiration with dashes of cold water.

Indelible Ink.—Some as argenti nit.

Indian Hemp.—Same as Cannabis Indica.

Iodine.—Emetics, starch or flour in water, barley water or other demulcent drinks.

Antidotes—*Continued*

Ivy Poisoning.—Apply soft soap freely to the affected parts; or bathe the poisoned skin frequently with a weak tincture of belladonna.

Laudanum.—Same as opium.

Lead.—Two ounces of Epsom salts in a pint of water, wineglass full every ten minutes until it operates freely. Afterward milk.

Lead Salts.—Same as lead.

Lead Water.—Same as lead.

Lobelia.—Stimulants externally and internally.

Lunar Caustic.—Same as argenti nit.

Lye.—Same as potash.

Mercury.—Same as corrosive sublimate.

Mineral Acid.—Same as acid, mineral.

Morphia.—Same as opium.

Muriatic Acid.—Same as acids, mineral.

Nitrate of Silver.—Same as argenti nit.

Nitre.—Same as saltpetre.

Nitric Acid.—Same as acids, mineral.

Nux Vomica.—Emetics, artificial respiration, linseed tea or barley-water; to an adult 30 drops of laudanum to relieve the spasms.

Oil of Bitter Almond.—Same as prussic acid.

Oil of Vitriol.—Same as acids, mineral.

Opium.—Emetics (10 grains of sulphate of copper if possible); after vomiting, which must be induced quickly, give plenty of strong coffee with brandy, put mustard plasters around calves of legs; keep patient aroused by walking around, dashing cold water in face, beating soles of feet or whipping body with towels wrung out in cold water. If the patient is allowed to go to sleep before the effect of the opium has passed off death will result.

Oxalic Acid.—Same as acids, mineral.

Paregoric.—Same as opium.

Paris Green.—Same as arsenic.

Phosphorus.—Emetics, large quantities of tepid water, with magnesia, chalk, whiting, or even flour stirred in it.

Potash.—Vinegar and water, oranges, lemons, sour beer, cider or sour fruit; then give oil, linseed or olive.

Prussic Acid.—Sal-volatile and water; apply smelling salts to nostrils; dash cold water in face; give stimulants.

Ratsbane.—Same as arsenic.

Red Precipitate.—Same as corrosive sublimate.

Red Lead.—Same as lead.

"Rough on Rats".—Same as arsenic.

Antidotes—*Continued*

Saltpetre.--Flour and water in large doses; linseed or sweet oil.

Salts of Tin.—Milk in large quantities.

Spanish Fly.—Same as Cantharides.

Spirits of Salts.—Same as acids, mineral.

Strychnine.—Same as nux vomica.

Sugar of Lead.—Same as lead.

Sulphuric Acid.—Same as acids, mineral.

Sulphate of Zinc.—Same as zinc salts.

Tartar Emetic.—Same as antimony.

Tartarized Antimony.—Same as antimony.

Tobacco Emetics.—Stimulants external and internal.

Verdigris.—Same as copper.

Vermilion.—Same as corrosive sublimate.

Volatile Alkali.—Same as potash.

White Precipitate.—Same as arsenic.

White Vitriol.—Same as zinc salts.

Zinc Salts.—Give milk with white of eggs, freely, afterward warm barley-water or linseed tea.

To Stop Vomiting

Drink freely of hot water, just as hot as can be borne.

Rattlesnake Bites

Whiskey is supposed to be the great cure-all. Give enough to cause intoxication.

Mad Dog Bites

See a physician at once if possible, or apply caustic potash at once to the wound. Give enough whiskey to cause sleep.

Cat Bites

Apply fat salt pork to the wound for a day or two, or until all the poison is all extracted.

Bites and Stings of Insects

Wash with a solution of water of ammonia.

Words of Wisdom for the People

If you would know what a dollar is worth, try to borrow one.
When the dog is down, everyone is ready to bite him.
Ask thy purse what thou shoulds't buy.
A good example is the best sermon.
A silent man's words are not brought into court.
A rich dress is not worth a straw to one who has a poor mind.
A father is a treasure, a brother a comfort, a friend is both.
A good fame is better than a good face.
A young man idle, and old man needy.
A bridle for the tongue is a necessary piece of furniture.
A civil denial is better than a rude grant.
A nice wife and a backdoor often make a rich man poor.
A good paymaster never wants workmen.
A good wife and health are a man's best wealth.
A man can never thrive who has a wasteful wife.
A man of words, and not of deeds, is like a garden full of weeds.
A lass that has many wooers oft fares the worst.
A handful of common sense is worth a bushel of learning.
A fool can make money; it requires a wise man to spend it.
A wealthy man who obtains his wealth honestly and uses it rightly
is a great blessing to the community.
An ounce of mother's wit is worth a pound of clergy.
A single fact is worth a shipload of argument.
A tree is known by its fruit.

Before thou marry be sure of a house wherein to tarry.
Be slow to promise, and quick to perform.
Better to be alone than in bad company.

Charity begins at home, but does not end there.
Confine your tongue, lest it confine you.
Constant occupation prevents temptation.

Daub yourself with honey and you will have plenty of flies.
Deeds are fruit, words are but leaves.
Delays are dangerous.
Dependence is a poor trade to follow.
Despise none, despair of none.
Diligence is the mistress of success.
Diseases are the interests paid for pleasures.
Do as you would be done by.

Words of Wisdom for the People—*Continued*

Do not halloo till you are out of the wood.
Do not rip up old sores.
Do not throw your opinions in everybody's teeth.
Don't run away with more than you can carry.
Don't value a gem by what it is set in.
Do what thou oughtest, and come what can.
Drunkenness reduces a man below the standard of a brute.

Empty vessels make the greatest sound.
Everybody's business is nobody's business.
Every couple is not a pair.
Every man is the architect of his own fortune.
Every one for himself, and God for us all.   -
Experience is the mother of science.
Experience teaches fools.

Faint heart never won fair lady.
False friends are worse than open enemies.
Forgive and forget.

God helps those who help themselves.
Good words cost nothing, but are worth much.
Gossiping and lying go hand in hand.

Half a loaf is better than no bread.
Hear twice before you speak once.
He is a wise man who speaks little.
He liveth long that liveth well.
He loses nothing for the asking.
He loseth nothing that keeps God for his friend.
He plays well that wins.
He that goes a-borrowing goes a-sorrowing.
He that is angry is seldom at ease.
He that lendeth loseth double (loses both his money and friends.)
He who knows himself best esteems himself least.
He who marries for wealth doth sell his liberty.
He who rises late never does a good day's work.
He who would reap well must sow well.
Hiders are good finders.
Humility is the foundation of all virtue.

Words of Wisdom for the People—*Continued*

Idle folks have the most labor.
Idleness is the root of all evil.
If you have too many irons in the fire, some of them will burn.
Ignorance is the parent of many injuries.
It is better to do well than to say well.
It is good to begin well, but better to end well.
It is never too late to learn.
It is a wise child that knows its own father.

Judge not of men or things at first sight.

Keep thy shop and thy shop will keep thee.

Least said soonest mended.
Life is half spent before we know what it is.
Live not to eat, but eat to live.
Look before you leap.
Look twice ere you determine once.

Make hay while the sun shines.
Marry in haste and repent at leisure.
Misfortunes seldom come alone.
Modesty is the handmaid of virtue.

Necessity is the mother of invention.
Never find any thing before it is lost.
Never sound the trumpet of your own praise.
Next to love, quietness.
None so blind as those who will not see.
Nothing venture, nothing win.

Of all studies, study your present condition.
One eye-witness is better than ten hearsays.
One is not so soon healed as hurt.
One never loses by doing a good turn.
One ounce of discretion is worth a pound of wit.
Opportunity makes the thief.
Our own opinion is never wrong.

Pay as you go.
Perfection is the point at which all should aim.
Possession is nine points of the law.
Poverty parts friends.
Prevention is better than cure.
Promise little and do much.

Reckless youth makes rueful age.

Seeing is believing.
Self-preservation is the first law of nature.
Show me a liar and I will show you a thief.
Silence does seldom any harm.
Sloth is the mother of poverty.
Sooner said than done.
Spare when you are young, and spend when you are old.
Speak the truth and shame the devil.
Strike while the iron is hot.
Study to be worthy of your parents.

Tell me the company you keep, and I'll tell you who you are.
Temperance is the best physic.
The more noble the more humble.
The path of virtue is the path of peace.
They love too much that die for love.
Too much familiarity breeds contempt.
Trade is the mother of money.
Two heads are better than one.

When all is consumed, repentance comes too late.
When fortune smiles on thee, take the advantage.
When poverty comes in at the door, love flies out at the window.
Where there is a will there is always a way.
While there's life there's hope.

You cannot take blood out of a stone.

Liberty Bell

In a room on the ground floor of the old State House, Philadelphia,
is the old bell that rang out, in conjunction with human voices, the
joyful tidings of the Declaration of Independence, in July, 1776. It
was cast by Pass & Stow, Philadelphia, and was hung in the belfry of the
State House early in June, 1753. It weighed 2,080 pounds, and around
it, near it's top, were cast the words, prophetic of it's destiny. *"Pro-
claim Liberty throughout all the Land, unto all the Inhabitants thereof. Lev.
xxv. 10."* PHLAD. MDCCLIII. When the British forces approached
Philadelphia, in 1777, the bell was taken down and carried to

Allentown, to prevent it's falling into the hands of the enemy. In 1781 it was placed in the brick tower of the State House, below the original belfry, which, being of wood, had become decayed. For more than fifty years the bell participated in the celebration of the anniversary of the Declaration of Independence, when it was cracked while ringing. An effort was made to restore it's sound, the crack was cut wider, but it was unsuccessful. A new steeple and a new bell were put up in 1828. For many years the old bell remained in silent dignity in the tower, when it was taken down and placed on a platform in Independence Hall, whence it was removed to a little room opposite in 1876, and there it remains.

Railway Signal Code

One whistle signifies "down brakes." Two whistles signify "off brakes." Three whistles signify "back up." Continued whistles signify "danger." Rapid short whistles "a cattle alarm." A sweeping parting of the hands on a level with the eyes, signifies "go ahead." Downward motion of the hands with extended arms signifies "stop." Beckoning motion of one hand signifies "back." Red flag waved up the track, signifies "danger." Red flag stuck up by the roadside, signifies "danger ahead." Red flag carried on a locomotive, signifies "an engine following." Red flag hoisted at a station, is a signal to "stop." Lantern at night, raised and lowered vertically, is a signal to "start." Lantern swung at right angles across the track is a signal to "start." Lantern swung in a circle signifies "back the train."

Time on Shipboard, divided into Three Watches

First watch, 1 bell, 12:30 o'clock; 2 bells, 1:00; 3 bells, 1:30; 4 bells, 2:00; 5 bells, 2:30; 6 bells, 3:00; 7 bells, 3:30; 8 bells, 4:00.

Second Watch, 1 bell, 4:30; 2 bells, 5:00; 3 bells, 5:30; 4 bells, 6:00; 5 bells, 6:30; 6 bells, 7:00; 7 bells, 7:30; 8 bells, 8:00.

Third watch, 1 bell, 8:30; 2 bells, 9:00; 3 bells, 9:30; 4 bells, 10:00; 5 bells, 10:30; 6 bells, 11:00; 7 bells, 11:30; 8 bells, 12:00.

A watch is that part of the officers and crew of a vessel who together attend to working her for an allotted time.

States and Territories, Capitals, Term of Office and Salaries of Governors

State	Capital	Yearly Salary	Term of Office
Alabama	Montgomery	$3,000	Two Years
Arizona Ty.	Prescott	2,600	Four Years
Arkansas	Little Rock	3,000	Two Years
California	Sacramento	6,000	Four Years
Colorado	Denver	5,000	Two Years
Connecticut	Hartford	2,000	Two Years
Delaware	Dover	2,000	Four Years
Florida	Tallahassee	3,500	Four Years
Georgia	Atlanta	3,000	Two Years
Idaho Ty.	Boise City	2,600	Four Years
Illinois	Springfield	6,000	Four Years
Indiana	Indianapolis	5,000	Four Years
Iowa	Des Moines	3,000	Two Years
Kansas	Topeka	3,000	Two Years
Kentucky	Frankfort	5,000	Four Years
Louisiana	Baton Rouge	4,000	Four Years
Maine	Augusta	2,000	Two Years
Maryland	Annapolis	4,500	Four Years
Massachusettes	Boston	5,000	One Year
Michigan	Lansing	1,000	Two Years
Minnesota	St. Paul	3,300	Two Years
Mississippi	Jackson	4,000	Four Years
Missouri	Jefferson City	5,000	Four Years
Montana	Helena	5,000	Four Years
Nebraska	Lincoln	2,500	Two Years
Nevada	Carson City	5,000	Four Years
New Hampshire	Concord	1,000	Two Years
New Jersey	Trenton	5,000	Three Years
New Mexico Ty.	Santa Fe	2,600	Four Years
New York	Albany	10,000	Three Years
North Carolina	Raleigh	3,000	Four Years
North Dakota	Bismark	3,000	Two Years
Ohio	Columbus	4,000	Two Years
Oregon	Salem	1,500	Four Years
Pennsylvania	Harrisburg	10,000	Four Years
Rhode Island	Newport	1,000	One Year
South Carolina	Columbia	3,500	Two Years
South Dakota	Pierre	2,500	Two Years
Tennessee	Nashville	4,000	Two Years
Texas	Austin	4,000	Two Years
Utah Ty.	Salt Lake City	2,600	Four Years
Vermont	Montpelier	1,000	Two Years
Virginia	Richmond	5,000	Four Years
Washington	Olympia	4,000	Four Years
West Virginia	Wheeling	2,700	Four Years
Wisconsin	Madison	5,000	Two Years
Wyoming Ty.	Cheyenne	2,600	Four Years
Alaska	Sitka	3,000	Four Years
Indian Ty.	Tahlequah	2,600	Four Years

The Governor of a Territory is appointed to the office by the President of the United States; but the Governor of a State is elected by the people directly.

KINGS AND QUEENS OF ENGLAND

Name	Saxons and Danes	Acc.	D.	Rgd.
Egbert	First King of all England	827	839	12
Ethelwulf	Son of Egbert	839	858	19
Ethelbald	Son of Ethelwulf	858	860	2
Ethelbert	Second son of Ethelwulf	858	866	8
Ethelred	Third son of Ethelwulf	866	871	5
Alfred	Fourth son of Ethelwulf	871	901	30
Edward the Elder	Son of Alfred	901	925	24
Athelstan	Eldest son of Edward	925	940	15
Edmund	Brother of Athelstan	940	946	6
Edred	Brother of Edmund	946	955	9
Edwy	Son of Edmund	955	958	3
Edgar	Second son of Edmund	958	975	17
Edward the Martyr	Son of Edgar	975	979	4
Ethelred II	Half-brother of Edward	979	1016	37
Edmund Ironside	Eldest son of Ethelred	1016	1017	1
Canute	By conquest and election	1017	1035	18
Harold I	Son of Canute	1035	1040	5
Hardicanute	Another son of Canute	1040	1042	2
Edward the Confessor	Son of Ethelred II	1042	1066	24
Harold II	Brother-in-law of Edward	1066	1066	0

The House of Normandy

William I	Obtained Crown by conquest	1066	1087	21
William II	Third son of William I	1087	1100	13
Henry I	Youngest son of Wm. I	1100	1135	35
Stephen	Third son of Stephen, Count of Blois, by Adela, fourth daughter of William I	1135	1154	19

The House of York

Edward IV	His grandfather was Richard, son of Edmund, fifth son of Edward III, and his grandmother, Anne, was great granddaughter of Lionel, third son of Edw. III.	1461	1483	22
Edward V	Eldest son of Edward IV	1483	1483	0
Richard III	Younger brother of Edw. IV	1483	1485	2

The House of Plantagenet

Name		Acc.	D.	Rgd.
Henry II	Son of Geoffrey Plantagenet by Matilda, only daughter of Henry I	1154	1189	35
Richard I	Eldest surviv'g son of Henry II.	1189	1199	10
John	Sixth and youngest son of Henry II	1199	1216	17
Henry III	Eldest son of John	1216	1272	56
Edward I	Eldest son of Henry III	1272	1307	35
Edward II	Eldest surviving son of Edward I.	1307	1327	20
Edward III	Eldest son of Edward II	1327	1377	50
Richard II	Son of the Black Prince, eldest son of Edward III	1377	1399	22

The House of Lancaster

Name		Acc.	D.	Rgd.
Henry IV	Son of John of Gaunt, fourth son of Edward III	1399	1413	14
Henry V	Eldest son of Henry IV	1413	1422	9
Henry VI	Only son of Henry V. died 1471.	1422	1461	39

The House of Tudor

Name		Acc.	D.	Rgd.
Henry VII	Son of Edmund, eldest son of Owen Tudor, by Katharine, widow of Henry V; his mother Margaret Beaufort, was great-granddaughter of John of Gaunt	1485	1509	24
Henry VIII	Only surviv'g son of Henry VII.	1509	1547	38
Edward VI	Son of Henry VIII, by Jane Seymour	1547	1553	6
Mary I	Daughter of Henry VIII, by Katharine of Arragon	1553	1558	5
Elizabeth	Daughter of Henry VIII, by Anne Boleyn	1558	1603	43

The House of Stuart

Name		Acc.	D.	Rgd.
James I	Son of Mary Queen of Scots, granddaughter of James IV and Margaret, daughter of Henry VII	1603	1625	22
Charles I	Only surviving son of James I.	1625	1649	24
Commonwealth	Commonw'lth declared May 19.	1649	1653	00
	Oliver Cromwell, lord protector.	1653	1658	00
	Richd Cromwell, lord protector.	1658	1659	00

The House of Stuart—Restored

Charles II	Eldest son of Charles I	1660	1685	25
James II	Second son of Charles I, died Sept. 16, 1701 (Interregnum, Dec. 11, 1688, Feb. 13, 1689)	1685 0000	1688 1701	3 00
William III and	Son of William, Prince of Orange, by Mary, daughter of Charles I	1689	1702	13
Mary II	Eldest daughter of James II	1689	1694	6
Anne	Second daughter of James II	1702	1714	12

The House of Hanover

George I	Son of Elector of Hanover, by Sophia, daughter of Elizabeth, daughter of James I	1714	1727	13
George II	Only son of George I	1727	1760	33
George III	Grandson of George II	1760	1820	60
George IV	Eldest son of George III	1820	1830	10
William IV	Third son of George III	1830	1837	7
Victoria	Daughter of Edw'd, fourth son of George III	1837	0000	00

What Royalty Costs England

As a sample of what royalty costs the people of Great Britain alone Whitaker gives the following annuities to the Royal family :

Her Majesty, privy purse.......................£	60,000
Salaries of household.........................	131,260
Expenses of household........................	172,500
Royal bounty, etc	13,500
Unappropriated........	8,540
	£385,800
	Equals, $1,929,000

Prince of Wales.............................£	40,000
Princess of Wales.......	10,000
Prince Albert Victor..........................	10,000
Ex-Empress of Prussia.....................	8,000
Duke of Edinburgh...........................	25,000
Princess Christian of Schleswig-Holstein...	6,000
Princess Louise (Marchioness of Lorne).........	6,000
Duke of Connaught...........................	25,000
Duke of Albany..............................	25,000
Duke of Cambridge	6,000
Duchess of Mecklenburg-Strelitz.............	3,000
Duke of Cambridge	12,000
Duchess of Teck..............................	5,000
	Grand Total £566,800
	Equals, $2,834,000

Salaries per Year of the British Cabinet

Secretary of Foreign Affairs and Lord of the Treasury, $50,000; Chancellor of the Exchequer, $25,000; Lord High Chancellor, $50,000; Lord Lieutenant of Ireland, $100,000; Lord President of Privy Council, $20,000; Secretary for Colonies, $25,000; Home Secretary, $25,000. Secretary of War, $25,000; Secretary of India, $25,000; First Lord of the Admiralty, $22,500; Lord Chancellor of Ireland, $30,000; President Board of Trade, $10,000.

THE BRITISH HOUSE OF COMMONS

The House of Commons dates since Edward II and is called the lower House. The English House of Commons, at the time of the union with Scotland in 1707, consisted of 513 members; 45 were then added for Scotland, and in 1801 100 for Ireland, making the total of 658. This total number was preserved by the Reform Act (1832), as well as by the recent one ('30 and '31, Vict. cap. 102), but in each case the apportionment was altered, and it now stands—England and Wales, 493 members; Scotland, 60; and Ireland, 105 members. By the Reform Act of 1867, 11 English boroughs were totally disfranchised and 23 others lost one member each; but 25 seats were bestowed on new boroughs and universities and 28 on counties. Four boroughs with 6 seats have since been disfranchised for corrupt practices, viz., Beverly, Bridgewater, Sligo and Cashel, and in eight others, representing 12 seats, the writs are suspended, making the present number of sitting members 640 in all.

FRENCH DYNASTIES AND SOVEREIGNS

The Merovingians

Clovis, "The Hairy," King of the Salic Franks.................. 428
Childeric III., last of the race...................................... 737

The Carlvovingians

Repin, "The Short," son of Charles Martel..... 752
Charlemagne, The Great Emperor of the West.................. 768
Louis V., "The Indolent," the last of the race.................. 986

The Capets

Hugh Capet, "The Great"................................... 987
Louis IX., "St. Louis"................................. ..1226
Charles IV., "The Handsome"............................1322

The House of Bourbon

Henry IV., "The Great," King of Navarre....................1589
Louis XIII., "The Just".................................1610
Louis XIV., "The Great," Dieudonni 1643
Louis XV., "The Well-beloved".............................1715
Louis XVI. (guillotined January 21, 1793)....................1774
Louis XVII. (never reigned)...............................1793

The House of Valois

Philip VI. de Valois, "The Fortunate".........................1328
Henry III., last of the race.................................1574

The First Republic

The National Convention First Sat..............September 21, 1792
The Directory Nominated...... ....November 1, 1795

The Consulate

Bonaparte, Cambacérès, and Lebrun..............December 24, 1799
Bonaparte, Consul for 10 years........................May 6, 1802
Bonaparte, Consul for life...........................August 2, 1802

The Empire

Napoleon I. decreed Emperor.........................May 18, 1804
Napoleon II. (never reigned) died ....July 22, 1832

The Restoration

Louis XVIII. re-entered Paris...........................May 3, 1814
Charles X., deposed July 30, 1830, died..............November 6, 1836
Heir-expectant, Henry, Comte de Chambord...September 29, 1820-24

The House of Orleans

Louis Philippe, King of the French....................... 1830
    (Abdicated February 24, 1848, died August 26, 1850.)
Heir-expectant, Comte de Paris, born...............August 19, 1848

The Second Republic

Provisional Government formed...................February 22, 1848
Louis Napoleon elected President.................December 19, 1848

The Second Empire

Napoleon III. elected Emperor..................November 22, 1852
    (Deposed, September 4, 1870, died January 9, 1873.)

Third Republic

Committee of Public Defense.......................September 4, 1870
L. A. Thiers, elected President......................August 31, 1871
Marshal MacMahon, elected President...................May 24, 1873
Jules Grévy elected President.....................January 30, 1879
M. F. S. Carnot elected President..................December 3, 1887

HIGHEST TOWER IN THE WORLD

The highest tower is Eiffel Tower, at Paris, France. The iron tower, of which engineer Eiffel was the designer, is erected on the banks of the Seine River, opposite the Trocadero Palace, as a feature of the Paris Exposition of 1889. This piece of work is extraordinary, not only on account of its height (300 metres, or 984 feet) which is nearly twice the height of the Washington Monument, formerly considered the highest artificial structure in the world, but because also it is entirely of iron. It is in the form of an open framework or latticework, standing on four great "legs" or columns, each placed at the angle of a square whose sides are 375 feet long. At a point 480 feet above the ground the legs meet at a landing and from this elevation up, tapers. The total weight of the tower is about 15,400,000 pounds, or 6,875 tons, and it cost $1,000,000.

LARGEST DEPOSIT OF ANTHRACITE COAL

The largest deposit of anthracite coal in the world is in Pennsylvania.

SEVEN WONDERS OF THE WORLD

A name given to seven very remarkable objects of ancient times.

The Pyramids of Egypt; Second, the Pharos or Watch Tower at Alexandria, Egypt, built by order of Philadelphus about 280 B. C.; it was built of white marble and could be seen at a distance of 100 miles·

Third, the Walls and Hanging Gardens of Babylon. Fourth, the Temple of Diana at Ephesus; it was supposed to have been 220 years in building. Fifth, the statue at Olympia, in Ellis, sculptured in ivory and gold by Phidias, the most eminent among the ancients. Sixth, the Tomb built for Mausolus, King of Caria, by Artemesia, his Queen. Seventh, the Colossus at Rhodes; it was a brazen statue of Apollo, 70 cubits high.

THE SEVEN DOLOURS OF THE VIRGIN MARY

The seven Dolours of the Virgin Mary: It is a feast in the Roman Catholic Church, and while it bears the name of devotion to the Virgin Mary, it in reality regards those incidents in the life and passion of Christ with which his mother is most closely associated. The seven incidents are as follows: First, the prediction of Simeon. Second, the flight into Egypt. Third, the loss of Jesus in Jerusalem. Fourth, the sight of Jesus bearing his cross toward Calvary. Fifth, the sight of Jesus upon the cross. Sixth, the piercing of his side with the lance. Seventh, his burial.

Seven in the Bible

Seven is frequently used as a mystical number in the Bible, as well as among the principal nations of antiquity, such as the Persians, Egyptians, Romans, Greeks, etc.

In the Bible we have the creation completed in seven days. Every seventh year was the Sabbatic year, and seven times seven ushered in the Jubilee.

We have the seven altars, seven green withes, seven locks, seven troubles, seven eyes, which are the seven spirits of God, the perfect Holy Spirit. In light we have the seven prismatic colors, which make the pure white light.

The Seven Sleepers

According to a legend of early Christianity, seven noble youths of Ephesus having fled from persecution to a certain cavern for refuge, where they were discovered, and walled in for a cruel death, were made to fall asleep, and in that state lived for two centuries. Their names are said to have been : Maximian, Malchus, Martinian, Denis, John, Serapion and Constantine.

Seven Wise Men of Greece

These men, distinguished for their practical sagacity and wise maxims on the principles of life, flourished in Greece in the sixth century B. C. Their names were Solon, Chilo, Pittacus, Bias, Periander, Cleobulus, and Thales.

Decisive Battles of the World

The Battle of Marathon, B. C. 490, in which the Athenians, under Miltiades, defeated the Persians under Datis.

The Battle of Syracuse, B. C. 413, in which the Athenians were defeated by the Syracusans and their allies.

The Battle of Arela, B. C. 331, in which the Persians, under Darius were defeated by the Macedonians and Greeks under Alexander the Great.

The Battle of Metaurus, B. C. 207, in which the Carthagenians, under Hasdrubul, were defeated by the Romans under the Consuls Caius, Claudius, Nero and Marcus Livius.

The Battle of Philippi, B. C. 42, in which Brutus and Cassius were defeated by Octavius and Antony. The fate of the republic was decided.

The Battle of Actium, B. C. 31, in which the combined fleets of Antony and Cleopatra were defeated by Octavius, and imperialism established in the person of Octavius.

The victory of the German Arminius over the Roman Legions under Varus, A. D. 9.

The Battle of Chalons, A. D. 451, in which the Huns, under Attila, called the "Scourge of God," were defeated by the confederate armies of Romans and Visigoths.

The Battle of Tours, A. D. 732, in which the Saracens were defeated by Charles Martel. Christendom was rescued from Islam.

The Battle of Hastings, A. D. 1066, in which Harold, commanding the English army, was defeated by William the Conqueror, of Normandy.

Joan of Arc's victory over the English at Orleans, A. D. 1429.

The defeat of the Spanish Armada by the English, A. D. 1588.

The Battle of Lutzen, A. D. 1632, which decided the religious liberties of Germany. Gustavus Adolphus was killed.

The Battle of Blenheim, A. D. 1704, in which the French and Bavarians, under Marshal Tallard, were defeated by the English and their allies under Marlborough.

The Battle of Pultowa, A. D. 1709, in which Charles XII of Sweden was defeated by the Russians under Peter the Great.

The victory of the Americans under General Gates over General Burgoyne at Saratoga, A. D. 1777.

The Battle of Valmy, A. D. 1792; in which an invading army of Prussians, Austrians and Hessians, under the command of the Duke of Brunswick, were defeated by the French under Dumouriez.

Decisive Battles—*Continued*

The Battle of Waterloo, A. D. 1815, in which the French under Napoleon were defeated by the allied armies of Russia, Austria, Prussia and England under the Duke of Wellington. The last battle of Napoleon. On the 21st of October, A. D. 1805, the Great Naval Battle of Trafalgar was fought. The English, under Lord Nelson, defeated the French and Spanish. It destroyed the hopes of Napoleon as to a successful invasion of England. Lord Nelson was killed.

NOTABLE BRIDGES OF THE WORLD

Brooklyn Bridge was commenced under the directions of J. Roebling in 1870 and completed in about thirteen years. It is 3,475 feet long and 135 feet wide. The cost was nearly $15,000,000.

The Cantilever Bridge, 1874, over the Niagara, is built almost of steel. Its length is 910 feet; the total weight is 3,000 tons, and the cost was $222,000.

The Niagara Suspension Bridge was built by Roebling in 1852–55, at a cost of $400,000. It is 245 feet above the water, 1,268 feet long.

The bridge at Havre de Grace, over the Susquehanna River, is 3,271 feet long and is divided into twelve wooden spans, resting on granite piers.

The Britannia Bridge, over the Menai Strait, Wales, at an elevation of 103 feet above high water. It is of wrought iron, 1,511 feet long, and was finished in 1850. Cost $3,008,000.

The Old London Bridge was the first stone bridge. It was commenced in 1176 and completed in 1209. Its founder, Peter of Cole Church, was buried in the crypt of the chapel erected on the center pier.

The new London Bridge is constructed of granite, from the designs of L. Rennier. It was commenced in 1824, and was completed in about seven years, at a cost of $7,291,000.

Coalbrookdale Bridge, England, is the first cast-iron bridge. It was built over the Severn in 1779.

The bridge at Burton, over the Trent, was formerly the longest bridge in England, being 1,545 feet. It is now partly removed. Built in the twelfth century.

The Rialto, at Venice, Italy, is said to have been built from designs of Michael Angelo. It is a single marble arch, 98½ feet long, and as completed in 1591.

Notable Bridges—*Continued*

The Bridge of Sighs, at Venice, over which condemned prisoners were transported from the hall of judgment to the place of execution, was built in 1589.

The bridge of the Holy Trinity at Florence, Italy, was built in 1569. It is 322 feet long, constructed of white marble, and stands unrivaled as a work of art.

The covered bridge at Pavia, Italy, over the Ticino, was built in the 14th century. The roof is held up by 100 granite columns.

Sublician bridge at Rome, the oldest wooden bridge known, was erected in the seventh century. Twice rebuilt, but ruins still of the structure remain.

Rush Street Bridge, Chicago, Ill., erected in 1884 at a cost of $132,000, is the largest general traffic drawbridge in the world. Its roadway will accommodate four teams abreast, and its foot passages are seven feet wide. It is swung by steam power and lighted by electric light.

Victoria Bridge, Montreal (tubular), 9,144 feet long; Louisville, over Ohio River (truss), 5,218 feet long; Trajans, over Danube River (stone), 4,770 feet long; Cincinnati, over Ohio River (suspension), 2,220 feet long; St. Louis, over the Mississippi (steel), 2,045 feet long; Highbridge, Harlem (stone), 1,460 feet long.

AVERAGE VELOCITY OF BODIES

Bodies	per hour	per second
A man walks	3 miles or	4 feet
A horse trots	7 "	10 "
A horse runs	20 "	29 "
A steamboat moves	18 "	26 "
A sailing vessel moves	10 "	14 "
Slow rivers flow	3 "	4 "
Rapid rivers flow	7 "	10 "
A moderate wind blows	7 "	10 "
A storm moves	36 "	52 "
A hurricane moves	80 "	117 "
A rifle ball moves	1,000 "	1,466 "
Sound moves	743 "	1,142 "

Light moves 192,000 miles per second.

Electricity moves 288,000 miles per second.

MASON AND DIXON'S LINE

A name given to the southern boundary line of the Free State of Pennsylvania which formerly separated it from the Slave States of Maryland and Virginia. It was run—with the exception of about twenty-two miles—by Charles Mason and Jeremiah Dixon, two English mathematicians and surveyors, between Nov. 15, 1763, and Dec. 26, 1767. During the excited debate in Congress, in 1820, on the question of excluding slavery from Missouri, the eccentric John Randolph of Roanoke made great use of this phrase, which was caught up and re-echoed by every newspaper in the land, and thus gained a celebrity which it still retains.

THE AGE WHICH VARIOUS ANIMALS ATTAIN

Name	Years	Name	Years
Whale, is said to live	1,000	Stag	45
Elephant	400	Hawks	40
Swan	300	Pelican	40
Parrots	100	Horse	30
Raven	100	Porpoise	30
Tortoise	100	Ox	30
Camel	100	Bear	20
Eagle	100	Cow	20
Crocodile	100	Deer	20
Geese	80	Rhinoceros	20
Lion	70	Wolf	20
Beaver	50	Swine	20
Leopards	25	Llamas	15
Jaguars	25	Monkey	16
Hyenas	25	Baboon	18
Chamois	25	Hens	16
Peacock	20	Pigeon	16
Cat	15	Nightingale	15
Dog	20	Sheep	10
Fox	15	Hare	8
Blackcap	15	Squirrel	7
Queen Bee	4	Rabbit	7
Drones (months)	4	Eel	10
Working Bees (months)	6	Wren	3

The Oldest Newspaper in the World

The oldest newspaper in the world is the *Imperial Gazette*, published in the Chinese language at Pekin, China. In August, 1882, its proprietors celebrated the 1,500th anniversary of its publication.

Duties of the Engineer
(About the boiler)

Water.—Before lighting fire, fill the boiler until water runs out of the lower gauge-cock and be careful, too, that the boiler is not full. Stationary boilers are usually filled from tanks elevated above them through the regular feed-water pipes, or through a separate pipe connected to the blow-off pipe or other convenient connection to the boiler. If there is no elevated tank they may be filled with buckets through the dome, by removing the safety valve or by a hand pump suitably connected.

Building Fire under a Cold Boiler.—Do this slowly and cautiously until the gauge shows five or ten pounds of steam. Then replenish the fire to the usual heat. Many boilers are injured by a quick, flashing fire, heating the boiler unevenly, causing a great strain on the tubes and rivets through unequal expansion.

Condition of Water and Fire.—Never unbank or replenish the fire before first ascertaining how high the water is in the water gauge.

In Case of Low Water.—Smooth the fire with ashes, dirt or fresh coal or draw it out of the furnace and wet it to extinguish fire. Never put water in the furnace.

Management of Fires and Draught.—Replenish the fire quickly and a little at a time, not enough to smother the fire and do not keep the door open long enough to cool the boiler. If burning coal, spread it thinly and evenly over the surface. Leave no air holes or dark spots. This will, in fact, apply to any kind of fuel, which is frequently wasted and the boiler injured through irregular firing and cold-air draughts through the doors. Too much draught or too little causes waste of fuel and just enough is essential to the best economy. Its management is of the greatest importance. A fireman who is painstaking and observant can save his wages to his employer by closely following the suggestion outlined above and keeping his boiler clean inside and out.

Clean Boiler.—Particular care should be taken to keep the flues or tubes and connections well swept and all sheets exposed to the fire

Leaks.—When discovered in the seams, rivets, valves, cocks or else-where should be repaired at once to avoid further damage.

Blisters.—When they appear, must be promptly trimmed or patched, as they may require.

Blowing Off.—Should never be done when the boiler is hot, as the hot iron would bake the sediment into a scale. The blow-off valve should be opened frequently while at work or before commencing work and just before leaving at night. This will keep the blow-off clear, and remove all the sediment that pressure can remove. The time required to open the valve and close it again is sufficient for the purpose.

Then every week or two, when the boiler is cold, let the water run out. Open the hand-hole, and clean all sediment from the sheets over the fire before filling again. When the boiler is new, or if there is mud or other sediment in the water, this should be done often.

Boiler Compounds.—For preventing or removing scale. There are several kinds on the market, but care should be taken in selecting, as they frequently contain acids injurious to iron. A good solvent is one part of gum gatechu, and two parts of soda. A couple of pounds once a week, introduced through the hand-hole, will be found sufficient. A half-gallon of molasses pumped into the boiler with the water a half a day before cleaning out will remove scale.

Safety Valve.—Raise it often, as it is liable to become fast to it's seat.

Pressure Gauge or Steam Gauge.—Should it at any time indicate the limit of pressure, see that the safety valve is blowing off steam.

Gauge Cocks and Gauge Glass.—Keep the connection to the glass clear, by frequently shutting one end and blowing the other, so you know that the passage is clear to both steam and water, and constantly use the try-cocks to prove the glass.

In Case of Foaming.—Close the throttle long enough to show true level of water. If water is too high, blow down to first gauge-cock, as shown when the throttle is closed, check the draft, and replenish fire; if possible, lighten the load on the engine until you can pump up and blow down a few times. Then carry a steady fire and high pressure of steam. This will, usually, stop the foaming; after which, improve the first opportunity to clean the boiler.

Important.—Never carry the water too high, but carry a steady level first and second gauge-cocks, thus avoiding wrecking the engine with water in the cylinder, and insuring best economy of fuel. Keep the gauges, cocks, etc., tight and in good order, and things generally about the engine and boiler in neat condition.

Thickness of Boiler Iron and Pressure allowed by United States Laws

Pressure equivalent to the standard for a boiler 42 inches in diameter, and ¼ inch thick.

Thickness in ₁₆ths	DIAMETERS						
	34 in. lbs.	36 in. lbs.	38 in. lbs.	40 in. lbs.	42 in. lbs.	44 in. lbs.	46 in. lbs.
5	169.9	160.4	152.	144.4	137.5	131.2	125.5
4½	158.5	149.7	141.8	134.7	128.3	122.5	117.2
4¼	147.2	130.1	131.8	125.1	119.2	113.7	108.8
4	135.9	128.3	121.6	115.5	110.	105.	100.
3¾	124.5	117.6	111.4	105.9	104.8	96.2	92.
3½	113.2	106.9	101.3	96.2	91.7	87.5	83.
3	101.9	96.2	91.2	82.6	82.5	78.7	75.1

Mechanical Horse-Power

A mechanical horse power is 33,000 pounds elevated one foot per minute, and is equal to elevating 3,957 gallons of water one foot per minute.

Animal-Power

Animal-Power ; working eight hours per day, in pounds raised one foot per minute

Horse or mule, large	- 22,000	Man, as in rowing -	- 4,000
Horse or mule, small	- - 18,000	Man, on tread-wheel -	3,100
Ox, average	- - - - 12,000	Man, turning a crank -	2,600
Ass, average - - - -	- 3,500	Mechanical Horse-Power	33,000

Horse-Power, Belting will Transmit with Safety

Width of Belt in Inches	Horse-Power, per 100 feet Velocity of Belt		Width of Belt in Inches	Horse-Power per 100 feet Velocity of Belt	
	Belt Single	Double Belt		Single Belt	Double Belt
1	.09	.18	12	1.09	2.18
2	.18	.36	14	1.27	2.55
3	.27	.55	16	1.45	2.91
4	.36	.73	18	1.64	3.27
5	.45	.91	20	1.82	3.64
6	.55	1.09	22	2.00	4.00
7	.64	1.27	24	2.18	4.36
8	.73	1.46	28	2.55	5.09
9	.82	1.64	32	2.91	5.82
10	.91	1.82	36	3.27	6.55
11	1.00	2.00	40	3.64	7.27

HORSE-POWER

The following table shows the indicated horse-power for each pound average pressure on a square inch for different diameters and speeds of pistons.

Diameter of Cylinder Inches	Speed of Piston in Feet a Minute				
	240	300	400	500	600
4	.091	.114	.152	.19	.228
4½	.115	.144	.192	.24	.283
5	.144	.18	.24	.30	.36
5½	.173	.216	.288	.36	.432
6	.205	.256	.342	.428	.513
6½	.245	.307	.409	.512	.614
7	.279	.348	.466	.583	.699
7½	.321	.401	.534	.669	.802
8	.365	.456	.608	.761	.912
8½	.413	.516	.688	.86	1.032
9	.462	.577	.77	.963	1.154
9½	.515	.644	.859	1.074	1.288
10	.571	.714	.952	1.190	1.428
10½	.63	.787	1.050	1 313	1.575
11	.691	.864	1.152	1.44	1.728
11½	.754	.943	1.257	1.572	1.886
12	.820	1.025	1.366	1.708	2.050
13	.964	1.206	1.608	2.01	2.412
14	1.119	1.398	1.864	2.331	2.797
15	1.285	1.606	2.131	2.671	3.212
16	1.461	1.827	2.436	3.045	3.654
17	1.643	2.054	2.739	3.424	4.108
18	1.849	2.312	3.083	3.854	4.624
19	2.061	2.577	3.436	4.295	5.154
20	2.292	2.855	3.807	4.759	5.731
21	2.518	3.148	4.197	5.247	6.296
22	2.764	3.455	4.607	5.759	6.911
23	3.021	3.776	5.035	6.294	7.552
24	3.209	4.111	5.482	6.853	8.223
25	3.569	4.461	5.948	7.436	8.923
26	3.861	4.826	6.435	8.044	9.652
27	4.156	5.199	6.932	8.666	10.399
28	4.477	5.596	7.462	9.328	11.193

RULES FOR CALCULATING SPEED OF PULLEYS

1. The diameter of the driver and driven being given, to find the number of revolutions of the driven:

RULE.—Multiply the diameter of the driver by its number of revolutions and divide the product by the diameter of the driven; the quient will be the number of revolutions.

2. The diameter and revolutions of the driver being given to find the diameter of the driven, that shall make any given number of revolutions in the same time.

RULE.—Multiply the diameter of the driver by its number of revolutions and divide the product by the number of revolutions of the driven; the quotient will be its diameter.

3. To ascertain the size of the driver:

RULE.—Multiply the diameter of the driven by the number of revolutions you wish to make and divide the product by the revolutions of the driver; the quotient will be the size of the driver.

BELTS

Leather belts must be well protected against water, and even moisture.

India-rubber is the proper substance for belts exposed to the weather, as it does not absorb moisture, and stretch and decay.

Leather belts run with grain side to the pulley will drive 30 per cent more than if run with flesh side. The belt, as well as the pulley, adheres best when smooth and the grain side adheres best because it is smoothest. It is desirable to run the grain (hair) side of leather belts on the pulley in order that the strongest part of the belt may be subject to the least wear.

The transmitting power of a double belt is to that of single belt as 10 is to 7. In ordering pulleys the kind of belt to be used should always be specified.

Belts should be kept soft and pliable. For this purpose blood-warm tallow, dried in by heat of fire or the sun, is advised. Castor Oil Dressing is also good.

The motion of driving should run with and not against the laps of the belts.

If too great a distance is attempted, the weight of the belt will produce a very heavy sag, drawing so hard on the shaft as to produce great friction in the bearing; while at the same time the belt will have an unsteady, flapping motion, which will destroy both the belt and the machinery.

If possible to avoid it, connected shafts should never be placed one directly over the other as in such case the belt must be kept very tight to do the work. For this purpose belts should be carefully selected of well-stretched leather.

It is desirable that the angle of the belt with the floor should not exceed 45°. It is also desirable to locate the shafting and machinery so that belts should run off from each shaft in opposite directions, as this arrangement will relieve the bearings from the friction that would result when the belts all pull one way on the shaft.

The diameter of the pulleys should be as large as can be admitted.

The pulley should be a little wider than the belt required for the work.

Having properly arranged the machinery for the reception of the belts, the next thing to be determined is the length and width of the belts.

When it is not convenient to measure with the tape-line the length required, apply the following rule: Add the diameter of the two pulleys together, divide the result by 2, and multiply the quotient by 3¼, then add this product to twice the distance between the centers of the shafts, and you have the length required.

The width of belt needed depends on three conditions:
1. The tension of the belt. 2. The size of the smaller pulley and the proportion of the surface touched by the belt. 3. The speed of the belt.

The working adhesion of a belt to the pulley will be in proportion both to the number of square inches of belt contact with the surface of the pulley and also to the arc of the circumference of the pulley touched by the belt. This adhesion forms the basis of all right calculation in ascertaining the width of belt necessary to transmit a given horse-power.

STRENGTH OF BELT LEATHER

The tensile strength of good ox-hide, well tanned, has been carefully examined with the following results:

The solid leather will sustain, per inches of width..675 lbs.
At the rivet-holes of the splices, per inches of width.382 lbs.
At the lacing, per inches of width...............210 lbs.
Safe-working tension, per inches of width........ 55 lbs.
The belts are assumed to be three-sixteenths of an inch thick.

SHRINKAGE OF CASTING

Pattern-maker's rule should be for	Cast-iron, 1–8	
" " " " "	Brass 3–16	
" " " " "	Lead..... 1–8	of an inch per linear foot
" " " " "	Tin. 1–12	
" " " " "	Zinc 3–16	

WEIGHT OF LIQUIDS PER GALLON

1 Gallon	Pounds	1 Gallon	Pounds
Ale	8.33	Oil of Turpentine	7.25
Acid, Nitric	10.58	Oil, Whale	7.25
Acid, Sulphuric	15.42	Petroleum	7.35
Acid, Muriatic	10.	Vinegar	8.43
Alcohol, Commerce	6.74	Salt Water	8.59
Alcohol, Proof Spirit	7.9375	Tar	8.43
Naphtha	7.08	Distilled Water	8.33
Oil, Linseed	7.75		

FACTS FOR BUILDERS

1,000 shingles laid 4 inches to the weather will cover 100 square feet of surface, and 5 pounds of shingle nails will fasten them on.

One-fifth more siding and flooring is needed than the number of square feet of surface to be covered, because of the lap in the siding and matching. 100 laths will cover 70 yards of surface, and 11 pounds of lath nails will nail them on. 8 bushels of good lime, 16 bushels of sand, and 1 bushel of hair will make enough good mortar to plaster 100 square yards.

A cord of stone, 3 bushels of lime, and a cubic yard of sand, will lay 100 cubic feet of wall.

Five courses of brick will lay one foot in height on a chimney, 8 bricks in a course will make a flue 4 inches wide and 12 inches long, and 16 bricks in a course will make a flue 8 inches wide and 16 inches long.

Cement, one bushel, and sand, two bushels, will cover 3½ square yards 1 inch thick, 4½ square yards ¾ inch thick, and 6¾ square yards ½ inch thick; 1 bushel cement and 1 bushel of sand will cover 2¼ square yards 1 inch thick, 3 square yards ¾ inch thick, and 4½ square yards ½ inch thick.

Number of Bricks Required in Wall per Square Foot Face of Wall

Thickness of Wall	No.	Thickness of Wall	No.
4 inches	7½	24 inches	46
8 "	15	28 "	52
12 "	22½	32 "	60¾
16 "	30	36 "	67
20 "	37½	42 "	75½

The Number of Bricks Required to Construct any Building

Reckoning 7 bricks to each superficial foot. Example—Required the number of bricks in 100 superficial feet of wall, 12 inches thick. Under 12 inch, and opposite 100, you will find the answer, 2,250, the number of bricks required.

Super-ficial Feet of Wall	Number of Bricks to Thickness of					
	4 inch	8 inch	12 inch	16 inch	20 inch	24 inch
1	7	15	23	30	38	45
2	15	30	45	60	75	90
3	23	45	68	90	113	135
4	30	60	90	120	150	180
5	38	75	113	150	188	225
6	45	90	135	180	225	270
7	53	105	158	210	263	315
8	60	120	180	240	300	360
9	68	135	203	270	338	405
10	75	150	225	300	375	450
20	150	300	450	600	750	900
30	225	450	675	900	1,125	1,350
40	300	600	900	1,200	1,500	1,800
50	375	750	1,125	1,500	1,875	2,250
60	450	900	1,350	1,800	2,250	2,700
70	525	1,050	1,575	2,100	2,625	3,150
80	600	1,200	1,800	2,400	3,000	3,600
90	675	1,350	2,025	2,700	3,375	4,050
100	750	1,500	2,250	3,000	3,750	4,500
200	1,500	3,000	4,500	6,000	7,500	9,000
300	2,250	4,500	6,750	9,000	11,250	13,500
400	3,000	6,000	9,000	12,000	15,000	18,000
500	3,750	7,500	11,250	15,000	18,750	22,500
600	4,500	9,000	13,500	18,000	22,500	27,000
700	5,250	10,500	15,750	21,000	26,250	31,500
800	6,000	12,000	18,000	24,000	30,000	36,000
900	6,750	13,500	20,250	27,000	33,750	40,500
1,000	7,500	15,000	22,500	30,000	37,500	45,000

VALUE OF A TON OF GOLD OR SILVER

A ton of pure gold is worth $602,799.21.
$1,000,000 gold coin weighs 3,685.8 pounds.
A ton of silver is worth $37,704.84.
$1,000,000 silver coin weighs 58,929.9 pounds.

Hints to Painter, Glazier and Paper-Hanger

One pound of paint will cover about four superficial yards the first coat and about six yards each additional coat.

About one pound of putty for stopping, will be required for every twenty yards.

One gallon of tar and one pound of pitch will cover about twelve yards of superficial the first coat, and about seventeen yards each additional coat.

White Paint

20 pounds white lead, 6 pints linseed oil, 2 pints turpentine and 1 pound litharge, will cover about 100 square yards.

Black Paint

28 pounds black paint, 10 pints linseed oil, 2 pints turpentine, and 1 pound litharge will cover about 160 square yards.

Distemper

112 pounds whiting, 28 pounds dry white lead, and 7 pounds glue, mixed with boiling water.

Slating

A square of slate or slating is 100 superficial feet.

In measuring, the width of the eaves is allowed at the widest part. Hips, valleys, and cutting are to be measured lineal, and six inches width extra is allowed.

The pitch of a slate roof should not be less than one inch height to four inches in length.

Table of Approximate Numbers in Decimals for Circles, Spheres, Squares, Cubes, etc.

Diameter of a circle multiplied by 3.1416 equals circumference.

Radius of a circle multiplied by 6.283185 equals circumference.

Square of the radius of a circle multiplied by 3.1416 equals area.

Square of the diameter of a circle multiplied by 0.7854 equals area.

Square of the circumference of a circle multiplied by 0.07958 equals area.

Half the circumference of a circle multiplied by half its diameter equals area.

Circumference of a circle multiplied by 0.159155 equals radius.

Square root of the area of a circle multiplied by 0.56419 equals radius.

Circumference of a circle multiplied by 0.31831 equals diameter.

Square root of the area of a circle multiplied by 1.12839 equals diameter.

Diameter of a circle multiplied by 0.86 equals side of inscribed equilateral triangle.

Diameter of a circle multiplied by 0.7071 equals side of an inscribed square.

Circumference of a circle multiplied by 0.226 equals side of an inscribed square.

Radius of a circle multiplied by 6.2832 equals circumference.

Circumference of a circle multiplied by 0.282 equals side of an equal square.

Diameter of a circle multiplied by 0.8862 equals side of an equal square.

Base of a triangle multiplied by one-half the altitude equals area.

Multiply both diameters and 0.7854 together equals area of an ellipse.

Surface of a sphere multiplied by one-sixth of its diameter equals solidity.

Circumference of a sphere multiplied by its diameter equals surface.

Square of the diameter of a sphere multiplied by 3.1416 equals surface.

Square of the circumference of a sphere multiplied by 10.3183 equals surface.

Cube of the diameter of a sphere multiplied by 0.5236 equals solidity.

Cube of the radius of a sphere multiplied by 4.1888 equals solidity.

Cube of the circumference of a sphere multiplied by 0.016887 equals solidity.

Square root of the surface of a sphere multiplied by 0.56419 equals diameter.

Square root of the surface of a sphere multiplied by 1.772454 equals circumference.

Cube root of the solidity of a sphere multiplied by 1.2407 equals diameter.

Cube root of the solidity of a sphere multiplied by 3.8978 equals circumference.

Radius of a sphere multiplied by 1.1547 equals side of an inscribed cube.

Square root of (⅓ of the square of) the diameter of a sphere equals side of inscribed cube.

Area of its base multiplied by ⅓ of its altitude equals solidity of a cone or pyramid whether round, square, or triangular.

Area of one of its sides multiplied by 6 equals surface of a cube.

Altitude of trapezoid multiplied by half the sum of its parallel sides equals area.

Square root of area of a circle multiplied by 3.54 equals circumference.

Radius multiplied by diameter of a circle multiplied by 1.57 equals area.

Number of degrees multiplied by radius multiplied by .0174 equals length of arc.

Square of diameter of sphere multiplied by .31416 equals convex surface.

Diameter of sphere multiplied by .806 equals dimensions of equal cube.

Diameter of sphere multiplied by .6667 equals length of equal cylinder.

Square inches multiplied by .00695 equals square feet.

Cubic inches multiplied by .00058 equals cubic feet.

Cubic feet multiplied by .03704 equals cubic yards.

Cylindrical inches multiplied by .0004546 equals cubic feet.

Cylindrical feet multiplied by .02909 equals cubic yards.

Degrees of Heat and Cold Required to Freeze, Melt, and Boil the Following Substances

Air furnace melts	3300	above zero.
Antimony melts	950	"
Bismuth melts	476	"
Brass melts	1900	"
Cadium melts	600	"
Cast Iron melts	3479	"
Copper melts	2160	"
Gold melts	1983	"
Glass melts	2377	"
Gutta Percha melts	150	"
Iron, wrought, melts	3980	"
Iron, bright red heat in the dark	752	"

Degrees of Heat, Etc.—*Continued*

Iron, red hot in twilight................ 884 above zero
Heat, cherry red........................1500   "
Heat, bright red................. 1860   "
Heat, red, visible by day..............1077   "
Heat, white...........................2900   "
Lead melts......................... 590   "
Lard melts............................ 96   "
Silver melts..........................1850   "
Steel melts...................... 2500   "
Platinum melts.......................3080   "
Tin melts............................ 424   "
Zinc melts............................ 740   "
Ice melts............................. 35   "

THE SPECIFIC GRAVITIES OF BODIES

Barometer, 30 inches; Fahrenheit's Thermometer, 60°

(From the Work of Drs. Thompson, Young and Ure)

Platinum................22.069	Steel.....................7.833
Gold....................19.360	Iron (cast) 7.645
Quicksilver..............13.568	Tin......................7.320
Lead....................11.352	Glass (crystal)...........3.150
Silver...................10.474	Granite..................3.000
Copper.................. 8.878	Marble (Parian)..........2.838
Brass 8.396	Flint....................2.570
Brick 2.000	Oak (English).............760
Nitre................... 1.900	Walnut...................671
Ivory 1.825	Cedar....................613
Brimstone 1.810	Elm.....................600
Coal.................... 1.250	Willow...................585
Boxwood................ 1.030	Fir......................550
Sea Water.............. 1.026	Poplar 383
Common Water.......... 1.000	Cork....................240

Degrees of Cold at which the following Articles Freeze

Milk freezes..................................29 above zero
Strong wine freezes..........................20   "
Water freezes................................32   "
Turpentine (spirits) freezes........... 15   "

Degrees of Heat at which the following Articles Boil

Alchohol boils.	175 above zero
Blood Heat.	98 "
Linseed Oil boils.	600 "
Petroleum boils.	305 "
Quicksilver boils.	622 "
Quicksilver volatilizes.	680 "
Water boils.	210 "
Water in vacuo boils.	98 "

WEIGHT OF A CUBIC FOOT OF EARTH, STONE, METAL, WOOD, ETC.

Article	Avoirdupois Pounds	Article	Avoirdupois Pounds
Air (at the sea level)	.07529	Alcohol	49
Alum	107	Antimony	418
Asbestos (starry)	192	Ash Wood	53
Bismuth (cast)	613	Brass (cast)	524
Bronze	513	Brass (wire)	534
Brick (common)	102	Brass (gun metal)	543
Beach Wood	46	Brandy	58
Bay Wood	51	Beer	65
Blood	66	Copper (cast)	549
Cobalt (cast)	488	Copper (sheet)	557
Clay	120	Copper (wire)	554
Cork	15	Coal, Lehigh	56
Charcoal (hardwood)	18.5	Coal, Lackawanna	50
Charcoal (softwood)	18	Coal, anthracite	89
Cider	35	Coal, cannel	77
Chestnut	38	Cedar Wood	35
Chalk	174	Earth (loose)	94
Ebony	83	Elm Wood	44
Firebrick	137	Gold (pure)	1.203¾
Granite	165	Gold (standard)	1.102
Grindstones	133	Gold (hammered)	1.210
Glass	180	Glass (window)	165
Hickory (pignut)	49	Hay (bale)	9
Hickory (shell-bark)	43	Hay (pressed)	25

Weight of a Cubic Foot, Etc.—*Continued*

Article	Avoirdupois Pounds	Article	Avoirdupois Pounds
Honey	90	Iron (wrought)	486
Ice	57.5	Iron (plates)	481
Lead (cast)	709	Iron (cast)	450
Lead (rolled)	711	Lignum Vitæ Wood	83
Limestone	165	Logwood	57
Mercury (fluid)	848	Marble	171
Mercury (solid)	977	Marble (Italian)	169
Millstone	155	Marble (Vermont)	165
Mud	102	Milk	64
Marl (mean)	109	Maple Wood	47
Mortar	110	Mahogany	66
Nickel (cast)	487	Oak (English)	52
Oil, Olive	57	Oak (Live, seasoned)	67
Oil, Whale	57.7	Oak (Canadian)	54
Oil, Linseed	59	Oak (American White)	45
Platinum (pure)	1.218	Port Wine	62
Platinum (hammered)	1.271	Paving Stone	151
Plaster of Paris	73.5	Pine (yellow)	38
Plumbago	131	Pine (white)	34
Peat	375 to 83	Pine (pitch)	43
Poplar Wood	46	Pine (red)	37
Rock Crystal	170	Red Lead	558
Red Hickory	52	Silver (pure)	654
Steel (soft)	489	Silver (hammered)	656
Steel (plates)	487	Silver (standard)	658
Slate	167	Sandstone	130
Sand	95	Sand (coarse)	112
Steel	490	Stone (common)	158
Sulphur	127	Steam (not under pressure)	.03689
Salt (common)	133	Spruce Wood	31
Tin	455	Type Metal	653
Tar	63	Tallow	59
Vinegar	67	Water (fresh)	62
Water (Dead Sea)	77	Water (sea)	64
Willow Wood	36	Zinc	429

Common Mining Terms (Dictionary)

Adit.—A level; a horizontal drift or passage from the surface into a mine.

Alluvium.—A deposit of loose gravel between the superficial covering of vegetable mold and subjacent rocks.

Amalgam.—Gold or silver combined with quicksilver.

Arastra (Mexican).—A circular combination in which ore is ground to powder by attrition of heavy stones.

Assaying.—Finding the percentage of a given metal in ore or bullion.

Assessment.—Amount levied on capital stock.

Barren Contract.—A contract vein, or a place in the contract vein, which has no mineral.

Base Bullion.—Precious metals contained in lead.

Bedrock.—The formation underlying pay-dirt.

Blende.—An ore of zinc, consisting of zinc and sulphur.

Blind Lode.—A lode having no outcrop.

Blossom Rock.—Float ore, found upon the surface or near where lodes or ledges outcrop, and from which they have become detached.

Bonanza.—Fair weather; a mine said to *en bonanza* when it is yielding a profit. It is a Spanish term meaning good-luck.

Breasting Ore.—Taking ore from the face, breast or end of a tunnel.

Bullion.—Precious metals, gold and silver, etc., not coined.

Cage.—The elevator used for hoisting and lowering the ore cars, men and materials of a mine.

Cap Rock.—Formation overlaying the ore or vein stone.

Carbonate.—A geological formation which carries silver ore, and from 5 to 70 per cent. of lead.

Carboniferous.—Containing coal.

Chlorides.—A compound of chlorine and silver.

Chute.—An inclined channel through which ore slides.

Chopping.—The rock that appears on the surface indicating the presence of a lode.

Claim.—A piece of land 25 to 300 feet wide and 1,500 feet long, which the government sells to the man who finds mineral within its limits.

Conglomerate.—Pudding stones, composed of gravel and pebble cemented together.

Contact.—A touching, meeting or junction of two different kinds of rock, a porphyry and slate.

Contact Vein.—A vein along the contact plane of, or between, two dissimilar rock masses.

Cord of Ore.—128 cubic feet of broken ore; about seven tons in quartz rock.

Country Rock.—Rock on either side of a lode or ledge, usually barren; the permanent rock inclosing a vein.

Crevice.—A narrow opening, resulting from a split or crack; a fissure.

Cribbing.—A timber or plank lining of a shaft; the confining of a wall-rock.

Cross Cut.—A level driven across the course of a vein.

Cupriferous.—Containing copper.

Debris.—Sediment from mines.

Denudation.—Rocks laid bare by running water or other agencies.

Deposit.—A body of ore distinct from a ledge.

Diggings.—Name applied to placers being worked.

Diluvium.—A deposit of superficial sand, loam, gravel, pebbles, etc.

Dip.—The slope, pitch or angle which a vein makes with the plane of the horizon.

Drift.—A horizontal passage underground.

Dump.—The pile of ore or debris taken from mines, or tailings from sluicing.

End Lines.—The lines bounding the ends of a claim.

Face.—End of level or tunnel against the ore or rock.

Fathom.—Six feet square on the vein.

Feeder.—A small vein joining a larger one.

Fissure Vein. A fissure or crack in the earth's crust filled with mineral matter.

Float.—Loose rock or isolated masses of ore, or ore detached from the original formation.

Flume.—A boxing or piping for carrying water.

Flux.—The flow of the ore in the furnace of the smelter.

Foot-wall.—The layer of rock immediately under the vein.

Forfeiture.—A failure to comply with the laws prescribing the quantity of work.

Free Gold.—Gold easily separated from the quartz or dirt.

Galena.—Lead ore; sulphur and lead.

Gangue.—The substance inclosing and accompanying the ore in a vein.

Gash Vein.—A vein wide above and narrow below.

Geode. A cavity studded around with crystals or mineral matter, a rounded stone containing such a cavity.

Grizzly.—Bars set in a flume to strain out the large stones used in hydraulic mining.

Gulch.—A ravine.

Hanging Wall.—The layer of rock or wall over a lode.

Heading.—The vein above the drift.

Headings.—In placer mining, the mass or gravel above the head of sluice.

High Grade Ore.—Ore which runs more silver than twenty ounces to the ton, with 50 or more per cent of lead.

Horse.—A mass of rock matter occurring in or between the branches of a vein.

Inch of Water.—About two and a half cubic feet per minute; the water that will run out of an opening one inch square.

Incline.—A slanting shaft.

Jumping a Claim.—Relocating a claim on which the required work has been done.

Level.—A tunnel cut on the vein from the main tunnel.   A drift.

Ledge.—A vein or lode.

Little Giant.—A movable nozzle attached to hydraulic pipes.

Locate.—To establish the possessory right to a mining claim.

Lode.—A metallic vein.

Low Grade Ore.—Ore which runs below twenty ounces of silver to the ton, fifty per cent of the ton being lead.

Mill Run.—A test of quality of ore after reduction.

Outcrop.—That portion of a vein appearing at the surface.

Pan or Panning.—Usually to wash the dirt from the free gold with a pan, the pan resembles an ordinary milk-pan.

Patch.—A small placer claim.

Petering.—The ore giving out.

Pitch.—The same as a dip.

Piping.—Washing gravel in a hydraulic claim by discharging water upon it through a nozzle.

Placer.—A gravelly place where gold is found; includes all forms of mineral deposits, excepting veins in place.

Pocket.—A rich spot in a vein or deposit; sometimes an entire claim contains but one or two pockets.

Porphyry.—A rock consisting of a compact base, usually feldspathic, through which crystals of feldspar are disseminated.

Primary or Primitive Rocks.—Consist of the various kinds of slate, quartz, serpentine, granite and gneiss; they are the lowest group of rocks, are irregularly crystallized, and contain a few animal relics.

Prospecting.—Hunting for mineral lodes or placers.

Pulp.—Pulverized ore in the lixiviation process.

Reducing.—Separating from foreign substances; the reduction of ores consists in extracting from them the metals they contain.

Salting a Mine.—Placing mineral or ore in barren places to swindle.

Shaft.—A vertical or inclined excavation for purpose of prospecting or working mines.

Side Lines.—The lines which bound the sides of a claim.

Slag.—Scum; dross; the excrement of a metal; vitrified cinders; waste from the smelters.

Slimes.—The finest of the crushed ore and gangue from mills.

Sluices.—Boxes or troughs through which gold-bearing gravel is washed.

Smelting.—Reducing the ores in furnaces to metals.

Soft Carbonate.—Silver-bearing mineral so soft that it can be readily taken out with a pick and shovel. It is usually sand impregnated with mineral, the mineral having been carbonated or oxydized.

Stamps.—Machines for crushing ores.

Stope.—A body or column of mineral left by running drifts about it.

Stoping.—The act of breaking down a stope and excavating it with a pick.

Strata.—A series of beds of rock.

Stull.—Platforms of timbers between levels for strengthening the mine by supporting the walls, and for storing ore and depositing wall rock and waste material upon.

Stull Timbers.—The large timbers placed across the vein or lode from one wall to another, to support the lagging upon which the ore or waste is placed.

Strike.—A fiud; a valuable mineral development made in an unexpected manner.

Sulphuret.—Combination of sulphur with a metallic, earthy or alkaline base.

Sump or Sumph.—A pit sunk at the bottom of a mine to collect the water. It can be the bottom of a shaft.

Tailings.—The auriferous earth that has once been washed and deprived of the greater portion of the gold it contained.

Tunnel. A level, driven at right angles to the vein which its object is to reach.

Vein.—Aggregations of mineral matter in fissures of rocks.

Walls.—The sides next to the lode.

Wash.—The first geological formation, being composed of earth, sand, gravel, and other mineral "washed" down from the mountains during a long series of ages.

Whim.—A machine for raising ores and refuse.

Wizen.—A shaft sunk from one level to the other.

Distances Sound May be Heard

Human Voice...................... .... 150 yards
Rifle Shot... ..... . 5,300 yards
Military Band Playing....... .... 5,200 yards
Cannon ....35,000 yards

Strength of Ice of Various Thicknesses

Ice two inches thick will bear men or infantry to walk on.

Ice four inches thick will bear cavalry or light guns.

Ice six inches thick will bear teams with moderate load or heavy field guns.

Ice eight inches thick will bear teams with very heavy loads, and sledges.

Ice ten inches thick will sustain a pressure of 1,000 pounds per square foot.

A cubic foot of ice weighs 57.5 pounds.

Dates of Dignities

The first English Duke was Edward, the Black Prince; he was created Duke of Cornwall by his father, Edward III, in 1337.

The title Marquis was first bestowed by Richard II on his favorite, Robert de Vere, Earl of Oxford, created Marquis of Dublin in 1386.

The Saxon titles of Alderman or Earl and Thane were changed into Earl and Baron by William I. The title of Viscount was long in use in France before it was bestowed on any person in England; the first person who held it was John Beaumont, created Viscount Beaumont and Count of Boulogne in France in 1440.

The order of Baronets was established by James I in 1611 and exists only in British Dominions.

The Saxons in the fifth and sixth centuries founded the Heptarchy, meaning the seven States, though there really were nine; these were all subdued by Egbert, King of Wessex, who, in consequence, took the title of King of England in 827.

The Norman Kings, beginning with William I in 1066, were also Dukes of Normandy.

Henry II, in 1172, styled himself Lord of Ireland, which title Henry VIII changed into King in 1541.

INVENTIONS AND DISCOVERIES

Accordeon—Invented by Damian, a Viennese, A. D. 1829.

Actinometer—Invented by Sir John Herschel, A. D. 1825.

Æolian Harp—Invented by Athanasius Kircher (German), A.D. 1653.

Air Brakes for railway cars—Invented by George Westinghouse, (American), A. D. 1871.

Air Gun—Invented by Marin, of Lesseau, Normandy, A. D. 1408.

Air Pump—Invented by Otto von Guericke, of Magdeburg, A. D. 1654.

Alum—Manufactured at Smyrna in the 13th century.

Aluminium—A metal, discovered by F. Wohler, A. D. 1827.

Anæsthesia—Discovered by Dr. Horace Wells, A. D. 1884.

Anchor—First forged in England, A. D. 578, invented by Anacharsis 594 B. C.

Anemometer—Invented by Wolfius, A. D. 1709.

Antimony—A metal, first extracted from the ore by Basilius Valentinus, A. D. 1490.

Arsenic—Discovered by Schroder, A. D. 1694.

Automatic Circuit Breaker—For Electro-Harmonic, in telegraphy, by C. Gray, A. D. 1876.

Automatic Valve Gear, for Newcomen steam engine, invented by Humphrey Patten, 1713.

Backgammon—Invented by Palamedes of Greece about 1224 B. C.

Balloon—The first inception, by Jesuit Francis Lana, A. D. 1670.

Bank—The first mention of it occurs at Rome 352 B. C.

Barometer—Was invented by Torricelli, A. D. 1643.

Bassoon—Invented by **Alfra**nio in A. D. 1539.

Bayonet—Invented in Bayonne, France, A. D. 1640.

Bellows—Invented by Anacharsis, 593 B. C.

Bismuth—A metal, by Basilius Valentinus in the 15th century.

Blood Circulation—Discovered by Dr. William Harvey, A. D. 1617.

Bombs—Invented at Venlo, Holland, in 1495.

Borax—Its chemical nature was discovered by Geoffrey, A. D. 1732.

Brandy—Manufactured in France early in the 14th century.

Bromine—Discovered by Balard of France, A. D. 1826.

Bullets—Made of stone were in use A. D. 1514.

Bullets—Made of iron are mentioned A. D. 1550.

Bullets—Made of lead before the 17th century.

Butter—Was used as food by the ancient Hebrews.

Butter, Artificial—Oleomargarine, invented by M. Mege Monries, Paris, A. D. 1869.

Cable Railways, Underground—Invented by A. S. Hallidie, San Francisco, Cal., A. D. 1871.

Cadmium—A metal discovered by Friedrich Stromeyer of Gottingen, A. D. 1818.

Caesium—A metal discovered by Kirchoff and Bunsen, A. D. 1860-61.

Calcium—A metal first isolated by Sir Humphrey Davy, A. D. 1808.

Caliper Compass—Invented in Nuremberg, A. D. 1540.

Calomel—Mentioned by Crollius in the 17th century, but undoubtedly known at an earlier period.

Camera Obscura—Said to have been invented in the 16th century by Baptisa Porta; invention claimed by some for Roger Bacon, A. D. 1290

Cannon—Said to have been used in the 12th and 13th centuries by the Moors; were used by the Spaniards, A. D. 1309, at the taking of Gibraltar; were used by Edward III of England, A. D. 1327, in his campaigns against the Scots; were used by the French, A. D. 1338, at the siege of Puy Guillaume. Cannon first made for iron balls A. D. 1440.

Mortars came into use, A. D. 1435, at the siege of Naples.

Howitzers came into use, A. D. 1697, at the siege of Ath.

Carronades were introduced about A. D. 1779.

Brass Cannon were cast in England by John Owen, A. D. 1535.

Camel Machine—·Invented by Bakker about 1688.

Carbon—Discovered by Antoine Lavoisier of France, A. D. 1788.

Carbonic Acid Gas—discovered by Dr. Black A. D. 1757; liquefied by Faraday, A. D. 1823.

Celluloid Billiard Balls—Invented by J. W. and I. S. Hyat, A. D. 1869.

Chloral—First obtained by Liebig, A. D. 1831.

Chlorine—First obtained by Scheele, A. D. 1774.

Chloroform—Discovered by Samuel Guthrie of Sacketts Harbor, N. Y., A. D. 1831.

Chromium—A metal discovered by Vauquelin, A. D. 1797.

Chronometer—First experiment with chronometers on a voyage to the coast of Guinea by Major Holmes, A. D. 1665.

Clarionets—Invented by John Christopher Denner of Leipsic, A. D. 1690.

Clock—Invented in the 6th century by Boethius.

Water Clocks—Invented by Scipio Nasica, 159 B. C.

Cobalt—Discovered as a metal by Brandt, A. D. 1733.

Coin—Brass money is spoken of by Homer as existing 1184 B. C.; bronze was coined in China 1120 B. C.; first copper and silver money was coined by Pheidon, King of Argos in Ægina, 895 B. C.; tin coin was coined by Dionysius of Syracuse; gold was first coined in Rome 207 B. C.; leaden coin is current in the Burman Empire; platinum was coined in Russia, A. D. 1828–1845.

Columbium—A metal discovered by Mr. Hatchett, A. D. 1801.

Cotton Gin—Invented by Eli Whitney, A. D. 1793.

Cyanogen—A gas discovered by Gay-Lussac, A. D. 1815.

Diamonds—The mines of Golconda, India, were discovered A. D. 1534.

Diamond Drills—Invented by Rudolphe Leschot, A. D. 1864.

Dice—Invented by Palamedes about 1224 B. C.　　·

Didymium—A metal discovered by Mosander, A. D. 1841.

Diving Bell—First used in Europe, A. D. 1509.

Drum—An Oriental invention introduced by the Moors into Spain, A. D. 713.

Dynamite—Invented by Ascagne Sobrero, 1846.

Electricity—The electrical properties of certain bodies were discovered about 600 B. C., by Thales of Miletus.

Electric Light—Invented by C. F. Bush, 1879; T. A. Edison, 1879.

Electric Light Carbon—Invented by M. Paul Jablochkoff, Paris, 1877.

Electric Railway—Invented by T. A. Edison, 1881.

Electrotype—Invented by Professor Jacobi in 1839.

Erbium—A metal discovered by Mosander, A. D. 1843.

Eudiometer—Invented by Dr. Priestly, A. D. 1772.

Flute—Known to the ancient Greeks.

French Horn—Was invented in the 18th century.

Galvanic Battery—First constructed by Volta, A. D. 1800.

Gas (Illuminating)—Made by Dr. Clayton about A. D. 1735.

Gas Meter—Invented by Mr. Clegg, A. D. 1815.

Geography—Known first as a study to the Romans.

Geometry—Origin ascribed to the Egyptians.

Glass—Discovered by the Phœnicians.

Glycerine—Discovered by Scheele, A. D. 1789.

Gold—A metal known as old as history.

Guillotine—Invented by J. I. Guillotin of Paris.

Gun Cotton—Discovered by Professor Schonbein of Basel, Switzerland, A. D. 1846.

Gunpowder—Known to some Hindoo tribes, B. C. 355.

Harmonium—Invented by Grenie, A. D. 1810.

Hats—First made by a Swiss at Paris, A. D. 1404.

Heliometer—Invented by Bouguer, A. D. 1747.

Hydraulic Ram—Invented by Montgolfier in the 18th century.

Hydraulic Press—Invented by Pascal; constructed by Joseph Bramak, A. D. 1796.

Hydrogen—Discovered in the 16th century by Paracelsus.

Indium—A metal discovered by Reich and Ritcher of Frieberg, Saxony, A. D. 1863.

Iridium—Discovered by Descotils, A. D. 1803.

Iron—A metal known to the ancients.

Lanthanium—A metal discovered by Mosander, A. D. 1841.

Lead—A metal known to the ancients.

Lightning Rods—Invented by B. Franklin, 1752.

Lithium—A metal first obtained by Day, A. D. 1818.

Locomotive—Invented by Watt, 1759.

Lyre—The earliest known of all stringed instruments.

Magic Lantern—Invented by Athanasius Kircher.

Magnesium—The metal first obtained by Bussy, A. D. 1830.

Magnet—The properties of the loadstone were discovered by the Greeks.

Manganese—First isolated by Gahn, A. D. 1774.

Mariner's Compass—Invention claimed by the Chinese for the Emperor Hong-ti, a grandson of Noah, about 2634 B. C.

Matches, Lucifer—Invented by Godfrey Hanckurtz, A. D. 1680.

Melodeon—Invented by Jeremiah Carhart, A. D. 1836.

Mercury—Known from the earliest ages.

Microscope—It was invented by Tansen, A. D. 1590.

Mirrors—Invented by the Venetians with a coating of tinfoil and mercury on the glass in the 16th century.

Mower and Reaper—Suggested by the ancients.

Musket—The first portable firearm, called the bombard, A. D. 1468. The Arquebuse came into use about A. D. 1480. The Musket was used A. D. 1521. The Wheel Lock was invented at Nuremberg about A. D. 1517. The Flint Lock came into use about A. D. 1692. Percussion Caps came into general use between 1820 and 1830.

Nails—First machine for cutting nails was invented in New York, A. D. 1794.

Nickel—A metal discovered by Cronstedt, A. D. 1751.

Nitric Acid—First obtained by Raymond Sully, A. D. 1287.

Nitrogen—Discovered by Rutherford, A. D. 1772.

Observatories—The Tower of Babel, erected 2247 B. C.

Omnibus—First appeared in Paris, A. D. 1825.

Oratorio—Origan ascribed to St. Philip Neri, A. D. 1550.

Organs—Invention ascribed to Archimedes about 220 B. C.

Osmiuno—A metal discovered by Tennant, A. D. 1803.

Oxygen—Discovered by Priestley in England, A. D. 1774.

Padlock—Invented by Bechar at Nuremberg, A. D. 1540.

Palladium—A metal discovered by Wollasten, A. D. 1803.

Paper—From fibrous matter by the Chinese, A. D. 95; first made from cotton, A. D. 1000; first paper made from rags, A. D. 1319.

Pens—From quills, used about A. D. 553; steel pens were first made by Mr Wise of England, A. D. 1803.

Phonograph—Invented by T. A. Edison, A. D. 1878.

Phonography—Invented by Isaac Pitman of England, A. D. 1837.

Photographing Objects in Motion—Invented by E. J. Muybridge of San Francisco, Cal., A. D. 1879.

Phosphorus—Discovered by Brandt of Hamburg, A. D. 1669.

Photography—First known in the 16th century; the Daguerreotype process discovered by M. Daguerre, A. D. 1839; producing negative photographs, invented by H. F. Tabbot, A. D. 1839; collodion was used by F. Archer, A. D. 1851.

Piano Forte—Invented by Cristofali, A. D. 1711.

Pistols—Known before the middle of the 16th century.

Platinum—Discovered by Don Antonio Ulloa, A. D. 1735.

Potassium—Obtained in a metallic state by Sir Humphrey Davy, A. D. 1807.

Printing—Was practiced by the Chinese 50 B. C.

Printing Press—The inventor of the hand press is unknown; cylinder press invented by Mr. Nicholson, A. D. 1790.

Prussic Acid—Discovered by Dissbach (German), A. D. 1709.

Pump—Invention of valve pump by Ctesibius of Alexandria, 224 B. C.

Quinine—Discovered by Pellitier and Caventou, A. D. 1820.

Rifle—Invented in the 15th century by Gaspard Zollner.

Rubidium—A metal discovered by Bunsen and Kirchoff, A. D. 1860.

Ruthenium—A metal observed by Professor Osman in the Ural Mountains.

Saddles—Were used first in the 13th century.

Safety Lamp—Invented by Sir Humphrey Davy, A. D. 1815.

Saw—According to Pliny, invented by Dædalus.

Screw—Known to the Greek.

Sewing Machine—Invented by Elias Howe, Jr., A. D. 1846.

Silver—Known to the ancients.

Soap—An invention of the Gauls.

Sodium—A metal first obtained by Sir Humphrey Davy, A. D. 1807.

Spectacles—Invented by Alexander de Spina, A. D. 1285.

Spinning Wheel—Invented 1330.

Spinning Jenny—Invented by Hargreaves, A. D. 1767.

Steamboat—Invented by Robert Fulton, 1807.

Steam Engine—James Watt invented the first perfect steam engine in England, A. D. 1764.

Steam Hammer—Invented by James Nasmyth, A. D. 1838.

Steel—Has been fabricated from the earliest times.

Steel Manufacture, Purification of Iron—Invented by H. Bessemer, 1856.

Stereoscope—Was known to Euclid, 300 B. C.

Stereotype—Invented by M. M. Didot in the 18th century.

Stethoscope—Invented by M. Laennec of Paris, A. D. 1823.

Strontium—A metal first obtained by Sir Humphrey Davy, A. D. 1808.

Swords—Were formed of iron by the Chinese, 1870 B. C.

Telegraph—Invented by Professor S. F. B. Morse, A. D. 1837.

Telescope—Was invented by Lifferbein in 1608. The first reflecting one was made by Isaac Newton, A. D. 1668.

Tellurium—A metal discovered by Kloproth, A. D. 1798.

Telephone—Invented by A. G. Bell, A. D. 1876.

Thallium—A metal discovered by Crookes, A. D. 1861.

Theatres—The first erected, the Bacchus at Athens, Greece, by Philos, 420 B. C.

Thermometer—The invention is generally credited to Galileo, A. D. 1596.

Threshing Machine—Invented by Michael Menizies at Edinburgh, A. D. 1732.

Thorium—A metal discovered by Berzelius, A. D. 1828.

Tinanium—A metal discovered by Gregoi in Cornwall, England, A. D. 1789.

Tin—Was known to the ancients.

Tobacco—Was discovered in San Domingo in 1496.

Torpedo—Invented by David Bushnell, 1777.

Trigonometry—Invented by the Greek astronomers at Alexandria.

Vaccination—Proposed by Dr. Edward Jenner, A. D. 1796.

Vanadium—A metal discovered by Sefstrom, A. D. 1830.

Velocipede—Invented by M. Drais, A. D. 1817.

Violin—Believed to have been invented by Ravana, King of Ceylon, 500 B. C.

Watch—Said to have been made first at Nuremberg, A. D. 1477.

Wire—The invention of drawing wire invented by Rodolph of Nuremberg, A. D. 1410.

Zinc—The ore from which the metal is made was by the Greeks.

Zirconium—A metal first obtained by Berzelius, A. D. 1824.

DICTIONARY OF ABBREVIATIONS

A

A. or @. At or to
A. B. Bachelor of Arts
Abbr. Abbreviated
A. C. Before Christ (*Ante Christum*)
Acct. Account
A. D. (*Anno Domini*). In the year of our Lord
Adjt.-Gen. Adjutant-General
Adm. Admiral, Admiralty
Admr. Administrator
Adv. Adverb
Agt. Agent
Alex. Alexander
A.M. Before Noon
Anon. Anonymous
Apr. April
Ariz. Ter. Arizona Territory
Atty. Attorney
A. U. C. In the year of Rome
Ave. Avenue

A. A. G. Assistant Adjutant-General.
Abb. Abbott, Abbess
Abp. Archbishop
Adj. Adjective
Adjt. Adjutant
A. D. C. Aide-de-camp
Ad. lib. At pleasure (*Ad libitum*)
Admx. Administratrix
Æt. (*Ætatis*). Of age, aged.
Ala. Alabama
A. M. Master of arts
Amt. Amount
Ans. Answer
A. R. Year of the reign
Ark. Arkansas
Atty.-Gen. Attorney-General
Aug. August
Avoir. Avoirdupois

B

b. Born
Bal. Balance
Bart. or Bt. Baronet
B. C. Before Christ
Bk. Bank; book
Bp. Bishop
Brig. Brigade; brigadier

B. A. British America
B.A. Bachelor of Arts
Bbl. Barrel
B.D. Bachelor of Divinity
Bot. Botany
Br. or bro. Brother
Brig.-Gen. Brigadier-General

C

Chap. Chapter
Cal. California
Cath. Catholic
C. C. P. Court of Common Pleas

C. or cent. (*centum*). A hundred
Capt. Captain
Cat. Catalogue
Cen. Century

Dictionary of Abbreviations.—*Continued*

C. H.   Court House
Chas.   Charles
Chron.   Chronicles
C. J.   Chief Justice
C. M.   Common Master
Colo.   Colorado
C. O. D.   Cash (or collect) on delivery
Conn. or Ct.   Connecticut
Cor. Mem.   Corresponding Member
Cor. Sec.   Corresponding Secretary

Chap.   Chaplain
Chem.   Chemistry
Cin.   Cincinnati
Cld. or cld.   Cleared
Co.   Company; county
Col.   Colonel; Colossians
Col.   Colorado.
Cor.   Corinthians; corner
Cr.   Creditor; credit
Cwt.   Hundredweight
Ct.   Connecticut; Count; Court

D

d.   Penny; pence
D.   Five hundred
D. C.   District of Columbia
D. C. L.   Doctor of Civil Law
Dea.   Deacon
Deft. or dft.   Defendant
Del.   Delaware
Dept.   Department
Diam.   Diameter
Dist.   District
Div.   Dividend
Dol.; dols.; $.   Dollars
Dr.   Doctor; debtor; dram

d.   Died; day
Dan.   Daniel; Danish
D. C. (*da capo*).   Again
D. D.   Doctor of Divinity
Dec.   December
Deg.   Degree or degrees
Dep.   Deputy
Deut.   Deuteronomy
Disc.   Discount
Dist.-Atty.   District-Attorney
Do. or do. (*ditto*).   The same
Doz. or doz.   Dozen
Dwt.   Pennyweight

E

E.   East
Ed.   Editor; edition
Edw.   Edward
e. g. (*exempli gratid*).   For example
Eliz.   Elizabeth
Eng.   England; English
Esd.   Esdras
Esq. or Esqr.   Esquire
Etc. or etc. or &c.   And so forth; and the like; and others.
Et seq. (*et sequentia*).   And what follows
Ex.   Exodus
Exec.   Executor

Eccl. or Eccles.   Ecclesiastes
Ecclus.   Ecclesiasticus
E. E.   Errors excepted
E. I.   East India or East Indies
E. N. E.   East-northeast
Eph.   Ephesians; Ephraim
E.S.E.   East-southeast
et. al. (*et alii*).   And others
Ex.   Example
Exch.   Exchequer
Ezek.   Ezekiel

Dictionary of Abbreviations.—*Continued*

F

Fahr.	Fahrenheit	Far.	Farthing
Feb.	February	Fem.	Feminine
Fig.	Figure	Fla.	Florida
Fol.	Folio	Fr.	French; France; Franc
Fri.	Friday	Ft.	Foot; feet; fort
Fur.	Furlong	Fir.	Firkin

G

Ga.	Georgia	Gal.	Galatians; gallon
G. B.	Great Britain	Gen.	Genesis; General
Gent.	Gentleman	Geo.	George
Geog.	Geography	Geol.	Geology
Geom.	Geometry	Ger.	German: Germany
Gov.	Governor	Gr.	Greek; gross
Gram.	Grammar	Gro.	Gross

H

H. or h. Hour

H. C. House of Commons

Heb. Hebrew

Hist. History; historical

H. I. H. His (or Her) Imperial Highness

H. M. S. His (or Her) Majesty's Steamer, Ship or Service.

Hon. Honorable

Hos. Hosea

H. B. M. His (or Her), Britannic Majesty

Hdkf. Handkerchief

Hhd. Hogshead

H. L. House of Lords

H. M. His (or Her) Majesty

Hort. Horticulture

H. R. H. His (or Her) Royal Highnesss

I

Ia. Iowa

Id. (*idem*). The same

Ill. Illinois

I. H. S. (*Iesus* (*or Jesus*) *Hominum Salvator*). Jesus the Savior of men.

Incog. (*incognito*). Unknown

Inst. Of this month; instant

I. N. R. I. Jesus of Nazareth, King of the Jews

Ire. Ireland

Ital. Italic; Italian

Ib. or ibid (*ibidem*). In the same place

I. e. or i. e. (*id est*). That is

In. or in. Inch; inches

Ind. Indiana; Index; Indian

Int. Interest

I. O. U. I owe you

Dictionary of Abbreviations.—*Continued*

J

J.	Judge or Justice	JJ.	Justices
Jam.	Jamaica	Jan.	January
Jap.	Japan; Japanese	Jas.	James
Je.	June	Jer.	Jeremiah
Jno.	John	Jona.	Jonathan
Jos.	Joseph	Josh.	Joshua
J. P.	Justice of the Peace	Jr.	Junior
Jul.	July	Jus.	Justinian

K

K.	King	Kan.	Kansas
K. B.	King's Bench	Ken. or Ky.	Kentucky
Knt. or Kt.	Knight		

L

L. l. £.	A pound sterling	La.	Louisiana
Lam.	Lamentations	Lat.	Latin
Lat.	Latitude	Lb. or lb.	Pound in weight
Ld.	Lord	Lea. or lea.	League
Lev.	Leviticus	L. I.	Long Island
Lieut. or Lt.	Lieutenant	L. L. B.	Bachelor of Laws
L. L. D.	Doctor of Law	Lon. or Long.	Longitude
L. S. (*Locus Sigilli*).	Place of the Seal		

M

M.	Noon, Meridian	M.	A thousand
M. or Mons.	Sir, Monsieur	M. A.	Master of Arts
Mac. or Macc.	Maccabees	Mad.	Madam
Maj.	Major	Maj.-Gen.	Major-General.
Mar.	March	Marq.	Marquis
Masc.	Masculine	Mass. or Ms.	Massachusetts
Matt.	Matthew	M. C.	Member of Congress
M. D.	Doctor of Medicine	M. D.	Maryland
Mdlle.	Mademoiselle	Me.	Maine
Mem.	Memorandum	Messrs. or M. M.	Gentlemen, Sirs

Dictionary of Abbreviations.—*Continued*

Mi. or Miss. Mississippi

Min. Minute

Mich. Michigan

Mlle. Mademoiselle

Minn. Minnesota

Mme. Madame

Miss. Misses

Mmes. Mesdames

M. M. Their Majesties

Mo. Missouri

M. M. Gentlemen

Mon. Monday

M. M. Messieurs

Mon. Monsieur or Sir

Mo. or mo. Month

M. P. Member of Parliament

Mr. Mister or Master

Mrs. Mistress or Missis

M. S. Manuscript

Mt. Mount or Mountain

MSS. Manuscripts

N

N. North

N. or n. Noun

N. A. North America

N. B. New Brunswick

N. B. Note well; take notice

N. C. North Carolina

N. E. New England; Northeast

Neb. Nebraska

Neh. Nehemiah

Nem. Con. No one contradicting

Nev. Nevada

Unanimously

N. H. New Hampshire

N. J. New Jersey

N. N. E. North-northeast

N. N. W. North-northwest

Nol. Pros. Unwilling to prosecute

No. or no. Number

Non. Seq. It does not follow

Nov. November

N. S. Nova Scotia

N. S. New Style (after 1752)

N. T. New Testament

Num. Number

N. W. Northwest

N. Y. New York

O

O. Ohio

Ob. or ob. (*Obiit*). Died

Obad. Obadiah

Obj. Objective

Oct. October

Olym. Olympiad

O. S. Old Style (previous to 1752)

O. T. Old Testament

Or. Oregon

Oz. or oz. Ounce

Dictionary of Abbreviations.—*Continued*

P

P. or p.   Page; part; pipe
Par.   Paragraph
Penn. or Pa.   Pennsylvania
Per. an. (*Per annum*).   By the year
Per. cent (*Per centum*).   By the hundred
Phil.   Philippians; Philemon
P. M. (*Post Meridian*).   Afternoon
P. O.   Postoffice
Pp. or pp.   Pages
Prof.   Professor
Pro. tem. (*Pro tempore*).   For the time being
Prox. (*proximo*).   Next (month)
P. S.   Postscript

Parl.   Parliament
P. E. I.   Prince Edward Island
Per. or pr.   By the
Ph. D.   Doctor of Philosophy
Plff.   Plaintiff
Phila.   Philadelphia
P. M.   Postmaster
Pop.   Population
Pres.   President
Prot.   Protestant
Prov.   Proverbs
Prus.   Prussia; Prussian
Ps.   Psalm or Psalms
Pt.   Pint, point, port
Pwt.   Pennyweight

Q

Q.   Question
Q. C.   Queen's Counsel
Q. M.   Quartermaster
Qr.   Quarter
Q. v. or q. v. (*quod vide*).   Which see
Qy.   Query

Q. or Qu.   Query; Question; Queen
Q. E. D.   Which was to be demonstrated
Q. M. G.   Quartermaster-General
Qt.   Quart

R

R.   Take Recipe
R. A.   Royal Academy
Regt.   Regiment
Rep.   Representative; Reporter
Rep.   Republican; Republic
R. N.   Royal Navy
Rom.   Roman; Romans
R. R.   Railroad
Russ.   Russia

R.   River; rood; rod
Rev.   Revelation; Reverend
Rev.   Review; Revolution
R. I.   Rhode Island
Richd.   Richard
Robt.   Robert
Rom. Cath.   Roman Catholic
Rt. Hon.   Right Honorable
Rt. Rev.   Right Reverend

Dictionary of Abbreviations. —*Continued*

S

S.	South; shilling
Sam.	Samuel
Sax.	Saxon
Schr.	Schooner
Scot.	Scotland
Sec.	Secretary
Sen.	Senate; Senator; Senior
Ser.	Series
Sing.	Singular
Sld. or sld.	Sailed
S. M.	Short meter
Soc.	Society
Sq. ft.	Square feet
Sq. in.	Square inches
Sq. yd.	Square yard
SS. or ss. (*scilicet*).	Namely
S. S. E.	South-southeast
St.	Saint; street; strait
S. T. D.	Doctor of Sacred Theology
Sun.	Sunday
Surg.	Surgeon; Surgery

S. A.	South America
Sat.	Saturday
S. C.	South Carolina
Scil. or Sc. (*scilicet*).	To wit
S. E.	Southeast
Sect.	Section
Sep, or Sept.	September
Serg.	Sergeant
S. J. C.	Supreme Judicial Court
S. Lat.	South Latitude
Sol.	Solomon
Sp.	Spain; Spanish
Sq. m.	Square miles
Sq. r.	Square rood
Sr.	Sir; Senior
SS. or ss. (*semis*).	Half
S. S. W.	South-southwest
Stat.	Statute
Ster., or Stg.	Sterling
Supt.	Superintendent
S.W.	Southwest

T

Ten. or Tenn.	Tennessee
Tax.	Texas
Thess.	Thessalonians
Thos.	Thomas
Tit.	Titus
Treas.	Treasurer
Trin.	Trinity

Ter.	Territory
Theo.	Theodore
Th. or Thurs.	Thursday
Tim.	Timothy
Tr.	Trustee
Trs.	Trustees
Tu. or Tues.	Tuesday

U

Ult. or ult. (*ultimo*).	Last, or of the last month
U. S. A.	United States of America
U. S. M.	United States Mail
U. S. V.	United States Volunteers

U. S.	United States
U. S. A.	United States Army
U. S. N.	United States Navy
U. S. S.	United States Senate
U. T.	Utah Territory

Dictionary of Abbreviations.—*Continued*

V

Va.   Virginia
Vice.-Pres.   Vice-President
Viz. or viz (*videlicet*).   Namely;
   To wit
V. R. (Victoria Regina).   Queen Victoria
Vs. or vs. (*versus*).   Against or in opposition

Ver.   Verse; Version
Vil.   Village
Vol.   Volume
Vt.   Vermont

W

W.   West
Wed.   Wednesday
W. I. or W. Ind.   West Indies
Wk.   Week
W. N. W.   West-northwest
W. S. W.   West-southwest
W T.   Wyoming Territory

Wash.   Washington
Whf.   Wharf
Wis. or Wisc.   Wisconsin
Wm.   William
W. S.   Writer of the Signet
W. Va.   West Virginia
Wt. or wt.   Weight

X

X. or Xt.   Christ

Xmas.   Christmas

Y

Yd. or yd.   Yard

Yrs.   Years

Z

Zach.   Zachary
Zeph.   Zephaniah
&.   and

Zech.   Zechariah
Zool.   Zoology
&c.   And the rest; and so forth

THE MOST VALUABLE GEM IN THE WORLD

The most valuable gem is a sapphire; weighs 12½ loth (a little over six ounces), and is valued at $16,000,000, it is the property of the Royal family of Germany, at Berlin.

VALUE OF DIAMONDS

Diamonds averaging one-half carat each, $60 per carat; diamonds averaging three-quarters carat each, $80 per carat; diamonds averaging one carat each, $100 per carat; diamonds averaging one and one-quarter carats each, $110 per carat; diamonds averaging one and one-half carats each, $120 per carat; diamonds averaging one and three-quarters carats each, $145 per carat; diamonds averaging two carats each, $175 per carat. In other words the value of the gem increases in the geometrical ratio of its weight. Four diamonds weighing together two carats are worth $120; but one diamond weigh. ing just as much is worth $350. Stones weighing over two carats are about the same price per carat as two-carat stones; they should be dearer, but they are not simply because the demand for them is limited· If the demand for diamonds were as imperative as the demand for flour or beef the geometrical ratio would again come into play, and five-carat stones would be valued in the thousands.

DIAMOND-CUTTING HOUSE

The largest diamond-cutting house in Amsterdam, Holland, is the Amsterdam where they employ 400 men. The famous Kohinoor diamond was cut there. The cutters make from $7 to $12 and even $14 per day.

BASEBALL PLATES DISTANCES

The distance from the home-plate to the pitcher's position is 50 feet, so that must be the distance the ball is pitched. The distance from the home-plate to the first base is 90 feet, and 127 feet 4 inches to second base.

CENTENARIANS

The most remarkable were :
Thomas Parr, died after a dinner party, in his 152d year.
The Countess of Desmond, killed by falling from a cherry-tree, in her 146th year.
John Riva of Venice, who chewed citron bark daily, died at the age of 116 years, leaving a son of 14 years.
Cardinal de Salis, who recommended daily exercise in all weathers, died in his 110th year.
Mrs. Ann Butler died at Portsmouth, England, January, 1883, at the age of 103 years.
Mrs. Betty Lloyd died at Ruabon, Wales, 1883, in her 107th year, her funeral being attended by two of her children aged over 80 years.

Weight of Large Bells of the World

Kremlin, Moscow, Russia	443,772 pounds
St. Ivan's, Moscow, Russia	127,830 "
Vienna, Austria	40,200 "
Olmutz, Bohemia	40,000 "
Rouen, France	40,000 "
"Big Ben," London, England	30,350 "
Montreal, Canada	28,560 "
City Hall, New York City	22,300 "
Fire Alarm, 33d St., New York City	21,612 "
St. Peter's, Rome, Italy	18,600 "
"Great Tom," Oxford, England	18,000 "
St. Paul's, London, England	11,470 "
Linden, Germany	10,854 "
Lewiston, Maine, United States	10,233 "
Worcester, England	6,600 "
York, England	6,384 "

Height of the Principal Monuments, Towers and Pyramids

Name	Height in feet
Eiffel, Paris, France	(300 metres) 984
Washington Monument, Washington, D. C., U. S.	555
Cologne Cathedral, Cologne, Germany	524
Old St. Paul's Church, London, England	505
Pyramid of Cheops, Egypt	486½
Antwerp Cathedral, Antwerp, Belgium	476
Strasburg Cathedral, Strasburg, Germany	474
Pyramid of Cephrenes, Egypt	456
St. Peter's Church, Rome, Italy	469
St. Stephen's Cathedral, Vienna, Austria	441
St. Martin's Church, Landshut, Germany	411
Salisbury Cathedral, England	404
Torazzo of Cremona, Cremona, Lombardy	396
Freiburg Cathedral, Freiburg, Germany	410
Florence Cathedral, Florence, Italy	272
Torre Asinelli, Bologna, Italy	370
St. Paul's Church, London, England	365
Cathedral of Seville, Seville, Spain	360
Pyramid of Sakkarah, Egypt	356

Height of Principal Mountains, Etc.—*Continued*

Utrecht Cathedral, Utrecht, Holland........................356
Milan Cathedral, Lombardy....................................355
Cathedral of Notre Dame, Munich, Germany................348
Church of St. Isaac, St. Petersburg, Russia...............336
Victoria Tower, Westminster, England.....................340
Bell Tower, St. Mark's, Venice, Italy......................323
Cathedral, Frankfort on Main, Germany....................326
Hotel des Invalides, Paris, France.........................344
Liberty Enlightening the World, New York Harbor (above water)..305
    "   "   "   " New York Harbor (above land).294
Boston Church, Lincolnshire, England.....................292
Trinity Church, New York, U. S............................284
St. Genevieva Church, Paris, France.......................274
Column at Delhi, Hindoostan, Asia.........................262
Porcelain Tower, Nankin, China............................260
Church of Notre Dame, Paris, France.......................224
Bunker Hill Monument, Massachusetts, U. S................221
York Cathedral, England...................................198
Leaning Tower of Pisa, Pisa, Italy........................188
Mosque of St. Sophia, Constantinople, Turkey.............182
Monument Place Vendome, Paris, France....................153
Trajan's Pillar, Rome, Italy..............................151
Pantheon, Rome, Italy.....................................145
Obelisk of Luxor, Paris, France...........................75
Egyptian Obelisk, New York, U. S.........................70
Washington Monument, Baltimore, U. S.....................175
City Column, London, England.............................202
Albert's Memorial, London, England.......................180
Alexander Column, St. Petersburg, Russia.................176
Tower of Water Works, Chicago, Ill., U. S................175
Nelson Column, London, England...........................171
Arc de Triomphe, Paris, France...........................162
Column of July, Paris, France.............................157
York Column, London, England.............................138
Nelson Column, Dublin, Ireland...........................134
Napoleon Column, Paris, France...........................132

How to Prove that the Earth Does Move

A simple and convincing mode of proving the assertion. It has puzzled the heads of a good many people to known how the earth turns round. A German educational journal published in Frankfort gives the following directions for proving that the earth "does move:" Take a good-sized bowl, fill it nearly full of water and put it upon the floor of a room which is not exposed to shaking or jarring from the street. Sprinkle over the surface of the water a coating of lycopodium powder, a white substance sometimes used for the purposes of the toilet and which can be obtained at almost any apothecary's. Then upon the surface of this coating of powder make with powdered charcoal a straight black line, say an inch or two in length. Having made this black mark with the charcoal powder on the surface of the contents of the bowl, lay down upon the floor close to the bowl a stick or some other straight object so that it will be exactly parallel with the mark. If the line happens to be parallel with a crack in the floor or with any stationary object in the room this will serve as well. Leave the bowl undisturbed for a few hours and then observe the position of the black mark with reference to the object that it was parallel with. It will be found to have moved about, and to have moved from east to west—that is to say in the direction opposite to that of the movement of the earth on its axis. The earth, in simply revolving, has carried the water and everything else in the bowl around with it, but the powder on the surface has been left behind a little. The line will always be found to have moved from east to west, which is perfectly good proof that everything else has moved the other way.

Two Natural Compasses

Allen Thompson, the old White Mountain guide, says: "When I am in the woods I never use a compass, in fact, I don't need any. There are three sure ways that I have for finding out the points of the compass. You will notice that three-fourths of the moss on trees grows on the north side; the heaviest boughs on spruce trees are always on the south side; and thirdly, the topmost twig on every uninjured hemlock tree tips to the east. You just remember this and you'll never get lost."

At any hour during the day-time, even in a dense fog or blinding snowstorm, the right direction may be readily ascertained by a very simple means of finding the position of the sun. All that is required is to place the point of a knife blade or a sharp lead-pencil on the thumb-nail, when a shadow will be cast directly from the sun, however dense may be the fog or snow.

How to Make a Compass at Home

Get from a druggist a common pasteboard pill-box of about one and three-fourths inches in diameter. Cut in the lid a round hole an inch in diameter. Cover the hole on the inside with a piece of window glass, which can be held in place by bits of sealing-wax at the corners.

Break off about three-eighths of an inch from the point of a sewing needle and affix it, point upward by means of sealing-wax, to the center of the bottom of the box. This is to be the pivot upon which the magnetic needle is to swing.

For a needle, use the permanent magnet made of a darning-needle. To adjust this to the pivot, cut out a piece of ivory or bone—the handle of an old tooth-brush is good material—a quarter of an inch square by a tenth of an inch thick. In the center of the square side bore a hole by means of an knife-blade or the handle end of a file, nearly through the piece.

The inner extremity of the hole must be smooth, with no small crevices or sharp edges. To the opposite surface attach by sealing-wax the needle, and after placing it upon the pivot, put the cover on the box. If the hole in the ivory be well made, one end of the needle will point to the north.

Place the compass near any large mass of iron as, for example, the kitchen stove, and see where it will point then.

News, the Derivation of the Word

The word "news" was not, as many suppose, derived from the adjective new, but from the fact that many years ago it was customary to put at the head of the periodical publications of the day the initial letters of the compass, thus:

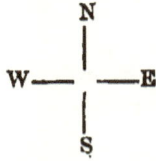

Signifying that the matter contained therein was from the four quarters of the globe. From the letters came the word "news."

ABBREVIATIONS USED BY PHYSICIANS IN PRE-SCRIPTIONS, MEDICAL BOOKS AND JOURNALS

ss. (*Semissis*). Half.
iss (*Sesqui*). One and a half.
A. āā. (*ana, utriusque*). Of each.
Abdom. Abdomen.
Abs. Febr. (*Absente febre*). In the absence of fever.
Ad. or Add (*Adde* or *Addator*). Add, or let there be added.
Ad Lib. (*Ad libitum*). At pleasure.
Altern. Hor. (*Alternis horis*). Every other hour.
Aq. (*Aqua*). Water.
Aq. Bull. (*Aqua Bulliens*). Boiling Water.
Aq. Comm. (*Aqua Communis*). Common water.
Aq. Ferv. (*Aqua fervens*). Hot water.
Aq. Font. (*Aqua fontis*). Spring water.
B. A. (*Balneum Arenæ*). A sand bath.
Bib. (*Bibe*). Drink.
Bis Ind. (*Bis indies*). Twice daily.
Bol. (*Bolus*). A large pill.
Bull. (*Bulliat*). Let it boil.
B. V. (*Balneum vaporis*). A vapor bath.
Cap. (*Capiat*). Let him take.
Chart. (*Chartula*). A small paper.
Cochl. (*Cochleare*). A spoonful.
Col. (*Cola*). Strain.
Collyr. (*Collyrium*). An eye water.
Comp. (*Compositus*). Compound.
C. or Cong. (*Congius*). A gallon.
Coq. (*Coque*). Boil.
Cort. (*Cortex*). Bark.
C. M. (*Cras Mane*). To-morrow morning.
C. N. (*Cras Nocte*). To-morrow night.
Crast. (*Crastinus*). For to-morrow.
D. (*Detur*). Let it be given.
Decub. (*Decubitus*). Lying down.
De D. in D. (*De die in diem*). From day to day.
Dig. (*Digeratur*). Let it be digested.
Dil. (*Dilutus*). Dilute.
Dim. (*Dimidius*). One-half.
Div. (*Divide*) Divide.
Enem. (*Enema*). A clyster.

Abbreviations, Etc.—*Continued*

F. (*Fiat*). Let it be made.

F. Pil. (*Fiat pilula*). Make into a pill.

Feb. Dur. (*Febre durante*). During the fever.

Fl. (*Fluidus*) Fluid.

Gr. (*Granum*). A grain.

Gt. (*Gutta*). A drop.

Gtt. (*Guttæ*). Drops.

Guttat. (*Guttatim*). By drops.

Hor. Decub. (*Hora decubitus*). At bedtime.

Lb. and Lib. (*Libra*). A pound weight.

Liq. Liquor.

M. (*Misce*). Mix.

Man. (*Minipulu*). A handful.

Mic. Pan. (*Mica Panis*). Crumb of bread.

Min. (*Minimum*). The sixtieth part of a drachm by measure.

Mist. (*Mistura*). A mixture.

Muc. (*Mucilago*). Mucilage.

O. (*Octarius*). A pint.

Ol. (*Oleum*). Oil.

Omn. Hor. (*Omni hora*). Every hour.

Omn. Man. (*Omni Mane*). Every morning.

Omn. Nocte. Every night.

Oz. (*Uncia*). An ounce.

P. Æ. (*Partes Æquales*). Equal parts.

Pil. (*Pilula*). A pill.

P. R. N. (*Pro re nata*). As occasion may require.

Pulv. (*Pulvis*). A powder.

Q. S. (*Quantum sufficit*). As much as is sufficient.

Rad. (*Radix*). Root.

Rep. (*Repetatur*). Let it be repeated.

S. (*Signa*). Write.

S. A. (*Secundum Artem*). According to art.

Sem. (*Semen*). Seed.

Si Non Val. (*Si non valeat*). If it does not answer.

Si Op. Sit. (*Si opus sit*). If there be need.

Sig. (*Sigulorum*). Of each.

Solv. (*Solve*). Dissolve.

Sp. (*Spiritus*). Spirit.

Sum. (*Sumat*). Let him take.

Sp. Vin. (*Spiritus vini*). Spirit of wine.

Syr. (*Syrupus*). Syrup.

Tr. Tinct. (*Tinctura*). Tincture.

V. S. (*Venæ sectio*). Venesection.

How Human Life is Spent

According to a French statistician, taking the mean of many accounts, a man of 50 years of age has slept 6,000 days, worked 6,500 days, walked 800 days, amused himself 4,000 days, was eating 1,500 days, was sick 500 days, etc. He ate 17,000 pounds of bread, 16,000 pounds of meat, 4,600 pounds of vegetables, eggs and fish, and drank 7,000 gallons of liquid, namely, water, tea, coffee, beer, wine, etc., altogether.

The Smallest Steam Engine in the World

The smallest steam engine in the world was built by Mr. D. A. A. Buck (American). The engine, boiler, governor and pumps stand in a space of seven-sixteenths of an inch square, or the area of a gold dollar and five-eighths of an inch high, composed of 148 distinct parts held together by 52 screws. Three drops of water fill the boiler to its proper capacity. Diameter of cylinder, one-sixteenth of an inch; length of stroke, three thirty-seconds of an inch; weight of engine, 15 grains.

The Smallest Locomotive in the World

A mechanic living in Jamestown, New York State, has constructed a perfect locomotive, which is said to be the smallest in the world. The engine is only eight and a quarter inches in length, with a tender ten inches long. The pumps throw one drop of water per stroke. As many as 585 screws were required to put the parts together. The engine itself weighs one and a half pounds, and the tender two pounds and two and a half ounces. The mechanic was at work on the locomotive for eight years, though intervals of time only were given to the labor of constructing it.

Jumbo, the Elephant

Jumbo, the famous elephant, was bought from a wandering band of Arabs—according to Sir Samuel Baker—when four years of age. Then was brought to the Jardin des Plantes, Paris, France, from there he was transferred to the London Zoological Gardens, in 1866, and remained there until bought by Barnum, Bailey & Hutchinson, in 1882. Jumbo was killed by a locomotive at Ontario, Canada, in 1885.

GENERAL COUNCILS

A. D.

Jerusalem, against Judaizers............................ ... 51
Arles, against the Donatists................................ 314
Nice, First Œcumenical Council............................ 325
Constantinople, Arian..................................... 337
Rome, Athanasian... 342
Sardis, against Arius...................................... 347
Constantinople, Second Œcumenical......................... 381
Ephesus, Third Œcumenical.......................... 431
Chalcedon, Fourth Œcumenical..................... 451
Constantinople, Fifth Œcumenical........................... 553
Constantinople, Sixth Œcumenical.......................... 681
·Nice, Seventh Œcumenical 787
Constantinople, Eighth Œcumenical.......................... 870
Rome, First Lateran.......................................1123
Rome, Second Lateran..................... 1139
Rome, Third Lateran......................................1197
Rome, Fourth Lateran....................................1215
Lyons, Emperor Frederick deposed..........................1243
Lyons, Temporary reunion of Greek and Latin Churches........1274
Vienne, Fifteenth Œcumenical..............................1312
Pisa, Popes elected and deposed............................1400
Constance, Huss condemned to be burnt.....................1414
Basle, Eighteenth Œcumenical..............................1431
Rome, Fifth Lateran...............................1512 to 1517
Trent, Nineteenth Œcumenical.....................1545 to 1563
Rome, Last Œcumenical...................................1870

LUCKY STONES

The stones sacred to the different months are:

January	Garnet	July	Ruby
February	Amethyst	August	Sardonyx
March	Bloodstone	September	Sapphire
April	Diamond	October	Opal
May	Emerald	November	Topaz
June	Agate	December	Turquoise

LIMIT OF PERPETUAL SNOW AT THE EQUATOR

The limit of perpetual snow is 15,200 feet above the sea level at the Equator

Highest Mountains in the World

Name	Feet High	Miles High
*Mt. Hercules, New Guinea	32,787	6 1-5
Mt. Everest, India, Thibet	29,002	5 3/4
Mt. Peterman, India, Thibet	28,156	5 1/3
Mt. Chumulri, India, Thibet	23,946	4 1/2
Mt. Sorato, Bolivia, S. Am.	21,284	4
Mt. Chimborazo, Ecuador, S. Am	21,149	4
Mt. Illimani, Bolivia, S. Am.	21,147	4
Mt. Hindoo-Koosh, Afghanistan, Asia	20,600	3 3/4
Mt. Demavend, Persia, Asia	19,998	3 2/3
Mt. Cotopaxi, Ecuador, South Am	19,495	3 2/3
Mt. Antisana, Ecuador, S. Am.	19,150	3 1/2
Mt. St. Elias, Alaska, N. Am	17,900	3 1/3
Mt. Popocatepetl, Mexico, N. Am	17,773	3 1/3
Mt. Ararat, Armenia, Asia	17,260	3 1/3
Mt. Roa Hawaii	16,000	3
Mt. Brown, British America, N. Am.	15,900	3
Mt. Blanc, Savoy, Europe	15,744	2 7/8
Monte Rosa, Switzerland, Europe	15,284	2 7/8
Mt. Whitney, California, N. Am	14,887	2 3/4
Mt. Fairweather, Alaska, N. Am	14,796	2 3/4
Mt. Shasta, California, N. Am	14,442	2 3/4
Mt. Ranier, Washington, N. Am.	14,444	2 3/4
Long's Peak, Colorado, N. Am	14,271	2 2/3
Pike's Peak, Colorado, N. Am	14,216	2 2/3
Mt. Ophir, Sumatra	13,800	2 5/8
Mt. Jungfrau, Switzerland, Europe	13,781	2 5/8
Fremont's Peak, Wyoming Ter., N. Am.	13,570	2 5/8
Mt. St. Helena, Washington, N. Am	13,400	2 1/2
Peak of Teneriffe, Canary Islands, Atlantic Ocean	12,236	2 1/3
Mt. Miltzin, Morocco, Africa	12,000	2
Mt. Hood, Oregon, N. Am.	11,225	2
Mt. Lebanon, Syria, Asia	10,600	2
Mont. Perdou, Spain, Europe	10,994	2
Mt. Etna, Sicily, Europe	10,874	2
Mt. Olympus, Greece, Europe	9,754	1 3/4
Monte Corno, Naples, Europe	9,523	1 3/4

*This mountain has only lately been estimated as to its height, but not yet measured by the Geographical Society; thus Mt. Everest is considered the highest mountain.

Highest Mountains—*Continued*

Name	Feet High	Miles High
Pass of Stelvio, Tyrol, Europe	9,177	1⅝
Grimsel Pass, Switzerland, Europe	8,400	1½
Mt. Sneehattan, Norway, Europe	8,115	1½
Mt. Pindus, Greece, Europe	7,677	1½
Great Pass of St. Bernard, Switzerland, Europe	7,173	1¼
Mt. Sinai, Arabia, Asia	6,985	1¼
Black Mountain, North Carolina, N. Am	6,707	1¼
Pass of Simplon, Switzerland, Europe	6,578	1¼
Mt. Washington, New Hampshire, N. Am	6,293	1¼
Mt. Marcy, New York, N. Am	5,402	1
Mt. Hecla, Iceland, Atlantic Ocean	5,095	1
Mt. Ben Nevis, Scotland, Great Britain	4,368	⅞
Mt. Mansfield, Vermont, N. Am	4,279	¾
Peak of Otter, Virginia, N. Am	4,260	¾
Mt. Vesuvius, Naples, Europe	3,932	¾
Mt. Round Top, New York, N. Am	3,804	¾
Macgillicuddy's Rocks, Ireland, Great Britain	3,404	⅝

RULERS OF GERMANY

House of Charlemange

	Time of Reign	Yrs
Charles I, the Great, second son of Pepin	800–814	14
Louis I, the Pious, son of Charles I	814–840	26
Charles II, the Bald, son of Louis I	840–843	3
Louis II, the German, son of Louis I	843–876	33
Charles III, the Fat, son of Louis II	880–887	7
Arnulf, grandson of Louis II	887–899	12
Louis III, the Child, Son of Arnulf	899–911	12

House of Franconia

	Time of Reign	Yrs
Conrad I, Duke of Franks, elected by the Princes of Germany	911–918	7

House of Saxony

	Time of Reign	Yrs
Henry I, the Fowler, Duke of Saxony	919–936	17
Otho I, the Great, son of Henry I	936–973	37
Otho II, son of Otho I	973–983	10
Otho III, son of Otho II	983–1002	19
Henry II, the Saint and the Lame, grandson of Henry I, Duke of Bavaria	1002–1024	22

Rulers of Germany—*Continued*

House of Franconia	Time of Reign	Yrs.
Conrad II, the Salic, elected to the throne	1024–1039	15
Henry III, the Black, son of Conrad II	1039–1056	17
Henry IV, son of Henry III	1056–1106	50
Henry V, son of Henry IV	1106–1125	19

House of Saxony

Lathaire II, the Saxon, Duke of Saxony	1125–1137	12

House of Hohenstaufen

Conrad III, son of Frederick of Swabia	1138–1152	14
Frederick I, Barbarossa, a nephew of Conrad III	1152–1190	38
Henry VI, son of Frederick I	1190–1197	7
Philip of Swabia, brother of Henry VI	1197–1208	11
Otho IV, son of Henry, the Lion	1197–1215	18
Frederick II, son of Henry VI	1215–1250	35
William of Holland, elected King of the Romans	1247–1256	9
Conrad IV, son of Frederick II	1250–1254	4

Interregnum

Wilhelm of Holland	1254–1256	2
Richard of Cornwall, brother of Henry III of England	1256–1273	17

House of Hapsburg

Rudolphus I, son of Albert IV, Count of Hapsburg	1273–1291	18

House of Nassau

Adolphus I, elected in opposition to Albert I	1292–1298	6

House of Hapsburg

Albert I. son of Rudolphus I	1298–1308	10

House of Luxemboug and Bavaria

Henry VII, Count Henry of Luxembourg	1308–1313	5
Louis IV, Louis of Bavaria	1313–1347	34
Charles IV, son of John King of Bohemia	1347–1378	31

Interregnum

Wenceslaus (deposed), son of Charles IV	1378–1400	22
Rupert, Count Palatine	1400–1410	10
Sigismund, brother of Wenceslaus	1410–1437	27

Rulers of Germany—*Continued*

House of Hapsburg	Time of Reign	Yrs.
Albert II, son of Albert IV of Austria................1438–1439		1
Frederick III, Duke of Styria and cousin of Albert II..1440–1493		53
Maximilian I, son of Frederick III....................1493–1519		26
Charles V (Chas. I of Spain), grandson of Maximilian I.1519–1556		37
Ferdinand I, brother of Charles V...................1558–1564		6
Maximilian II, son of Ferdinand I..................1564–1576		12
Rudolphus II, son of Maximilian II.................1576–1612		36
Matthias I, brother of Rudolphus II................1612–1619		7
Ferdinand II, cousin of Matthias I..................1619–1637		18
Ferdinand III, son of Ferdinand II.................1637–1657		20
Leopold I, son of Ferdinand III....... 1658–1705		47
Joseph I, son of Leopold I...........................1705–1711		6
Charles VI, brother of Joseph I................... 1711–1740		29

House of Bavaria

Charles VII, Charles Albert, electoral Prince of Bavaria.1742–1745		3

House of Hapsburg—Lorraine

Francis I, son of Leopold, Duke of Lorraine.........1745–1765		20
Joseph II, son of Francis I..........................1765–1790		25
Leopold II, brother of Joseph II.............. 1790–1792		2
Francis II, son of Leopold II......................1792–1806		14

Interregnum

Confederation of the Rhine.........................1806–1815		9
German Bund.......................... 1815–1866		51
North German Confederation......................1866–1871		5

House of Hohenzollern

William I, King of Prussia (see Prussia) 1871–1888		17
Frederick III, son of William I....................1888–1888		¼
William II, son of Frederick III...................1888		

RULERS OF PRUSSIA

Frederick I, son of Frederick William of Brandenburg.1701–1713		12
Frederick William I, son of Frederick I..............1713–1740		27
Frederick II, the Great, son of Frederick William I..1740–1786		46
Frederick William II, nephew of Frederick II.......1786–1797		11
Frederick William III, son of Frederick William II..1797–1840		43
Frederick William IV, son of Frederick William III..1840–1861		21
William I, brother of Frederick William IV.........1861		

WEIGHT OF THE EARTH

It has been estimated that the average weight of the material of the earth is 354 pounds to the cubic foot. In the earth are about 259,800,000,000 cubic miles. As computed from those figures the weight of the earth is 6,768,838,943,539,200,000,000 tons.

TURF TERMS (DICTIONERY)

Aged Horses—Usually applied to horses on the running turf that are over six years of age.

Beefy—A horse with too much fat.

Barney—A race in which there has been a "cross" or "sell-out."

Bar—When a horse is prohibited from running or trotting in a certain class or entering for any special purse (he is said to be barred).

Beat Out—Beaten by a distance or from the start.

Bolt—To give up the race by running to one side.

Boots—Canvas or leather appliances to protect the ankles or knees.

Break—In trotting, to change to a run or skip.

Breaker—A horse is said to be a good or bad breaker as regards his ability to get quickly back to the proper gait.

Broke Down—When the tendons supporting the cannon-bones give way the horse is said to be broken down.

Brush—A short contest on the road or track.

By a Throatlatch—When a horse wins by a head he is sometimes said to have won by a throatlatch.

Carom—So called when one horse in a race jostles another so as to interfere with the latter.

Collar—To catch up with the leading horse.

Colt—Usually applied to a male horse until he has completed his fourth year.

Crack (To)—This is said of a horse that gives way and falls behind the moment he is caught up with.

Cross—It is a double cross where the party who agrees to lose either wins or tries to win without giving warning to his confederates.

Campaign—To make a tour through the country during the racing season.

Catch—To fall quickly into the proper stride.

Caution—To admonish a jockey or driver against any infraction of the rules.

Turf Terms—*Continued*

Circuit—A number of tracks associated together, such as the Western Circuit, Eastern Circuit, etc.

Claim—To protest; to claim a name for any horse.

Cluck—To make a clucking sound to encourage a horse to greater exertion.

Collar—To draw upon an antagonist.

Colors—The caps or costumes worn by jockeys or drivers to distinguish one from another.

Combination—A pool formed by jockeys or drivers to "fix" an event.

Convert—A term used by trainers; to change a horse's gait, such as a pacer to a trotter.

Cup—When a track is so moist that the horse's feet make deep impressions it is said to "cup."

Cut Down—To run a horse into another and injure his limbs so as to disable him.

Cut In—To take advantage of an opening.

Cut Out—To lead the others from the start; to set the pace.

Daisy Cutter—A horse that keeps his feet near the ground in trotting or running.

Dash—A single heat of one or more miles.

Dead Beat—Beaten to a standstill.

Dead Heat—When two or more horses cross the score at the same instant.

Dead One—A horse that will not run or has no chance to win, or is not meant to win.

Distance—In races of mile heats, 80 yards; of two mile heats, 150 yards; of three mile heats, 220 yards; of mile heats, 3 in 5, 100 yards. Horses in these positions are declared "distanced" when the leading horse or horses have crossed the score.

Dosed—When a horse has been given a drug to cause him to lose a race he is said to have been dosed.

Drawn—Withdrawn before or during a race.

Duffer—A horse which loses heart or refuses to exert himself during a race.

Entry—The posting of the names of an owner and horse intending to participate in a race.

End to End—A race in which the pace is forced from start to finish,

Filly—Usually, a mare continues to be so called until she has completed her fourth year.

Fixed—A race which is decided, before coming off, to go a certain way is said to have been "fixed."

Turf Terms—*Continued*

Feather Weight—Seventy-five pounds. If all the contestants in a race were privileged to "feather" it would be a race at "catch weight," although ordinarily "catch weight" means that the owner of a horse can place any weight upon him that he chooses, and he is presumed to choose the lightest practicable.

Flag—The signal used by the judge to shut out or distance a horse.

Fluke—So said when a horse has won a race through an accident.

Free handicap—It is called a free handicap race in which the owner. if he does not like the weight imposed by the handicaper, may withdraw his horse without paying forfeit.

For Blood—An expression used by drivers when they drive to win.

Forfeit--To pay forfeit; nonfulfillment of the conditions.

Gad—To whip or lash a horse.

Gentleman Rider—An amateur, or one who does not ride for pay.

Get Away—To rush from the score.

Go As They Please—To wagon, harness, or under saddle, as the owner pleases.

Gone Wrong—Out of condition, off the feed, or incapacitated from further use or turf training.

Got At—To poison a horse on the eve of a race or otherwise unfit him.

Handicaped—Weighted according to age, or the distance to be run or trotted.

Hands Down—A horse that wins without the aid of his jockey, and by the sheer force of his own speed is said to "win with [his jockey's] hands down."

Harness—When a horse trots to sulky he is said to go in "harness."

Headed—To lead the way by a head; to be lead by a head.

Heat—A division of the distance of a race, such as half-mile heats, mile heats, etc.

Hippodrome—A race that aims at gate money only, while professing to be for a stake, purse, or prize.

Homestretch—The last quarter of a track.

Hull Down—A nautical term, which, in its application to the turf, means that a horse is so far out of sight (behind) that he has no chance to win.

Hurdle—A fence-like arrangement used in hurdle races for horses to jump over.

Turf Terms—*Continued*

In Condition.—A term used by trainers to express a horse's being in good form, or condition for racing.

Jock.—Jockey, driver, or horse-dealer.

Jog.—Generally used where a horse has won easily.

Left at the Post.—A term used on the running turf, where a horse scores for races, but refuses to go on.

Levanted.—Applied to a word-cf-mouth bettor, who disappears as soon as he ascertains that he has lost.

Level-headed.—Steady. The opposite of flighty.

Lift.—A term used by drivers when manipulating the reins to rouse a horse to greater exertion.

Maiden.—A horse that has never won a running race.

Match Race.—One made expressly between horses, usually not more than two, in contradistinction to a race for a purse.

Mile and Repeat.—A race in which a mile is trotted and then repeated, the horse winning each mile being the winner.

Mixed-gaited.—When a horse changes from a trot to a pace, or runs in front and trots behind, he is said to be mixed-gaited.

Moral.—"A moral" is a "sure thing." It is a contraction of "a moral certainty."

Mount.—A jockey who is engaged to ride a horse in a race is said to have been given the mount.

Musician.—A horse that roars.

Naming at Post.—Naming the starters at the starting-post; used on the running turf.

Nobble—To poison a horse on the eve of a race, or otherwise unfit him.

Nomination—The entry or naming of a horse or embryo foal for a race.

Off—Out of condition; off the feed.

Office—The same thing as the tip, which is secret information as to the condition of a horse or the purpose in the race of those who have him in charge. It is called "the straight tip" when the information comes from owner, trainer or rider.

On—To be "on" is to back a horse. A person is also "on" who fancies he knows what will be the outcome of a race that other persons believe is to be conducted squarely.

Open The Gap—To draw away from the others.

Outsiders—All persons who do not, in one way or another, thrive by means of racing.

Turf Terms—*Continued*

Permission—Assent from the judges to dismount or get out of the sulky.

Plates—Light shoes worn by horses for racing.

Play or pay—Either start or lose the money paid for entry.

Pole—The inside or inside fence of a track.

Pole-Horse—One of a double team; the one having the inside of the track.

Pool—A combination or aggregation of bets. A clique.

Protest - A complaint made to the judges for having been fouled or otherwise obstructed; a complaint against a horse-driver or jockey who is not qualified to enter in a certain race or go upon a certain track.

Pulled—When a horse is prevented by his driver from winning a race, he is said to have been pulled.

Pulling a Horse—Riding or driving to lose, by repressing the speed of a horse. The same thing is popularly but erroneously called "hippodroming."

Punting—When a man backs a horse for small stakes he is called " a punter;" and if he uses the money he wins on one race to bet on the one next succeeding, he is said to be "playing on velvet." That is, as he cannot lose, he has "a soft thing."

Quarter-Horse—In running turf parlance, a horse good for a short distance only.

Quarter-Pole—The first dividing line of a mile track.

Quitter—A horse that loses heart in a race; a "duffer" or bolter.

Racker—A horse having a gait between a pace and a trot.

Rattle-Headed—Unsteady, flighty, unreliable.

Recall—A call back after a false start.

Record—The time made by a horse, under the rules; more specifically, his best time.

Right Off the Reel—Winning in straight heats.

Ringer—A running or trotting horse that is entered for or participates under an alias in races slower than those of his class.

Road-Horse—A horse used for road-driving.

Roarer—A horse that is broken-winded or breathes laboriously.

Ruled Off—Banished from a track or all tracks for infraction of rules.

Rules to Govern—The National Association Rules are generally meant when this expression is used.

Ruck—The main body of horses in a running race, neither the leaders nor the tailers, the latter of whom are termed whippers in.

Sandwiched—When running and trotting races are alternated at the same meeting, the events are said to be sandwiched.

Turf Terms—*Continued*

Score—The starting-point on a track; to score for a start.

Scratch—When a horse won a race through an accident.

Season—The duration of racing or stud service for the year.

Scut—Driven to win, or driven fast.

Set Back—When a horse has finished first in a heat through an infraction of the rules, the second horse is given his place, this is called a "set back."

Shake up—To rouse or encourage a horse.

Shut Out—A horse that is distanced or prevented from getting ahead of the others.

Side-Wheeler—A pacer.

Skip—A short break.

Spin—A short burst of speed; a sharp drive; used by road-riders.

Split Heats—Heats divided among the contestants.

Spoked—Having the spokes taken out of a wheel by the hub of another's vehicle.

Square Away—To get away steady from the start.

Square Gaited—Of level, steady action.

Starter—The person who sees that the horses are in proper positions and that they get away together.

Stayer—A horse that maintains steadiness and has the ability to go a long race without distress.

Steady—Pure-gaited, level-headed; to keep a horse well in hand.

Steeplechase—A running race in which fences, ditches and other obstructions are to be jumped.

Straight Heats—Heats of any race which are won in succession by one horse. As a technicality the race is not one of straight heats if the first heat is "dead" or is lost by a horse that wins the race in the next consecutive heats.

Stride—The distance from the point where a horse's hind foot leaves the ground to where it is put down.

Sugared—Bribed or paid to throw a race or heat.

Suspended—Ruled off a track or tracks for a time.

Sweepstakes—A race in which the winner of first and second horses takes the stakes, each owner contributing an equal amount.

Swerve—Going out of the regular course, such as cutting in ahead of an opponent.

Ticker.—Stop-watch.

Time-bar.—A record which bars a horse from entering into a slower class.

Turf Terms—*Continued*

Tip.—Is secret information as to the condition of a horse or the purpose in the race of those who have him in charge. It is called the "straight tip" when the information comes from owner, trainer, or rider.

Track Horse.—A horse used exclusively for racing.

Train on.—When a horse is able to race season after season, and improve.

Trial.—A private test of a horse's speed.

Turned Out.—Withdrawn from the turf and stabled or pastured.

Touts.—Hangers-on around stables for the purpose of picking up information and selling it.

Unplaced.—On the running turf, where a field of more than four start, the first four are numbered as they cross the score at the finish; the rest are unplaced.

Untried Horse.—Said of a stallion or a mare whose progeny has not yet been a winner.

Wagon (To).—To be driven to a skeleton four-wheeled vehicle.

Walk Over.—A race in which all the contestants but one are withdrawn.

Weaver.—A pacer is sometimes called a weaver from the peculiar motion of the head and neck while in motion.

Weight-for-Age.—The handicap or weight apportioned to a horse according to age.

Weighing-in—Weighing the jockeys with their whips and saddles, or drivers in a handicap race, before the start.

Weights—Metal appliances for a horse's feet, to steady him or convert from one gait to another. A bar of metal carried by a driver to bring him to the required weight.

Wearing Silk—Said of a jockey when he has donned the full suit of his stable.

Welcher—One who bets with no intention or means of paying if he loses.

Welter Weights—Heavy weights.

Whippers-in—The main body of horses in a running race—neither the leaders nor the tailers, the latter of whom are termed whippers-in.

Winded—Blown out, exhausted.

Winning Straight—See "Straight Heats."

Wire—The line from the judge's stand which marks the score.

Word—The signal from the judges for a fair start.

WHAT CONGRESS COSTS

There are just 414 members of the House and of the Senate, and to wait upon and run errands and hold open the doors as they pass in and out, and carrying cards of their callers, and taking care of the thousands of bills they put in, they have employed about 400 people, who are paid the snug little sum of $684,000 for doing so. Every member has one employe, and for the service of the same there is paid an average of about $1,800 each. A total of $420,000 is required to pay the salaries of the Senators, and for the compensation of the members of the House $1,695,000 is to be provided, and this brings the salaries of our national law-makers to a total of over $2,000,000 per year. It costs a little less than $150,000 per session to pay the mileage of the members, and the country pays $50,000 to purchase the stationery for the members and officers of the House alone in any one session. The treasury pays $52,000 for reporting the debates, whether Congress sits for one month or for 12, as the official reporters, like most of the clerks, are paid by the year, though they seldom do more than 12 months' work in the 24 months that make a Congressional term.

SALARY OF THE PRESIDENT OF THE UNITED STATES

Most people believe that the $50,000 a year which the president gets as his salary is the total sum. This is a mistake. $36,064 is given him, in addition to his salary of $50,000, to pay the salaries of his subordinates and clerks. His private secretary is paid $3,250; his assistant secretary $2,250; his stenographer $1,800; five messengers, each $1,200; a steward $1,800; two doorkeepers, each $1,200; four other clerks at good salaries; one telegraph operator; two ushers $1,200 and $1,400; a night usher $1,200; a watchman $900; and a man who takes care of the fires who receives $864 a year. In addition to this, there is given him $8,000 for incidental expenses such as stationery, carpets, and the care of the presidental stables. And under another heading there is given him nearly $40,000 more. Of this $12,500 is for repairs and refurnishing the White House; $2,500 is for fuel; $4,000 is for the green-house; $15,000 is for gas, matches, and the stable. The White House, all told, costs the country in connection with the president considerably over $125,000 yearly.

SALARIES OF THE PRINCIPAL UNITED STATES OFFICERS

Legislative

Rank	Salary per Annum
President	$50,000
Vice-President	8,000
Secretary of State	8,000
Secretary of Treasury	8,000
Secretary of Interior	8,000
Secretary of Navy	8,000
Secretary of War	8,000
Postmaster-General	8,000
Attorney General	8,000
Speaker of House of Representatives	8,000
United States Senators	5,000
Representatives in Congress	5,000

SALARIES OF UNITED STATES MINISTERS TO FOREIGN COUNTRIES

Country	Salary per Annum
England	$17,500
Germany	17,500
France	17,500
Russia	17,500
Italy	12,000
China	12,000
Brazil	12,000
Spain	12,000
Japan	12,000
Mexico	12,000
Central America	10,000
Chili	10,000
Peru	10,000
Venezuela	7,500
Turkey	7,500
Sweden and Norway	7,500
Netherlands	7,500
Denmark	5,000
Greece	5,000
Uruguay	5,000
Portugal	5,000
Switzerland	5,000
Siberia	4,000

United States Judges' Salaries

Office	Per annum
Chief Justice U. S. Supreme Court	$10,500
Associate Judges	10,000
United States Circuit Judges	6,000
United States District Judges from $3,500 to	5,000
Judge of U. S. Court of Claims	4,500

The Periods of Gestation

The periods of gestation are the same in Horse and Ass, 11 months each; Camel, 12 months; Elephant, 2 years; Lion, 5 months; Buffalo, 12 months; Cow, 9 months; Sheep, 5 months; Reindeer, 8 months; Monkey, 7 months; Bear, 6 months; Sow, 4 months; Dog, 9 weeks; Cat, 8 weeks; Rabbit, 4 weeks; Guinea Pig, 3 weeks; Wolf, 90 to 95 days; Parrots sit 40 days; Swans, 42 days; Goose, 30 days; Ducks, 30 days; Pea Hens, 28 days; Turkeys, 28 days; Hens, 21 days; Pigeons, 14 days; Canaries, 14 days.

The periods of gestation are subject to considerable variation, especially in domestic animals, and various conditions modify the period, of which the above are only the averages.

Fecundity of Fish

A codfish has been found to produce 3,686,760 eggs; a flounder, weighing 24 ounces to produce 1,357,403 eggs; Herring, weighing from 4 to 6 ounces to produce from 21,285 to 36,960 eggs; Ling to produce 19,248,652 eggs; Lobsters, weighing from 14 to 36 ounces to produce 21,699; a mackerel, weighing 20 ounces to produce 454,061 eggs; a prawn, to produce 8,800 eggs; a shrimp to produce 2,800 to 6,800 eggs; Soles, weighing 4½ ounces to produce 100,362.

Fecundity of Birds

Eagle, lay at a sitting 2 to 3 eggs; Falcon lay from 2 to 4 eggs; Fowl, domestic, lay from 6 to 20 eggs; Hawk, from 2 to 4 eggs; Owl, from 2 to 6 eggs; Partridge, from 14 to 20 eggs; Pheasant, from 10 to 20 eggs; Wren, from 10 to 16 eggs; Sparrow, from 4 to 6 eggs; Sparrow Hawk, from 2 to 5 eggs; Stork, from 2 to 3 eggs; Swallow, from 5 to 6 eggs.

LIFE PERIOD OF BIRDS

Blackbird, lives from 10 to 12 years; Blackcap, lives 15 years; Canary (if it does not couple), lives 24 years; Chaffinch, lives from 20 to 24 years; Crane, lives 24 years; Crow, lives 100 years; Eagle, lives 100 years; Fowl (common), lives 10 years; Goldfinch, lives from 10 to 15 years; Goose, lives 50 years; Heron, lives 60 years; Lark, lives from 16 to 18 years; Linnet, lives from 14 to 23 years; Nightingale, lives from 16 to 18 years; Parrot, lives 10 years; Partridge, lives 15 years; Peacock, lives 24 years; Pelican, lives from 40 to 50 years; Pheasant, lives 15 years; Pigeon, lives 20 years; Raven, lives 100 years; Robin, lives from 10 to 12 years; Skylark, lives from 10 to 30 years, Sparrow Hawk, lives 40 years; Starling, lives from 10 to 12 years; Swan, lives 100 years; Thrush, lives from 8 to 10 years; Titlark, from 5 to 6 years; Wheatear, lives 2 years; Wren, lives from 2 to 3 years.

HOW BIRDS AND BEASTS ARE GROUPED

A covey of Partridges; a nide of Pheasants; a wish of Snipe; a bevy of Quails; a flight of Doves; a flight of Swallows; a muster of Peacocks; a siege of Herons; a building of Rooks; a brood of Grouse; a plump of Wild Fowls; a strand of Plovers; a watch of Nightingales; a clattering of Choughs; a flock of Geese; a cast of Hawks; a trip of Dottrell; a swarm of Bees; a school of Whales; a shoal of Herrings; a herd of Swine; a skulk of Foxes; a pack of Wolves; a drove of Oxen; a sounder of Hogs; a troop of Monkeys; a pride of Lions; a sleuth of Bears.

THE GREAT CANALS IN THE WORLD

The longest canal is the Imperial Canal of China; it is over 1,000 miles long. In the year 1681 was completed the greatest undertaking of the kind on the European Continent, the Canal Languedoc or the Canal du Midi, to connect the Atlantic Ocean with the Mediterranean Sea; its length is about 148 miles; it has over 100 locks, and about 50 aqueducts, and its highest point is not less than 600 feet above the sea level; it is navigable for vessels of upward of 100 tons. The largest ship canal in Europe is the great North Holland Canal, completed in 1825; it is 125 feet wide at the water surface, and 31 feet wide on the bottom, and has a depth of 20 feet; it extends from Amsterdam to the Helder, in all 51 miles.

The Caledonia Canal in Scotland is 60 miles long, which includes three lakes. The Suez Canal is 88 miles long, of which 66 miles is actual canal. The Erie Canal is 350½ miles long and cost over $7,000,000. The Ohio Canal from Cleveland to Portsmouth is 332 miles long, and cost nearly $5,000,000. The Miami and Erie Canal is 291 miles long, and cost nearly $4,000,000. The Wabash and Erie Canal is 379 miles long.

ELEVATION OF LOCALITIES ABOVE THE SEA LEVEL

Place	Location	Feet Above Sea Level
Tunnel, C. & O. R. R.	Peru, S. Am.	15,645 feet
City of Potosi	Bolivia, S. Am.	13,330 "
Lake Titicaca	Peru, S. Am.	12,846 "
City of Cuzco	Peru, S. Am.	11,380 "
City of La Paz	Bolivia, S. Am.	10,883 "
City of Quito	Ecuador, S. Am	9,543 "
City of Chuquisaca	Bolivia, S. Am.	9,343 "
City of Bogota	U. S. of Colombia, S. Am.	8,732 "
Montezuma	Colorado, N. Am	10,295 "
City of Leadville	Colorado, N. Am.	10,200 "
City of Sherman	Wyoming Ter., N. Am.	8,242 "
Hospice Great St. Bernard	Alps, Europe	7,963 "
City of Arequipa	Peru, S. Am.	7,852 "
City of Mexico	Mexico, N. Am	7,471 "
City of Puebla	Mexico, N. Am.	7,200 "
Summit C. P. R. R.	California, N. Am	7,042 "
City of Valladolid	Mexico, N. Am.	6,395 "
City of Cabul	Afghanistan, Asia	6,360 "
Lake Tahoe	California, N. Am.	6,216 "
City of Cheyenne	Wyoming Ter., N. Am.	6,041 "
City of Popayan	U. S. of Colombia, S. Am.	6,000 "
City of Kelat	Beloochistan, Asia	6,000 "
City of Truckee	California, N. Am	5,866 "
City of Cashmere	India, Asia	5,000 "
City of Ogden	Utah, N. Am	4,340 "
City of Jalapa	Mexico, N. Am.	4,340 "
Great Salt Lake	Utah, N. Am.	4,220 "
City of Teheran	Persia, Asia	4,137 "
Pyramid Lake	Nevada, N. Am	4,000 "
City of Jerusalem	Syria, Asia	2,730 "
City of Madrid	Spain, Europe	1,995 "
City of Munich	Germany, Europe	1,764 "
Lake Neufchatel	Switzerland, Europe	1,437 "
Gibraltar	Spain, Europe	1,400 "
Lake Lucerne	Switzerland, Europe	1,380 "
Lake Zurich	Switzerland, Europe	1,363 "
Lake Constance	Switzerland, Europe	1,250 "
City of Geneva	Switzerland, Europe	1,230 "
City of Moscow	Russia, Europe	928 "
Lake Superior	United States, N. Am.	587 "
Lake Huron	United States, N. Am.	574 "
Lake Erie	United States, N. Am.	555 "
Lake Ontario	United States, N. Am.	282 "
City of Paris	France, Europe	115 "
City of London	England, Europe	64 "

LAKE AND SEAS BELOW THE SEA LEVEL

Name.	Location.	Feet Below the Sea Level
Dead Sea	Syria, Asia	1,317 feet
Lake Gennesaret	Syria, Asia	653 "
Caspian Sea	Between Europe and Asia	83 "

PLANETS, DISTANCE FROM THE SUN

Planet	Distance in Miles
Neptune	2,745,998,000 miles
Uranus	1,822,360,000 "
Saturn	872,132,000 "
Jupiter	480,000,000 "
Mars	145,000,000 "
Earth	92,000,000 "
Venus	68,000,000 "
Mercury	37,000,000 "
Earth's Moon distant from the earth	240,000 "

The enormous distance from us of the fixed stars, which are supposed to be suns for other planets, are beyond conception. One of these Sirius (the Dog Star), is supposed to be twenty trillion miles away.

The Size of Planets and Number of Moons.

Planet	Number of Moons It Has	Diameter in Miles
Sun		882,000 miles
Jupiter	4 Moons	91,000 "
Saturn	8 Moons	71,903 "
Neptune	1 Moon	38,000 "
Uranus	6 Moons	34,331 "
Venus		7,621 "
Mars	2 Moons	4,222 "
Mercury		2,984 "
Earth	1 Moon	8,000 "
Earth's Moon		2,162 "

The Velocity of Speed of Planets

The velocity cf speed with which the various planets move through space as they move around the sun is shown in the following:

Planet	Miles in One Hour
Mercury	110,725 mile
Venus	80,000 "
Earth	68,000 "
Jupiter	30,000 "
Saturn	22,309 "
Uranus	15,000 "
Neptune	12,000 "

Light moves at the rate of 192,000 miles a second, and yet passing with that velocity it would take three years and nine months to reach Alpha, the nearest star, which is nineteen trillions of miles away.

Time in Which Various Planets Revolve Around the Sun

The following is the time of revolution of the various planets around the sun:

Neptune	164½ years
Uranus	84 "
Saturn	29½ "
Jupiter	12 "
Mars	1 year 10½ months
Earth	1 yea
Venus	224⅔ days
Mercury	88

The Length of Days of the Planets

The length of days of the various planets is indicated by the following table, which shows the length of time required for revolution on its axis:

Planet	Time of Daily Revolution
Mars	24 hours, 39 minutes, 2½ seconds
Mercury	24 " 5 " 28 "
Earth	24 "
Venus	23 " 21 " 7 "
Saturn	10 " 30 "
Jupiter	9 " 56 "
Uranus	7 " 5 "

The sun revolves upon its own axis at the rate of 4,564 miles per hour, and yet it requires 25¼ days to complete one entire revolution.

Height of Cascades and Waterfalls

Name	Location	Height of Fall in feet
Sentinel	Yosemite Valley, Cal., N. Am	3,270 feet
Yosemite	Yosemite Valley, Cal., N. Am	2,634 "
Royal Arch	Yosemite Valley, Cal., N. Am	2,000 "
Cascade	Alps Mountains, Europe	2,400 "
Arve	Savoy, Europe	1,600 "
Montmorency	Canada, N. Am	250 "
Niagara	U. S. and Canada, N. Am	164 "
Missouri	Montana, N. Am	94 "
Missouri	Montana, N. Am	80 "
Missouri	Montana, N. Am	50 "
Potomac	Virginia and Maryland, N. Am	74 "
Passaic	New Jersey, N. Am	74 "
Mohawk	New York, N. Am	68 "
Cataracts of the Nile	Egypt, Africa	40 "

How Long it Would Take a Railroad to Reach the Sun

If a railway were built to the sun, and trains upon it were run at the rate of sixty miles an hour, run day and night without a stop, it would require 175 years to make the journey from the earth to the sun, distance 92,000,000 miles.

For Cleaning Various Substances

Black Silk

Brush and wipe it thoroughly, lay on table with the side intended to show, up; sponge with hot coffee strained through muslin; when partially dry, iron.

Alabaster

Use strong soap and water.

To Remove Stains or Grease from Oil Paint

Use bisulphide of carbon, spirits of turpentine, or if dry and old, use chloroform. These and tar spots can be softened with olive oil and lard.

Rust from Steel

Take half-ounce of emery powder mixed with one ounce of soap, and rub well.

Fruit Spots from Cottons

Apply cold soap, then touch the spot with a hair pencil or feather dipped in chlorate of soda, then dip immediately in cold water.

Stains, Iron Rust or Ink from Vellum or Parchment

Moisten the spot with a solution of oxalic acid; absorb the acid quickly by blotting-paper or cloth.

Grease from Silks

Take a lump of magnesia, rub it wet on the spot, let it dry, then brush the powder off.

Iron Rust from White Goods

May be removed from white goods by sour milk.

Scorch Stains from White Linen

Lay in bright sun.

Mildew

Moisten the spot with clean water; rub on it a thick coating of Castile soap mixed with chalk scrapings; rub with end of finger, then wash off.

Oil Marks on Wall Paper

Apply paste of cold water and pipe clay, leave it on all night, brush off in the morning.

To Renovate Plush Goods

Sponge carefully with chloroform. This is also excellent for restoring the color to goods that are faded.

Spoons Discolored by Cooked Eggs

May be brightened by a vigorous rubbing with common salt.

Paint Spots from Clothing

Saturate with equal parts turpentine and spirits of ammonia.

To Extract Stains from Silver

Salamoniac one part, vinegar sixteen parts, mix well and use this liquid with a piece of flannel, then wash the plate in clean water.

To Cleanse House Paper

Rub with a flannel cloth dipped in oatmeal.

To Cleanse Black Cloth

Mix one part of spirits of ammonia with three parts warm water, rub with sponge or dark cloth, clean with water; rub with the nap.

Ink and Rust Stains

Are removed easily by a solution containing ten parts each of tartaric acid, alum and distilled water. The solution has the trade name of Encrivior.

Ink Stains from White Cloth and Hands

Ripe tomatoes will remove ink stains from white cloth, also from the hands.

Cleanse Chromos

Go over lightly with a damp cloth.

Cleanse Furniture of Finger Marks

Rub with a soft rag and sweet oil.

Cleanse Zinc

Rub with a piece of cotton cloth dipped in kerosene, afterwards with a dry cloth.

Cleanse Hands from Vegetable Stains

Rub with a slice of raw potato.

To Clean Tinware

Common soda applied with a moistened newspaper and polish with a dry piece will make it look like new.

To Clean Window Glass

Paint can be removed by a strong solution of soda.

How to Prevent Iron from Rusting or to Remove Rust.

Apply kerosene with a rag when you are about to put your stove away for the Summer and it will prevent it from rusting. Treat your hardware and farming implements in the same way before you lay them aside in the Fall. To remove rust immerse the articles in kerosene oil and let them remain for some time; the rust will become so much loosened as to come off very easy.

How to Preserve Eggs

To each pailful of water add two pints of fresh slaked lime and one pint of common salt, mix well. Fill your barrel half full with this fluid, put your eggs down in it any time after June and before January, and they will keep two years if desired.

How to Keep Fresh Meat a Week or Two in Summer.

Any one can keep fresh meat very nicely for a week or two by putting it into sour milk or buttermilk (to be covered over with it) placing it in a cool cellar. The bone or fat need not be removed. Rinse well when used.

Prevent Decay of Farming Implements

When not in use have them sheltered from the sun, wind, rain and snow. By this means sleighs, carts, wagons, ploughs, harrows, threshing-machines and the like would last twice as long as they would if left in the open air, swelling from moisture one week and shrinking the next from the influence of the sun and wind.

Destroy Moss on Trees

Paint them with whitewash made of quicklime and wood ashes.

— 137 —

Protect Fruit Trees from Attack of Mice, etc.

Paint with tar, 1 part; tallow, 3 parts; mix; apply hot to the bark of a tree with a paint brush.

Prepare Flannel from Shrinking

Put new flannel into clean cold water and let it remain a week, changing the water frequently, then wash well in warm water using a little soap to remove the oily matter. Flannel prepared in this way will never shrink or get hard.

Clean Feathers

Feathers may be cleansed with a lather of soap and hot water and pearl ash. When it is a little cool wash the feathers in it, gently squeezing it, rinse it well in cold water, shaking well before the fire, but not too near. Curl it by drawing each fibre over the blunt edge of a fruit knife.

To Revive Withered Cuttings of Flowers, Rosebuds, etc.

Mix four drops of spirits of camphor with one ounce of water and place withered cuttings of flowers, rosebuds, etc., after carrying in the hands, and they will revive. Keep the stems in the fluid for half a day in a dark place.

How to Make Corks Good for Stoppers

Corks which you steep in vaseline are an excellent substitute for glass stoppers. They are not in the least affected by acids, and never become fixed through long disuse.

Polish for Fine, Hard Wood

Take shellac, 3 pounds; wood naptha, 3 pints; another recipe, 2 pounds shellac; 1 ounce each of powdered gum mastic and gum sandarac, one-half pint of copal varnish, mixed well and shaken until dissolved in one gallon spirits of nitre.

Walnut Stain

One and one-half ounces common soda, two and one-half ounces Vandyke brown and one-quarter ounce bichromate of potassium, dissolved in one quart water, boil the ingredients together for ten minutes; it makes a fine walnut stain.

THE LONGEST RIVERS IN THE WORLD

Name and Location	Miles Long
Missouri (with the Mississippi,) United States	4,500
Nile (Stanley's), Africa	4,100
Nile (Old Survey), Africa	3,000
Amazon, Brazil, S. Am	3,994
Mississippi (Proper), United States	3,200
Missouri, United States	2,900
Murry, Australasia	3,000
Yang-tze-Kiang, China, Asia	2,990
Hoang-Ho, China, Asia	2,800
Yenesei, Siberia, Asia	2,580
Lena, Siberia, Asia	2,500
Niger, Soudan, Africa	2,500
Mackenzie, British North America	2,500
Obi, Siberia, Asia	2,800
Congo, Central Africa	2,500
Volga, Russia, Europe	2,030
St. Lawrence, Canada, N. Am	2,060
Madeira, Brazil, S. Am	2,000
Amoor, Siberia, Asia	2,300
Parana with Platte, Argentine Republic	2,130
Rio Grande, United States, N. Am	1,800
Indus, Hindostan, Asia	1,795
Danube, Russia, Europe	1,630
Sandes, Hindostan, Asia	1,600
Brahmapoota, Thibet, Asia	1,500
St. Francisco, Brazil, S. Am	1,400
Columbia, United States, N. Am	1,090
Colorado, United States, N. Am	1,000
Yellowstone, United States, N. Am	1,000
Ohio, United States, N. Am	980
Rhine, Germany, Europe	810
Arkansas, United States, N. Am	900
Tennessee, United States, N. Am	800
Red River of the North, United States, N. Am	700
Cumberland, United States, N. Am	600
Alabama, United States, N. Am	600
Susquehanna, United States, N. Am	500
James, United States, N. Am	500
Connecticut, United States, N. Am	450
Seine, France, Europe	425
Delaware, United States, N. Am	400
Potomac, United States, N. Am	400
Hudson, United States, N. Am	325
Kenebec, United States, N. Am	160
Thames, England, Europe	233
Shannon, Ireland, Europe	200

Fine Decorative Work Paste

Take seventy-five parts of India-rubber, dissolved in sixty parts of chloroform, with fifteen parts gum mastic added makes a purely transparent paste which can be used in the most delicate kind of decorative work.

SIZE OF THE OCEANS

Name	Square Miles	Name	Square Miles
Pacific	77,000,000	Antarctic	13,000,000
Atlantic	31,000,000	Arctic	7,000,000
Indian	21,000,000		

SIZE AND LENGTH OF SEAS

Name	Location	Area Sq. Miles	Length in Miles
Mediterranean	Bet. Europe and Africa	977,000	2,000
Behring	Bet. North America and Asia	567,000	
Caribbean	South America	200,000	1,800
China	Asia		1,700
Red	Bet. Africa and Asia	185,000	1,400
Japan	Asia		1,000
Black	Europe	185,000	932
Caspian	Asia	156,000	640
Baltic	Europe	154,570	600
Okhotsh	Asia		600
White	Europe	4,500	450
Aral	Asia	26,900	250
Dead	Asia	400	

SIZE OF LAKES

Name	Location	Length Miles	Width Miles	Area Sq. Miles
Superior	North America	380	120	32,000
Michigan	North America	330	60	22,400
Baikal	Asia	360	35	8,000
Huron	North America	250	90	21,000
Great Slave	North America	300	45	12,800
Erie	North America	270	50	9,600
Winnipeg	North America	240	40	8,500
Athabasca	South America	200	20	4,600
Ontario	North America	180	40	6,300
Great Bear	North America	150	40	14,000
Maracaybo	South America	150	60	6,500
Ladoga	Europe	125	75	6,804
Champlain	North America	123	12	15,000
Lake of the Woods	North America	70	25	7,650
Geneva	Europe	50	10	336
Constance	Europe	45	10	200
George	North America	36	3	114
Cayuga	South America	36	4	100
Great Salt Lake	North America			46

FACTS ABOUT THE PLANET EARTH

Diameter at the Equator, 7,925 miles, diameter at the Poles, 7,899 miles; mean diameter, 7,916 miles; circumference at the Equator, 24,899 miles; surface of the Earth, in round numbers : Land, 54,500,- 000 square miles; water, 142,000,000 square miles; total, 196,000,000 square miles. Mean annual temperature: Poles, 30°; Polar regions, 36°; Torrid Zone, 75°; Equator, 82°; Globe, 50°. Mean annual rainfall, 36 inches. Specific gravity, 5.450 to 5.000.

AREA AND POPULATION OF THE EARTH BY CONTINENTS

(According to Behm and Wagner's estimate, 1884.)

Continental Divisions	Area in Sq. Miles	Inhabitants Number	Per Sq. Mile
Asia	17,832,340	795,591,000	44.0
America	15,389,250	100,410,400	6.5
Africa	11,929,300	205,823,200	17.0
Europe	3,802,234	327,743,400	84.0
Australasia	3,581,140	4,232,000	1.1
Polar Regions	1,791,280	82,500	
Total	54,415,544	1,433,887,500	26.3

An estimate of the population of the earth made in 1886 by Professor E. Levasseur for the International Statistical Institute is as follows: Asia, 789,000,000; America, 112,000,000; Africa, 197,000,000; Europe, 347,000,000; Oceania, 38,000,000; total, 1,483,000,000.

POPULATION OF THE EARTH ACCORDING TO RACE

(Estimate by John Bartholomew, F. R. G. S., Edinburgh.)

Race	Location	Number
Indo-Germanic or Aryan	Europe, Persia, etc	545,500,000
Mongolian or Turanian	Greater part of Asia	630,000,000
Semitic or Hamitic	North Africa, Arabia	65,000,000
Negro and Bantu	Central Africa	150,000,000
Hottentot and Bushmen	South Africa	150,000
Malay and Polynesian	Australasia and Polynesia	35,000,000
American Indian	North and South America	15,000,000
Total		1,440,650,000

Distance Around the World in Traveling (Statute Miles)

From San Francisco, Cal., to Yokohama, Japan...........4,764 miles
" Yokohama to Hong Kong, Hong Kong Island.......1,620 "
" Hong Kong to Singapore, Asia....................1,150 "
" Singapore to Calcutta, India, Asia................1,200 "
" Calcutta to Bombay, India, Asia...................1,409 "
" Bombay to Aden, Arabia, Asia....................1,664 "
" Aden to Suez, Egypt, Africa......................1,308 "
" Suez to Alexandria, Egypt, Africa................. 250 "
" Alexandria to Marseilles, France, Europe...........1,900 "
" Marseilles to Paris, France, Europe................ 536 "
" Paris to London, England, Europe................. 316 "
" London to Liverpool, England, Europe............. 205 "
" Liverpool to New York, United States.............3,000 "
" New York to San Francisco, Cal., United States.....3,311 "

Principal Exports of Countries

Argentine Republic.—Condensed meats, hides, horsehair, oil, tallow, wool.

Austria.—Salt, meerschaum pipes, flax, cutlery, linens.

Australasia.—Tin, copper, coal, hides, wool, gold, silver.

Arabia.—Coffee, gum arabic, aloes, alum, almonds, frankincense, myrrh, balsam.

Belgium.—Cotton, linen and woolen manufactures, iron, marble, mats, mirrors.

Brazil.—Coffee, diamonds, drugs, hides, sugar, rum, tobacco, dye-woods, crude rubber.

Canada, Nova Scotia, and New Brunswick.—Corn, flour, fish, furs, gold, leather, hides, lumber.

Cape Colony.—Brandy, wine, ostrich feathers, hides, tallow.

Central America.—Logwood, cochineal, coffee, rice, sugar, mahogany, indigo, cocoa, tobacco.

China.—Camphor, cassia, chinaware, lead, mercury, opium, pearls, rice, silk, raw and manufactured, tea, sugar, zinc.

Colombia Republic.—Coffee, gold, indigo, Peruvian bark.

Denmark.—Butter, cheese, cattle, feathers, horses, grain, jute, wool, beef, pork.

Exports—*Continued*

Eastern, Western, and Southern Africa.—Gold, ivory, ostrich feathers, palm oil, fruit.

Egypt.—Asafœtida, cotton, grain, hemp, hides, linseed, gum, silk, tobacco, indigo, fruit, sugar.

Ecuador.—Cocoa, coffee, cotton, India-rubber, Peruvian bark, sugar, indigo.

France.—Brandy, butter, chinaware, cotton, linen, silk and woolen manufactures, drugs, artificial flowers, hair, hats, millinery goods, jewelry, wine, olive oil, paper, perfumery, leather goods, toys.

Germany.—Linen, cotton, silk and woolen manufactures, copper, hops, zinc, jewelry, cutlery, hardware, toys, perfumery, chemical products, flax, beer, wine, leather.

Great Britain and Ireland.—Iron, cotton, linen, silk and woolen manufactures, ale, alkali, arms, coal, chemical products, hardware, earthenware, cutlery, copper, horses, tin, porter, lace, machinery.

Greenland.—Whale oil, whalebone, sealskins.

Greece.—Cotton, currants, figs, olive oil, honey, leather, silk, soap, wine, zinc.

Holland.—Fine linen, woolens, butter, cheese, fish, cattle.

India.—Coffee, cotton, gum, hides, indigo, jute, opium, pearls, precious stones, saffron, pepper, shawls, sugar, tea, silk, raw and manufactured.

Italy.—Alabaster, brimstone, almonds, chemical products, fruit, hemp, olive oil, sumac, silk, wine, spirits.

Iceland.—Fish, train oil.

Japan.—Silk and cotton goods, copper, iron, glass, chinaware, varnish, tea, silk, raw and manufactured.

Java.—Arrack, cinnamon, rice, indigo, coffee, cloves, cochineal, gold, pepper, sago, pearls, tin, tobacco.

Liberia.—Coffee, gold, palm oil, gum, rice, sugar.

Mexico.—Gold, silver, sugar, cochineal, vanilla, copper, mahogany, dyewood, indigo, jalap, hides, lead.

Madagascar.—Cattle, cotton, hides, indigo, maize, rice.

Morocco.—Almonds, beans, fruit, gum, Morocco leather, oil, skins, wool.

Paraguay.—Cassava, sugar, corn, tobacco.

Persia.—Asafœtida, carpets, rugs, madder, opium, pearls, shawls, silk, tobacco, rhubarb, swords.

Peru.—Silver, gold, Peruvian bark, saltpetre, quinine, borax, cubic-nitre, guano, copper, alpaca-wood.

Exports—*Continued*

Chili.—Copper, gold, hides, wheat, flour, silver, sugar, wool.

Portugal.—Cork, fruit, oil, fish, saffron, salt, wine.

Russia.—Bristles, hemp, iron, linen, grain, cordage, flax, copper, caviar, flour, linseed, furs, corn, potash, skins, hides, stearine, timber, tallow, tar, wool, platina.

Sandwich Islands.—Hides, rice, salt, skins, sugar, tallow, wool, fruit.

Spain.—Copper, cork, fish, fruit, grain, lead, olive oil, quicksilver, rice, saffron, sheep, skin, wine, wool.

Sweden and Norway.—Iron, steel, copper, timber, fish, bones, butter, cheese, cattle, nickel, jute, tar.

Switzerland.—Cheese, cotton, linens, watches, jewelry, laces, silks, machines.

Turkey.—Currants, figs, gum, goat's hair, carpets, hides, maize, mastic, meerschaum, oil, opium, raisins, saffron, shawls, silk, muslin, swords.

Transvaal.—Gum arabic, gold, ivory, ostrich feathers.

United States.—Butter, cattle, cheese, coal, coal oil, corn, cotton, canned fruits, meats and fish, flour, furs, gold, grain, ham, hardware, hides, hogs, iron, lard, lead, copper, leather, lumber, machinery, meat, molasses, pork, quicksilver, raisins, silver, skins, tobacco, watches, wine, linen, woolen and cotton goods, machinery of all kinds.

Uruguay and Argentine Republic.—Condensed meat, guano, hides, horsehair, oil, skins, tallow, wool.

Venezuela.—Balsam, cocoa, coffee, copper, cotton, hides, tobacco.

West Indies.—Alum, arrow root, cochineal, cocoa, ginger, tobacco, sugar, molasses, rum, coffee, indigo, pepper.

MARRIAGE AGE IN DIFFERENT COUNTRIES

In Austria, 14 years for both sexes; Belgium, the man 18 years and the woman at 15 years; France, the man at 18 years, the woman at 15 years; Germany, the man at 18 years, the woman at 14 years; Greece, the man at 14 years, the woman at 12 years; Hungary—the Catholics, the man at 14 years, the woman at 12 years; the Protestants, the man at 18 years, the woman at 15 years; Portugal, the man at 14 years, the woman at 12 years; Russia, the man at 18 years, the woman at 16 years; Saxony, the man at 18 years, the woman at 16 years; Spain, the man at 14 years, the woman at 14 years; Switzerland, the man at 14 years, the woman at 12 years; Turkey at puberty; United States, the man at 21 years, the woman at 18 years.

SIZE OF ANIMALS

Antelope, 3¼ feet
Armadillo and tail, 5 feet
Anteater, 1 foot
Badger, 2½ feet
Barbary Ape, 3½ feet
Bottle-nosed Seal, 11 to 18 feet
Civet, 2 feet
Chamois, 3 feet
Common Bat, 4 or 5 inches
Common Seal, 4 to 6 feet
Dormouse, 6 inches
Dog-faced Baboon, 5 feet
Dromedary, 6 to 7 feet
Elephant, 10 or 11 feet
Elephant (high), 6 or 7 feet
Ermine, 10 inches
Ferret, 14 inches
Flying Squirrel, 6 inches
Fox, 1½ to 2 feet
Giraffe, 15 to 16 feet (high)
Great Anteater, 4 feet
Hedgehog, 10 inches
Hyena, 3 feet
Stag, 4 to 5 feet
Sable, 11 inches
Spectrum Bat, 7 inches
Tiger, 8 to 9 feet
Tiger (high), 4 feet
Tapir, 6 feet

Hippopotamus, 10 to 20 feet
Ichneumon, 15 inches
Jackal, 2½ feet
Kangaroo, 3 to 4 feet
Lion, 6 to 8 and 9 feet
Lynx, 4 feet
Lioness, 5 to 7 feet
Mole, 6 inches
Marmot, 10 inches
Musk Deer, 3¼ feet
Maned Seal, 10 to 14 feet
Opossum, 15 to 18 inches
Ordinary Squirrel, 8 inches
Otter, 3¼ feet
Orang-outang, 4½ to 5½ feet
Pigmy Antelope 10 inches
Pigmy Ape, 3½ feet
Polecat, 17 inches
Porcupine, 2½ feet
Roebuck, 3¾ feet
Raccoon, 2 feet
Rhinoceros, 12 feet
Rhinoceros (high), 6 to 7 feet
Vampire, 6 to 12 inches
Vaulting Monkey, 13 inches
Wolf, 2½ to 3 feet
Weasel, 7½ inches
Wild Cat, 2 to 5 feet
Walrus or Morse, 15 to 18 feet

BAIT FOR DIFFERENT GAME

Badger—Mice or flesh of any kind.
Beaver—Fresh roots.
Fox—Fowl, flesh, fish, toasted cheese.
Marten—Head of fish, piece of meat or fowl.
Mink—Fowl, flesh or roasted fish.
Muskrat—Carrots, potatoes, apples, etc.
Opossum—Nuts, corn, mice, piece of fowl.
Otter—Fish, piece of a bird or otter mush.
Raccoon—Chicken, frog or fish.
Skunk—Mice, meat, piece of a fowl.
Squirrel—Grain, nuts, or ear of corn.
Wolf—Waste part of tame or wild game.
Woodchuck—Roots, fruit, corn or bread.

How Fast Rabbits Increase

One Pair of Rabbits in four years, if none are killed or die, will be increased to 1,250,000 rabbits.

Shortest and Longest Verse in the Bible

Shortest verse, St. John, 11th chapter, 35th verse; longest verse, Esther, 8th chapter, 9th verse.

Large Families

Lucas Saez returned to Spain in June, 1883, from the United States with 37 children, 79 grandchildren, and 81 great-grandchildren—in all 197 people, 107 males and 90 females, his eldest son being 70 years of age.

Tedor Vassileff, of Moscow, Russia, in 1782, had 83 children living when pensioned by the Czar. He had 69 children by his first wife, at 27 births; and, after her death, had 18 more by his second wife, in 8 births.

Parent	Place	Number of Children	Date
Mme. Frescobaldi	Florence, Italy	52	1570
David Wilson	Indiana, United States	47	1850
Mr. Greenhill	Abbots Langley, Europe	39	
Rev. Dr. Erskine	Scotland, Europe	33	1760

Mme. Frescobaldi had never less than three children at a birth.

Heaviest Men

Miles Darden (the Tennessee Giant), height 7 feet 6 inches, and weighed over 1,000 pounds.

Daniel Lambert (English), was 5 feet 11 inches high, and weighed 739 pounds.

Small People or Dwarfs

Smallest woman, Lucia Zarate, height 20 inches, born in Mexico in 1865.

Smallest man, General Mite, height 21 inches, born in New York in 1864.

Che Mah (the Chinese dwarf), if living is nearly 50 years of age, he is 25 inches high.

Tom Thumb, height 28 inches.

Commodore Nutt 32 inches.

TALLEST MEN (GIANTS)

The Giant Og. (in Bible), 16 feet high.
The Giant Goliah (in Bible), 10 feet high.
Hans Bar (Hungarian Soldier), 11 feet high.
Chang (the Chinese Giant), 8 feet 2 inches high.
Brustard, the Giant, 7 feet 9 inches high.
Miles Darden (the Tennessee Giant), 7 feet 6 inches high.

A LADY'S CHANCE TO MARRY

Every lady has some chance to marry, it may be one to fifty, or it may be ten to one that she will. Representing her entire chance at one hundred at certain points of her progress in time, it is found to be in the following ratio:

Ladies between the ages of			15 and 20 years		....	$14\frac{1}{2}$	per cent	
"	"	"	"	20 " 25 "	....	52	"	"
"	"	"	"	25 " 30 "	....	18	"	"
"	"	"	"	30 " 35 "	....	$15\frac{1}{2}$	"	"
"	"	"	"	35 " 40 "	....	$3\frac{3}{4}$	"	"
"	"	"	"	40 " 45 "	....	$2\frac{1}{2}$	"	"
"	"	"	"	45 " 50 "	....	$\frac{3}{4}$ of 1	"	"
"	"	"	"	50 " 55 "	....	$\frac{1}{4}$ of 1	"	"

HEIGHT AND WEIGHT OF LADIES

It is often asked how thick a lady ought to be in proportion to her height. A very young girl may becomingly be thinner than a matron, but the following table gives a fair indication of proper proportions:

Height	Weight in Pounds	Height	Weight in pounds
Four feet, 7 inches	about 73	Five feet, 6 inches	about 144
Four feet, 10 inches	" 90	Five feet, 7 inches	" 150
Five feet	" 100	Five feet, 8 inches	" 155
Five feet, one inch	" 106	Five feet, 9 inches	" 163
Five feet, two inches	" 113	Five feet, 10 inches	" 169
Five feet, three inches	" 119	Five feet, 11 inches	" 176
Five feet, four inches	" 130	Six feet	" 180
Five feet, five inches	" 138	Six feet, one inch	" 186

THE WEDDING ANNIVERSARY

At end of first year comes the.........................Cotton Wedding
At end of second year comes the....................Paper "
At end of third year comes the...................Leather "
At end of fifth year comes the....................Wooden "
At end of seventh year comes the....   ....Woolen "
At end of tenth year comes the.........................Tin "
At end of twelfth year comes the.......Silk and Fine Linen "
At end of fifteenth year comes the.................Crystal "
At end of twentieth year comes the.................China "
At end of twenty-fifth year comes the..............Silver "
At end of thirtieth year comes the... ....Pearl "
At end of fortieth year comes the................... Ruby "
At end of fiftieth year comes the..................Golden "
At end of seventy-fifth year comes the...........Diamond "

WEIGHT OF VARIOUS BREEDS OF POULTRY

	pounds	ounces
Black Polish cock, 3 years old weighs.	5	3
" " hen, 3 years old weighs	3	4
" Spanish cock, 4 months old weighs	2	11
" " pullet, weighs....	2	11
Cochin-China cock, 16 mo. old (Moulting) weighs..	6	5
" " hen weighs	4	6
Dorking cock weighs	7	
" hen weighs	6	8
Game cock weighs	4	10
" hen weighs	3	
Golden Polish cock weighs	5	
" " hen weighs	3	8
Malay cock, 16 months old weighs	6	14
" hen, 16 months old, weighs	4	8
Pheasant Malay cock, 2 years old, weighs	7	
" " hen weighs	5	1
" " pullet, 17 months old, weighs....	5	3
Silver Hamburg hen weighs	3	1
" Polish hen weighs	3	4
Turkey (cock), 16 months old, weighs	16	
" (hen), 3 to 4 years old, weighs	8	6
White China gander, 6 years old weighs	12	13
" " goose, weighs	11	13

SPEED OF BIRDS

Hawks fly at the rate of 150 miles per hour.
Ducks "   "   "   90 "   "   "
Crows "   "   "   25 "   "   "
Falcons "   "   "   75 "   "   "
Sparrows   "   "   92 "   "   "

BIBLE FACTS AND FIGURES

The Old Testament contains 2,728,100 letters, 592,493 words, 23,214 verses, 929 chapters, and 39 books. The New Testament contains 838,380 letters, 181,253 words, 7,959 verses, 260 chapters and 27 books. The total for Old and New Testament, 3,566,480 letters. 773,746 words, 31,173 verses, 1,189 chapters and 66 books. The Bible contains 3,500,000 ems (compositor's measure).

The word Reverend occurs but once, which is in the 9th verse of the 111th Psalm.

The middle verse of the Bible is the 8th verse of the 118th Psalm.

The 21st of the 7th chapter of Ezra contains all the letters of the alphabet except the letter J.

The 19th chapter of II Kings and the 37th chapter of Isaiah are alike.

The longest verse is the 9th verse of the 8th chapter of the Book of Esther.

The shortest verse is the 35th verse of the 11th chapter of the Book of St. John.

There are no words or names of more than six syllables.

MOST NORTHERN AND SOUTHERN POINTS
REACHED BY EXPLORERS

The following table shows the farthest points of north latitude by Arctic Explorers up to and including the Greely expedition:

Year	Explorers	North Latitude
1607	Hudson.............................	80 deg., 23 min., 00 sec.
1773	Phipps (Lord Musgrove)............	80 " 48 " 00 "
1806	Scoresby	81 " 12 " 42 "
1827	Parry.............................	82 " 45 " 30 "
1874	Meyer (on land)...................	82 " 9 " 00 "
1875	Markham (Nare's expedition).......	83 " 20 " 26 "
1876	Payer.............................	83 " 7 " 00 "
1884	Lockwood (Greely's party).........	83 " 24 " 30 "

The farthest point reached south was by Rose in February, 1842, was 78 degrees, 11 minutes, south latitude; and the farthest points north was by Lockwood in May, 1882, was 83 degrees, 24 minutes, 30 seconds north latitude.

The Longest Tunnels in the World

The longest tunnel in the world is the Mount St. Gothard Tunnel, Italy. It is 48,840 feet long or nearly 10 miles long.

The Mount Cenis Tunnel, Italy, is next, is 39,840 feet long or about 7 miles long.

The Hoosac Tunnel, Mass., is 25,080 feet long or about 4½ miles long, the longest in the United States.

The Nochistongo Tunnel is 21,659 feet long, or about 4 miles long.

The Sutro Tunnel is 21,120 feet long or about 4 miles long.

The Thames and Medway Tunnel, England, is 11,880 feet long, or about 2 miles long.

Herschel's Weather Table

For Foretelling the Weather, Throughout all the Lunations of Each Year, Forever

This table and the accompanying remarks are the result of many years' actual observation, the whole being constructed on a due consideration of the attraction of the Sun and Moon, in their several positions respecting the Earth, and will, by simple inspection, show the observer what kind of weather will most probably follow the entrance of the Moon into any of its quarters, and that so near the truth as to be seldom or never found to fail:

If the New Moon, First Quarter, Full Moon, or Last Quarter Happens Between

	In Summer	In Winter
Midnight and 2 o'clock	Fair	Frost unless wind Southwest.
2 and 4 morning	Cold and showers.	Snow and stormy
4 and 6 "	Rain.	Rain.
6 and 8 "	Wind and rain.	Stormy.
8 and 10 "	Changeable	Cold rain if wind W, snow if E
10 and 12 "	Frequent showers	Cold and high wind
12 and 2 afternoon	Very rainy	Snow or rain.
2 and 4 "	Changeable	Fair and mild.
4 and 6 "	Fair.	Fair.
6 and 8 "	Fair if wind NW.	Fair and frosty if wind N or NE
8 and 10 "	Rainy if S or SW.	Rain or snow if South or SW.
10 and midnight	Fair.	Fair and frosty.

Observations.—1. The nearer the time of the Moon's change, first quarter, full and last quarter are to *midnight*, the fairer will be the weather during the next seven days.

Weather Table—*Continued*

2. The space for this calculation occupies from ten at night till two next morning.

3. The nearer to *midday* or *noon* the phases of the moon happen, the more foul or wet weather may be expected during the next seven days.

4. The space for this calculation occupies from ten in the forenoon to two in the afternoon. These observations refer principally to the Summer, though they affect Spring and Autumn nearly in the same ratio.

5. The Moon's change, first quarter, full and last quarter, happening during six of the afternoon hours, *i. e.*, from four to ten, may be followed by fair weather; but this is mostly dependent on the *wind*, as is noted in the table.

6. Though the weather, from a variety of irregular causes, is more uncertain in the latter part of Autumn, the whole of Winter, and the beginning of Spring, yet in the main the above observations will apply to those periods also.

7. To prognosticate correctly, especially in those cases where the *wind* is concerned, the observer should be within sight of a good *vane*, where the four cardinal points of the heavens are correctly placed.

FRENCH PASTE DIAMONDS

French paste used in making artificial diamonds is a kind of glass with a mixture of oxide of lead. Imitation stones are now so nearly perfect that the market of real diamonds is beginning to suffer.

French chemists now reproduce the dichroism of the sapphire, and the composition of rubies of which the base is phosphate of lime.

DENSITY OF POPULATION

The population per square mile of the different countries is as follows:

Belgium	451	China	110
England and Wales	389	Scotland	109
Holland	291	Portugal	108
Italy	237	Spain	90
Japan	209	Greece	73
Germany	193	Sweden and Norway	21
Switzerland	175	Turkey	20
Ireland	169	United States	11
Austro-Hungary	158	Russia	10
France	150	Mexico	9
Denmark	111	Brazil	3

Different Nations, Names of their People and the Language they Speak

Name of Nation	Name of People	Language Spoken
Abyssinia	Abyssinians	Abyssinian.
Afghanistan	Afghans	Persian and Hindoostanee.
Algeria	Algerine	Chiefly Arabic.
Arabia	Arabs, Arabians	Arabic.
Australasia	Australasians	Dutch, English and various native languages are spoken.
Austria	Austrians	German, Hungarian, Slavonic.
Belgium	Belgians	Flemish and French.
Beloochistan	Beloochees	Beloochee and Hindoostanee.
Bolivia	Bolivians	Spanish
Brazil	Brazilians	Portuguese.
Canada	Canadians	English and French.
Chile	Chileans	Spanish.
China	Chinese	Chinese.
East Indies	East Indians	Hindoostanee, Bengalee, Siamese, Malay, etc.
Egypt	Egyptians	Chiefly Arabic and Italian.
France	French	French.
Germany	Germans	German.
Greece	Greeks	Greek.
Greenland	Greenlanders	Danish and Esquimaux.
Hindoostan	Hindoos	Hindoostanee and others.
Holland	Dutch	Dutch.
Iceland	Icelanders	Icelanderic.
Ireland	Irish	English and Irish.
Italy	Italians	Italian.
Japan	Japanese	Japanese.
Mexico	Mexican	Spanish.
Norway	Norwegians	Danish.
Paraguay	Paraguayans	Spanish.
Peru	Peruvians	Spanish.
Poland	Poles	Polish.
Persia	Persians	Persian.
Portugal	Portuguese	Portuguese.
Prussia	Prussians	German.
Russia	Russians	Russian.
Sweden	Swedes	Swedish.
Scotland	Scotch	English and Gaelic.
Siam	Siamese	Siamese.
Siberia	Siberians	Russian mostly.
Spain	Spaniards	Spanish.
Switzerland	Swiss	German, French and Italian.
Turkey	Turks	Turkish.
United States	American	English.
Venezuela	Venezuelans	Spanish.
Wales	Welsh	English and Welsh.
West Indies	West Indians	Spanish.

THE HUMAN FAMILY

The human family living to-day consists of about 1,450,000,000 individuals. In Asia, where man was first planted there are now about 800,000,000 souls, on an average 120 to the square mile. In Europe there are about 320,000,000 souls, averaging 100 to the square mile. In Africa there are about 210,000,000. In America, North and South, there are about 110,000,000, relatively thinly scattered and recent. In the islands, large and small, are probably 10,000,000 souls. The extremes of the white and black are five to three, the remaining 700,-000,000 intermediate brown and tawny. Of the human race 500,000,000 are well clothed, that is wear garments of some kinds and live in houses partly furnished with the appointments of civilization; 700,000,000 are semi-clothed, living in huts and caves with no furnishing; 250,000,000 are practically naked, having nothing that can be called a home, are barbarous and savage. The range is from the topmost round—the Anglo-Saxon civilization, which is the highest known—down to naked savagery. The portion of the race lying below the line of human condition is at the very least three-fifths of the whole or 900,000,000. All the people now living in the world, say 1,450,000,000, could find standing room within the limits of a field 100 miles square. In a field 200 miles square they could all be comfortably seated.

GOLD LEAF THICKNESS

Gold leaf is the 254-248th part of an inch in thickness, which is common work of the gold-beater. Sheets have been beaten the 367,-500th part of an inch in thickness. One ounce of gold can be beaten out so as to cover 160 square feet of surface.

AGE AND MORTALITY

The following table which years of experience of scientific men has proven, settles the death-rate. One of the following number of persons may die within one year:

At 10 years	1 in 134	At 45 years	1 in 90
At 15 "	1 in 131	At 50 "	1 in 73
At 20 "	1 in 129	At 55 "	1 in 54
At 25 "	1 in 124	At 60 "	1 in 35
At 30 "	1 in 119	At 65 "	1 in 25
At 35 "	1 in 112	At 70 "	1 in 17
At 40 "	1 in 103		

BLEEDING WOUNDS. HOW TO STOP IT.

If blood spurts from the wound, an artery is divided; bind limb tightly above wound with India-rubber tubing, strap, handkerchief or scarf; or, bend the limb forcibly at next joint above wound; or, press flat hand or stone where blood is flowing. If blood flows freely, but does not spurt, a vein is divided; then apply same measures as in case wounded artery, but below the wound. If scalp wounded, make a pad of cloth or waste, and bandage very tightly over wound with folded pocket handkerchief. Send for a physician then.

BURNS AND SCALDS—TREATMENT

Apply lint, cotton, wool or waste, soaked in oil, or oil and lime water, and bind the same on with handkerchief or cloth. If necessary to remove clothes, cut them off by running knife or scissors along seams. Send for a physician then.

BROKEN LIMBS

Broken Leg—Treatment

Pull on leg steadily and firmly until it is of same length as sound one. Roll up a coat or empty sack into form of a cushion; carefully place leg upon it; then bind two together with scarves or handkerchiefs. Do not lift patient from the ground until stretcher is close at hand. Take great pains by carefully lifting to prevent broken bone coming through skin.

Broken Thigh—Treatment

Take hold of ankle and by steady traction, pull limb to same length as sound one; another person must then tie knees together, and afterward the ankles. Both limbs should then be laid over a sack of straw, or folded coat, so as to bend the knees. Patient should on no account be moved until stretcher or cart is close at hand. Send for a doctor then.

Broken Arm—Treatment

Pull arm to length of sound one. Apply splints, one outside and the other inside, binding them firmly on with cloth or handkerchiefs. The best splints are made by folding newspapers to necessary length, binding them above and below seat of fracture; anything hard and light, of suitable size, would act equally well, for instance, wood, pasteboard, twigs, leather, etc. Send for a doctor then.

Broken Ribs—Treatment

Broken Ribs cause intense pain when patient breathes; bind roller towel firmly round chest, fastening with pins, or sewing. Send for a doctor.

Broken Collar Bone—Treatment

Bend arm over front of chest; place it in a sling; bind it in that position by scarf going round chest outside sling. Send for doctor then.

TREATMENT FOR VARIOUS CAUSES

Flesh Wounds

Uncover wound; wash it with clean water; wring out a clean handkerchief, or lint, in cold water, and lay it over the wound. Then bind in position with handkerchief. On no account use tobacco or cobweb.

Fainting

From heat, exhaustion, or loss of blood. Keep head low; undo clothing about neck; plenty of fresh air; dash cold water on face and chest; smelling-salts carefully used; a little brandy when sensibility has returned, excepting in cases of sunstroke, and where means have not been taken to prevent further bleeding.

Fits

1. If snoring and face flushed, undo clothing around neck, keep head raised and dash cold water on top of head; hot-water bottles to feet. Send for doctor. Do not give brandy.

2. If foaming at mouth and convulsed, undo clothing, apply smelling-salts and prevent the patient from hurting himself or herself until conscious again.

Rupture or "Break of the Body"

Try and push it back with flat hand; keep man on his back. Cold, wet cloths laid over rupture will, perhaps, aid its return. Send for doctor then.

Suffocation

Suffocation from breathing noxious vapors from wells, coal gas or charcoal flumes.—Remove the patient to fresh air, sprinkle cold water on face and head, rub strong vinegar about nostrils, give drink of vinegar and water; to excite breathing, apply rules given in case of drowning. Unless a candle will burn with a clear flame in a well near the water, it is unsafe for persons to go down. Air may be purified by showering water into the well.

Drowning

Freely expose the face, neck and chest in the breeze, except in very severe weather. Turn the patient on face (let some one hold head so that the face does not touch the ground) and elevate the body so that the water in the lungs may flow out at the nose and mouth. First turn the patient slightly on his side, apply snuff or ammonia to the nostrils, dash cold water in the face, rubbing the body briskly until it is warm. To imitate respiration, throw the patient on his face, then turn the body gently but completely on the side and a little beyond, repeating these measures deliberately, efficiently and perseveringly fifteen times a minute in all. This number of thoracic movements per minute acts with the natural order of respiratory thoracic dilations and contractions, corresponds with the slow movement of the heart, averaging something less than sixty pulsations per minute. When the prone position is resumed, make equable but efficient pressure along the spine; remove it immediately before rotation on the side. (The first measure augments expiration; the second commences inspiration.) To induce circulation and warmth, continue these measures, rubbing the limbs upward with a firm pressure and with energy, using handkerchiefs, etc. Replace the patient's wet clothing by such other as can be soonest procured· To incite inspiration, let the surface of the body be briskly slapped with the hand or let cold water be dashed briskly on the surface, previously rubbed dry and warm.

Frozen Limbs

Rub with snow or place in cold water until sensation returns. Warm very gradually.

A Shock

If faint and cold, give stimulant in small doses, once in fifteen or twenty minutes, and secure warmth by external application or rubbing.

Composition of the Human Body

A man of 154 pounds weight contains 116 pounds of water, and 38 pounds of dry matter. Of the dry matter 28 pounds are organic, and 10 pounds are mineral matter. The blood of a fully grown and healthy man weighs, in a liquid state, about 20 pounds, consisting of about 15¾ pounds of water and 4⅓ pounds of solid matter.

Ten Laws of Health

1. Pure air is the food of the lungs. This is obtained by scientific ventilation, which consists in admitting currents or movements of air in the apartments through two or more apertures.

2. Good and properly cooked food, not food seasoned to cover up decay, partial or complete.

3. Water, not iced, but cooled by being placed upon ice, either in pitchers or bottles.

4. Adequate exercise in the open air, in order to help the skin throw off effete matter.

5. The sun bath. No sitting or reading in darkened rooms, or those lighted by gas. Gas burns up oxygen very rapidly. Sitting under a gas jet turns the hair gray, and by overheating the scalp destroys its vitality, and causes the hair to fall out.

6. Proper and sufficient clothing: that which is loose, light and warm. Light colors for Summer, and dark for Winter. In Winter wear a flannel bandage around the abdomen.

7. Occupations which are of an outdoor character; eight hours for work, eight hours for sleep, eight hours for rest.

8. Personal cleanliness is essential. Bathe once a week. Baths to be of the same temperature as the body. Bathing enables the skin to throw off effete matters, causing the dead and useless epidermis to peel off.

9. No marriage with a near relative.

10. Avoid wine, whiskey, beer and tobacco. Keep thy soul and body clean.

The Heart

The heart is six inches in length and four inches in diameter. It beats 70 times per minute. It forces out 2½ ounces of blood at each beat; 10 pounds 15 ounces of blood per minute.

The Lungs

The lungs are inflated on an average of 19 times per minute; 1,140 times per hour. At each inspiration about 26 cubic inches of air are inhaled; 2⅛ gallons of air per minute.

To Remove a Particle From the Eye

Take a horsehair and double it, leaving a loop. If the object can be seen, lay the loop over it, close the eye, and the mote will come out as the hair is withdrawn. If the irritating object cannot be seen, raise the lid of the eye as high as possible, and place the loop as high as you can, close the eye, and roll the ball around a few times, draw out the hair, and the substance which caused the pain will be sure to come with it.

The Pulse in Health

New born infants from 140 down to 130 per minute.
During 1st year from 130 down to 115 per minute.
During 2d year from 115 down to 100 per minute.
During 3d year from 105 down to 95 per minute.
During 7th to 14th year from 90 down to 80 per minute.
During 14th to 21st year from 85 down to 75 per minute.
During 21st to 60th year from 75 down to 70 per minute.
In old age from 75 up to 80 per minute.

Ventilation

Each person requires at least from three to four cubic feet of air per minute. Ordinary windows allow about 8 cubic feet a minute to pass. Sleeping apartments require 1,000 feet to each occupant.

An ordinary gas flame requires as much air as nine persons.

A neat, clean, fresh aired, sweet, cheerful, well-arranged house, exerts a moral influence over its inmates, and makes the members of a family peaceable and considerate of each other's feelings; on the contrary, a filthy, squalid, noxious dwelling, contributes to make its inhabitants selfish, sensual, and regardless of the feelings of others.

Never sleep in a small, close bedroom, either during Summer or Winter, without free ventilation from door or windows, unless otherwise supplied with abundance of fresh air. It will be seen that a person's house usually corresponds with his character.

How Fast a Person Grows

At birth the mean length of boys is 18½ inches, and of girls is 18⅓ inches. Growth is most rapid immediately after birth and continually diminishes until about five years of age, from then until 16 years the annual growth is 2 1-5 inches; during the next year, 1½ inches, and during the next two years, one inch only. The mean height of man has been estimated at 5 feet 4 inches.

A man is taller in the morning than at night by half an inch

The Ten Seven Years of Life

Seven years in childhood's sport and play, 7,
Seven years in school from day to day, 14
Seven years at trade or college life, 21
Seven years to find and place a wife, 28
Seven years to pleasure's follies given, 35
Seven years by business hardly driven, 42
Seven years for fame, a wild-goose chase, 49
Seven years for wealth, a bootless race, 56
Seven years for hoarding for your heir, 63
Seven years in weakness spent, and care, 70
Then die and go you know not where.

What to Do When the Clothes Take Fire

Three out of four persons rush up to the burning individual and begin to paw with their hands without any definite aim. It is useless to tell the victim to do this or that, or to call for water. In fact, it is generally best to say not a word, but seize a blanket from a bed, or a cloak of any woolen fabric—if none is at hand take any woolen material—hold the corners as far apart as you can, stretch them out higher than your head, and running boldly to the person make a motion of clasping in the arms, mostly about the shoulders. This instantly smothers the fire and saves the face. The next instant throw the unfortunate person on the floor. This is an additional safety to the face and breast, and any remnant of flame can be put out more leisurely.

MUSCLES, HEAT AND FAT, WATER PROPERTIES OF FOOD

Name of Food	100 parts of each Water, etc.	Muscle making	Heat and Fat making
Apples	84.0	5.0	10.0
Barley	14.0	15.0	68.8
Beans	14.8	24.0	57.7
Beef	50.0	15.0	30.0
Buckwheat	14.2	8.6	75.4
Butter			all
Cabbage	90.0	4.0	5.0
Cheese	10.0	65.0	19.0
Chicken	46.0	18.0	32.0
Corn	14.0	12.0	73.0
Cucumbers	97.0	1.5	1.0
Eggs, white of	79.0	17.0	none
Eggs, yolk of	53.0	15.0	27.0
Lamb	50.5	11.0	35.0
Milk, cow's	86.0	5.0	8.0
Mutton	44.0	12.5	40.0
Oats	13.6	17.0	66.4
Peas	14.0	23.4	60.0
Pork	38.5	10.0	50.0
Potatoes	75.2	1.4	22.5
Rice	13.5	6.5	79.5
Turnips	94.4	1.1	4.0
Veal	68.5	10.1	16.5
Wheat	14.0	14.6	69.4

TO DETERMINE THE WEIGHT OF LIVE CATTLE

Measure in inches girth around breast just behind shoulder-blade and the length of back from tail to fore part of shoulder-blade. Multiply girth by length and divide by 144. If girth is less than three feet, multiply the quotient by 11; if between three and five feet, multiply by 16; if between five and seven feet, multiply by 23; if between seven and nine feet, multiply by 31. If animal is lean, deduct one-twentieth from result, or take girth and length in feet, multiply square of girth by length, and multiply product by 3.36. Live weight multiplied by .605 gives net weight, nearly.

CARRYING CAPACITY OF A FREIGHT CAR

This table applies to Ten Ton Cars

Apples.	370 bushels	Hogs........50 to	60	head
Barley............	300 "	Lime.............	70	barrels
Bran........	1,000 "	Lumber...........	6,000	feet
Butter............	20,000 pounds	Oats	680	bushels
Cattle........18 to	20 head	Potatoes..........	430	"
Corn	400 bushels	Salt............. ..	70	barrels
Eggs ....130 to	160 barrels	Sheep ....80 to	100	head
Flaxseed..........	360 bushels	Wheat...........	340	bushels
Flour	90 barrels	Whiskey.........	60	barrels
Flour.............	200 sacks	Wood............	6	cords

OILS, CLASSIFIED

Drying Oils	Non-Drying Oils
Linseed Oils	Almond Oil
Cress-seed Oil	Castor Oil
Poppy Oil	Colza Oil
Sunflower Oil	Oil of Mustard
Walnut Oil	Rape-seed Oil
Tobacco-seed Oil	Olive Oil, etc.

Essential Oils

Oil of Anise	Oil of Lemon
Oil of Bergamot	Oil of Mint
Oil of Carraway	Oil of Myrrh
Oil of Cassia	Oil of Nutmeg
Oil of Cedar	Oil of Peppermint
Oil of Cloves	Oil of Rose
Oil of Lavender	Oil of Turpentine

ANCHORS A VESSEL MUST CARRY

A vessel of 2,000 tons must carry anchors weighing 18 tons with two-inch chain cables 300 fathoms long, and pro rata for larger or smaller vessels. All vessels carry seven anchors.

NAME OF ALLOYS OR COMPOSITION OF METALS

Name of Metal	Alloys
Aluminium bronze	Copper and Aluminium
Bell metal	Copper and Tin
Brass	Copper and Zinc
Britannia metal	Antimony and Tin
Bronze	Copper and Tin
Dutch metal	Copper and Zinc
German Silver	Copper, Nickel and Zinc
Gold currency	Gold and Copper
Gun metal	Copper and Tin
Mosaic gold	Copper and Zinc
Ormolu	Tin and Lead
Pewter	Silver and copper
Silver currency	Lead and Arsenic
Shot	Antimony and Tin
Solder	Lead, Antimony and Bismuth
Stereotype metal	Lead and Antimony (also copper
Type metal	at times)

Metal combine with Chlorine and produce Chlorides.
Metal combine with Sulphur and produce Sulphides.
Metal combine with Oxygen and produce Oxides

WHAT THERE IS IN A TON OF COAL

From one ton of ordinary gas coal may be produced 1,500 pounds of coke, 20 gallons of ammonia water, and 140 pounds of coal tar.

By destructive distillation the coal tar will yield 69.6 pounds of pitch, 17 pounds of creosote, 14 pounds heavy oils, 9.5 pounds of naphtha yellow, 6.3 pounds of naphthaline, 4.75 pounds of naphthol, 2.25 pounds of alazarin, 2.4 pounds of solvent naphtha, 1.5 pounds of phenol, 1.2 pounds of aurine, 1.1 pounds of benzine, 1.1 pounds of analine, 0.77 of a pound of toluidine, 0.46 of a pound of anthracine and 0.9 of a pound of toluene. From the latter is obtained the new substance known as saccharine, which is 230 times as sweet as the best cane sugar, one part of it giving a very sweet taste to a thousand parts of water.

BALLOONS, REMARKABLE ASCENSIONS

The most remarkable ascents on record are those of Montgolfier, who ascended to the height of 2,000 yards from Lyons, France, in 1783. Guy Lussac, in 1804, from Paris, France, to the height of 7,700 yards. Cox and Glaisher, in 1862, from Wolviston, England, to the height of 12,333 yards.

During the Siege of Paris, France, from September 1870, to February 1871, 64 balloons were sent up, with 91 passengers, 354 pigeons, and 3,000,000 letters, weighing nine tons.

BUSINESS LAW IN DAILY USE

It is a fraud to conceal a fraud.

Ignorance of the law excuses no one.

The acts of one partner bind all the rest.

A note or contract made with a minor or lunatic is void.

An agreement without consideration is void unless fully executed.

Signatures made with a lead pencil are good in law.

The law compels no one to do impossibilities.

A receipt for money paid is not legally conclusive.

Contracts made on Sunday cannot be enforced.

Contracts for advertising in Sunday newspapers are invalid.

Each individual in a partnership is responsible for the whole amount of the debts of the firm, except in case of special partnership.

Principals are responsible for the acts of their agents.

Agents are responsible to their principals for errors.

A note given by a minor is void.

A note drawn on Sunday is void.

It is not legally necessary to say on a note " for value received."

A note obtained by fraud, or from a person in a state of intoxication, cannot be collected.

If a note be lost or stolen, it does not release the maker; he must pay.

The indorser of a note is exempt from liability if not served with notice of its dishonor within twenty-four hours of its non-payment.

Notes bear interest only when so stated.

Checks or drafts must be presented for payment in reasonable time.

An indorsee has the right of action against all whose names were on the bill when he received it, unless an indorsement be such as would free the indorser from liability.

Part payments of a debt which has passed the time of statutory limitations revives the whole debt.

An indorsee may prevent his own liability to be sued by writing "without recourse" or similar words.

If the letter containing a protest of non-payment be put into the post-office, any miscarriage does not affect the party giving notice.

An oral agreement must be proved by evidence, a written agreement proves itself. The law prefers written to oral evidence because of its precision.

An indorsement should be written on the back of a bill or note.

The payee should be distinctly named in a note, unless payable to bearer.

No consideration is sufficient in law if it be illegal in its nature.

A bill may be written upon any paper or substitute for it, either with ink or pencil.

If two or more persons as partners are jointly liable on a note or bill, due notice to one of them is sufficient.

All claims which rest upon written contracts must be sued within four years from the time when they are due.

If the time of payment of a note is not inserted, it is payable on demand.

Notes falling due Sunday, or on a legal holiday, must be paid the day previous. Notes dated Sunday are void.

Altering a note in any manner, by the holder, makes it void.

If a note is transferred as security, or even as payment of a pre-existing debt, the debt revives if the note be dishonored.

The holder of a note may give notice of dishonor to all previous indorsers, or only to one of them. Releasing a prior indorser releases all who follow him. Indorsers are liable in their order; and each has twenty-four hours after receiving his own notice to give notice to those whom he wishes to hold liable.

The maker of an "accommodation" bill or note, that is to say, one for which he has received no consideration, having lent his name or credit for the accommodation of the payee, is not bound to the person accommodated, but is bound to all parties into whose hands it may subsequently fall in due course of business, precisely as if there was a good consideration.

Useful Information—Law

Every citizen is entitled to inspect and copy public writings.

When an instrument consists partly of written words and partly of a printed form, and the two inconsistent, the former controls the latter.

The language of a writing is to be interpreted according to the meaning it bears in the place of its execution.

A married woman who is adjudged a sole trader is responsible and liable for the maintenance of her minor children.

The husband of a sole-trader is not liable for any debts contracted by her in the course of her sole-trader business, unless agreed by contract.

If original pleadings or papers be lost, the court may authorize a copy thereof to be filed and used in place of the original.

When debts are incurred by any person or his wife or family for the common necessaries of life, one half of his earnings for personal services rendered at any time within thirty days next preceding attachment or execution, are subject to execution, garnishment or attachment, to satisfy debts so incurred.

Legal holidays are every Sunday, the first day of January, 22d of February, 30th of May, 4th of July, and 25th of December.

If the 1st of January, 22d of February, 30th of May, 4th of July, or 25th of December fall on Sunday, the Monday following is a holiday. The day of the state elections, or by order of the President or Governor.

The Knot and the Mile

The "knot" and the mile are terms often used interchangeably, but erroneously so. The fact is that a mile is less than 87 per cent of a knot. Three and one-half miles are equal, within a very small fraction to three knots. The knot is 6,082.66 feet in length. The statute mile is 5,280 feet. The result of the difference is that speed in miles per hour is always considerably larger than when stated in knots, and if a person forgets this and states the speed at so many knots, when it was really so many miles, he may be giving figures verging on the incredible.

A CENTENNIAL CALENDAR

For ascertaining any Day of the Week for any given time within the Present Century.

Years 1801 to 1900

Years											31 Jan.	28 Feb.	31 Mar.	30 Apr.	31 May	30 June	31 July	31 Aug.	30 Sept.	31 Oct.	30 Nov.	31 Dec.
1801	1807	1818	1829	1835	1846	1857	1863	1874	1885	1891	4	7	7	3	5	1	3	6	2	4	7	2
1802	1813	1819	1830	1841	1847	1858	1869	1875	1886	1897	5	1	1	4	6	2	4	7	3	5	1	3
1803	1814	1825	1831	1842	1853	1859	1870	1881	1887	1898	6	2	2	5	7	3	5	1	4	6	2	4
1805	1811	1822	1833	1839	1850	1861	1867	1878	1889	1895	2	5	5	1	3	6	1	4	7	2	5	7
1806	1817	1823	1834	1845	1851	1862	1873	1879	1890	......	3	6	6	2	4	7	2	5	1	3	6	1
1809	1815	1826	1837	1843	1854	1865	1871	1882	1893	1899	7	3	3	6	1	4	6	2	5	7	3	5
1810	1821	1827	1838	1849	1855	1866	1877	1883	1894	1900	1	4	4	7	2	5	7	3	6	1	4	6

Leap Years

Leap Years				31 Jan.	28 Feb.	29	31 Mar.	30 Apr.	31 May	30 June	31 July	31 Aug.	30 Sept.	31 Oct.	30 Nov.	31 Dec.
1804	1832	1860	1888	7	3		4	7	2	5	7	3	6	1	4	6
1808	1836	1864	1892	5	1		2	5	7	3	5	1	4	6	2	4
1812	1840	1868	1896	3	6		7	3	5	1	3	6	2	4	7	2
1816	1844	1872	......	1	4		5	1	3	6	1	4	7	2	5	7
1820	1848	1876	......	6	2		3	6	1	4	6	2	5	7	3	5
1824	1852	1880	......	4	7		1	4	6	2	4	7	3	5	1	3
1828	1856	1884	......	2	5		6	2	4	7	2	5	1	3	6	1

Days of the Week

Day	1	2	3	4	5	6	7
1	M	T	W	T	F	S	S
2	T	W	T	F	S	S	M
3	W	T	F	S	S	M	T
4	T	F	S	S	M	T	W
5	F	S	S	M	T	W	T
6	S	S	M	T	W	T	F
7	S	M	T	W	T	F	S
8	M	T	W	T	F	S	S
9	T	W	T	F	S	S	M
10	W	T	F	S	S	M	T
11	T	F	S	S	M	T	W
12	F	S	S	M	T	W	T
13	S	S	M	T	W	T	F
14	S	M	T	W	T	F	S
15	M	T	W	T	F	S	S
16	T	W	T	F	S	S	M
17	W	T	F	S	S	M	T
18	T	F	S	S	M	T	W
19	F	S	S	M	T	W	T
20	S	S	M	T	W	T	F
21	S	M	T	W	T	F	S
22	M	T	W	T	F	S	S
23	T	W	T	F	S	S	M
24	W	T	F	S	S	M	T
25	T	F	S	S	M	T	W
26	F	S	S	M	T	W	T
27	S	S	M	T	W	T	F
28	S	M	T	W	T	F	S
29	M	T	W	T	F	S	S
30	T	W	T	F	S	S	M
31	W	T	F	S	S	M	T

NOTE.—To ascertain any day of the week in any year of the present century, first look in the table of years for the year required, and under the months are figures which refer to the corresponding figures at the head of the columns of days below. *For Example:* To know what day of the week Sept. 2d will be on in the year 1873, in the table of years look for 1873, and in a parallel line under Sept. is fig. 1, which directs to col. 1, in which it will be seen that Sept. 2d falls on Tuesday.

This table will give the day of the week on which a person was born.

Bankers' Table

Showing the number of days from any date in one month to the same date in any other month.

FROM TO	Jan.	Feb.	Mar.	Apr.	May	June	July	Aug.	Sep.	Oct.	Nov.	Dec.
January	365	31	59	90	120	151	181	212	243	273	304	334
February	334	365	28	59	89	120	150	181	212	242	273	303
March	306	337	365	31	61	92	122	153	184	214	245	275
April	275	306	334	365	30	61	91	122	153	183	214	244
May	245	276	304	335	365	31	61	92	123	153	184	214
June	214	245	273	304	334	365	30	61	92	122	153	183
July	184	215	243	274	304	335	365	31	62	92	123	153
August	153	184	212	243	273	304	334	365	31	61	92	122
September	122	153	181	212	242	273	303	334	365	30	61	91
October	92	123	151	182	212	243	273	304	335	365	31	61
November	61	92	120	151	181	212	242	273	304	334	365	30
December	31	62	90	121	151	182	212	243	274	304	335	365

Example—How many days from May 5th to October 5th? Look for May at the left hand and October at the top; in the angle is 153. In leap year add one day if February is included.

Bills of Exchange

A Bill of Exchange or Draft is an order drawn by one person or firm upon another, payable either at sight or at a stated future time.

It becomes an "Acceptance" when the party upon whom it is drawn writes across the face "Accepted" and signs his name thereto; and is negotiable and bankable the same as a note and is subject to the same laws.

In many States both Sight and Time Drafts are entitled to three days' grace, the same as notes; but if made in form of a bank check, "pay to," without the words "at sight," it is payable on presentation without grace.

Financial Crises

1837—United States "Wild Cat" crisis, all banks closed.

1839—Bank of England saved by Bank of France. Severe in France where 93 companies failed for six millions.

1844—England, State loans to merchants. Bank of England reformed.

1847—England, failures, 20 millions; discount, 13 per cent.

1857—United States, 7,200 houses failed for 111 millions.

1866—London, Overend-Gurney crisis; failures exceeding 100 millions.

VALUE OF FOREIGN COINS IN U. S. MONEY

(Proclaimed by the Secretary of the Treasury, January 1, 1889)

Country	Standard	Monetary Unit	Value in U. S. Mon.
Argentine Rep.	Double	Peso	$0.96,5
Austria	Single silver	Florin	.33,6
Belgium	Double	Franc	.19,3
Bolivia	Single silver	Boliviano	.68
Brazil	Single gold	Milreis of 1,000 reis	.54,6
British N. Amer.	Single gold	Dollar	1.00
Chili	Double	Peso	.91,2
Cuba	Double	Peso	.92,6
Denmark	Single gold	Crown	.26,8
Ecuador	Single silver	Sucre	.68
Egypt	Single gold	Pound (100 piastres)	4.94,3
France	Double	Franc	.19,3
German Empire	Single gold	Mark	.23,8
Great Britain	Single gold	Pound sterling	4.86,6½
Greece	Double	Drachma	.19 3
Guatemala	Single silver	Peso	.68
Hayti	Double	Gourde	.96,5
Honduras	Single silver	Peso	.68
India	Single silver	Rupee of 16 annas	.32,3
Italy	Double	Lira	.19,3
Japan	*Double	Yen {Gold	.99,7
		{Silver	.73,4
Liberia	Single Gold	Dollar	1.00
Mexico	Single silver,	Dollar	.73,9
Netherlands	Double	Florin	.40,2
Nicaragua	Single silver	Peso	.68
Norway	Single gold	Crown	.23,8
Peru	Single silver	Sol	.68
Portugal	Single gold	Milreis of 1,000 reis	1.08
Russia	Single silver	Rouble of 100 kopecks	.54,4
Spain	Double	Peseta of 100 centimes	.19,3
Sweden	Single gold	Crown	.26,8
Switzerland	Double	Franc	.19,3
Tripoli	Single silver	Mahbub of 20 piastres	.61,4
Turkey	Single gold	Piastre	.04,4
U. S. Colombia	Single silver	Peso	.68
Venezuela	Single silver	Bolivar	.13,6

*Gold the nominal standard. Silver practically the standard. The value of the Shanghai taels based on the price of silver used in estimating the value of foreign silver coins, as above, is $1.005.

NOTE.—The "Standard" of a given country is indicated as follows, namely: *Double*, where its standard silver coins are unlimited legal tender, the same as its gold coins; *Single gold* or *single silver*, as its standard coins of one or the other metal are unlimited legal tender. The par of exchange of the monetary unit of a country with a single gold, or a double, standard is fixed at the value of the gold unit as compared with the United States gold unit. In the case of a country with a single silver standard, the par of exchange is computed at the mean price of silver in the London market for a period commencing October 1st and ending December 24th, as per daily cable despatches to the Bureau of the Mint.

Brokers' Technicalities

A "Bull" is one who operates to raise the value of stocks, that he may buy for a rise.

A "Bear" is one who sells stock for future delivery which he does not own at the time of sale.

A "Corner" is when the bears cannot buy or borrow the stock to deliver in fulfillment of their contracts.

"Overloaded" is when the bulls cannot take and pay for the stock they have purchased.

"Short" is when a person or party sells stocks when they have none and expect to buy or borrow in time to deliver.

"Long" is when a person or party has a plentiful supply of stocks.

A "Pool or Ring" is a combination formed to control the price of stocks.

A broker is said to carry stocks for his customer when he has bought and is holding it for his account.

A "Wash" is a pretended sale by special agreement between buyer and seller, for the purpose of getting a quotation reported.

A "Put and Call" is when a person gives so much per cent. for the option of buying or selling so much stock on a certain fixed day, at a price fixed the day the option is given.

Navy Yards of the United States

1. Brooklyn Navy Yard, Brooklyn, N. Y.
2. Charlestown Navy Yard, Boston, Mass.
3. Gosport Navy Yard, near Norfolk, Va.
4. Kittery Navy Yard, opposite Portsmouth, N. H.
5. League Island Navy Yard, seven miles below Philadelphia, Pa.
6. Mare Island Navy Yard, near San Francisco, Cal.
7. New London Naval Station, New London, Conn.
8. Norfolk Navy Yard, Norfolk, Va.
9. Pensacola Navy Yard, Pensacola, Fla.
10. Washington City Navy Yard, Washington, D. C.

There are naval stations at New London, Conn., Port Royal, S. C., and Key West, Fla., and a torpedo station and naval war college at Newport, R. I.

United States Naval Academy is at Annapolis, Md.

Principal Countries of the World, their Population, Area in Square Miles and Capitals

Country	Population	Area Sq. M.	Location	Capital
Abyssinia	3,000,000	129,000	Africa	Gondar
Afghanistan	4,000,000	279,000	Asia	Cabul
Anam Kingdom	12,000,000	202,600	Asia	Hul
Algeria	3,310,412	161,476	Africa	Algiers
Arabia	6,000,000	887,442	Asia	Mecca
Andorra	5,800	175	Europe	Andorra
Argentine Confederation	3,026,000	1,125,086	S. Am.	Buenos Ayres
Australia	3,200,000	3,091,897	Oceanica	Melbourne
Austro-Hungary	39,206,052	261,591	Europe	Vienna
Belgium	5,720,807	11,373	Europe	Brussels
Beloochistan	1,000,200	140,000	Asia	Kelat
Bolivia	2,327,000	481,600	S. America	La Paz
Brazil	10,200,000	3,219,000	S. Am.	Rio de Janeiro
British India	199,755,993	874,220	Asia	Calcutta
British Honduras	27,542	7,562	C. America	Belize
Bulgaria	2,007,919	24,360	Europe	Sophia
Burmah Kingdom	5,000,520	176,568	Asia	Mandalay
Canada	4,500,200	3,425,743	N. America	Ottawa
Cape Colony	1,029,168	229,815	Africa	Capetown
China Empire	404,180,000	4,179,559	Asia	Pekin
Chili	2,271,949	256,399	S. America	Santiago
Colombia, U. S. of	4,000,000	331,420	S. America	Bogota
Congo Free State	8,000,021	1,056,200	Africa	
Corea	10,227,885	82,000	Asia	Seoul
Costa Rica	190,000	26,040	C. America	San Jose
Denmark	2,045,179	13,784	Europe	Copenhagen
Ecuador	1,146,000	248,370	S. America	Quito
Egypt	6,806,381	394,240	Africa	Cairo
France	37,672,048	204,177	Europe	Paris
German Empire	45,234,061	212,028	Europe	Berlin
Great Britain and Ireland	35,246,568	120,908	Europe	London
British Empire	315,885,000	8,991,254		London
Greece	1,979,453	25,111	Europe	Athens
Guatemala	1,278,311	46,774	C. Am.	N. Guatemala
Hayti	93,200	9,830	W. In.	Port-au-Prince
Dominican Republic	300,000	20,596	W. In.	San Domingo

Principal Countries, Etc.—*Continued*

Country	Population	Area Sq. M.	Location	Capital
Honduras	458,000	42,658	C. Am.	Tegucigalpa
Ireland	5,174,836	32,531	Near Europe	Dublin
Italy	28,459,451	114,411	Europe	Rome
Japan Empire	36,700,118	148,456	Near Asia	Tokio
Liberia	1,140,000	14,300	Africa	Monrovia
Madagascar	3,000,000	228,570	Nr. Africa	Antanarivo
Mexico	10,097,000	748,953	North America	Mexico
Montenego	245,380	13,486	Europe	Cetigne
Morocco	6,500,000	319,000	Africa	Morocco
Natal	416,219	21,150	Afa.	Pietermaritzburg
Nicaragua	400,900	51,660	C. America	Managua
Netherlands	28,459,628	12,648	Europe	The Hague
Norway	1,806,900	122,869	Europe	Christiania
Nubia	400,000	35,000	Africa	Dongola
Orange Free State	133,518	70,000	Africa	Bloemfontein
Paraguay	476,000	91,970	S. A.	Asuncion
Persia	7,653,600	635,949	Asia	Teheran
Peru	2,970,000	503,718	South America	Lima
Portugal	4,306,554	36,510	Europe	Lisbon
Roumania	5,376,000	48,307	Europe	Bukharest
Russia	86,486,959	2,041,402	Europe	St. Petersburg
Russian Empire	102,970,000	8,644,100		St. Petersburg
San Salvador	554,000	7,225	C. Am.	San Salvador
San Marino	7,816	32	Europe	San Marino
Sandwich Islands	66,097	6,667	Pacific O.	Honolulu
Servia	1,820,000	18,800	Europe	Belgrade
Scotland	3,815,753	29,820	Nr. Europe	Edinburgh
Siam	5,700,000	28,554	Asia	Bangkok
Spain	16,061,859	191,100	Europe	Madrid
Sweden	4,603,595	170,979	Europe	Stockholm
Switzerland	2,846,102	15,992	Europe	Bern
United States	58,442,060	3,602,990	N. Am.	Washington
Uruguay	520,536	73,538	S. Am.	Montevideo
Turkey	4,490,945	63,850	Europe	Constantinople
Turkey	16,172,981	729,350	Asia	Constantinople
Transvaal	800,000	114,360	Africa	Pretoria
Tunis	2,100,000	42,000	Africa	Tunis
Venezuela	2,121,988	632,695	S. Am.	Caracas
Zanzibar	300,000	625	Africa	Zanzibar

Navies of the World

Country	Vessels	Men	Country	Vessels	Men
Great Britain	556	87,427	Turkey	64	4,200
France	507	42,848	Brazil	59	4,323
Russia	410	31,000	Portugal	55	4,908
Italy	175	13,328	Norway	50	1,260
China	124	8,935	Argentine Republic	38	1,500
Netherlands	120	7,204	Japan	36	4,500
Spain	114	22,000	Greece	35	2,864
Austro-Hungary	110	9,775	Egypt	29	2,100
United States	107	12,114	Chili	18	1,988
Denmark	92	1,500	Roumania	16	1,247
Germany	79	16,995	Canada	7	1,200
Sweden	68	5,927	Mexico	5	510

Presidents of the Continental Congresses

Peyton Randolph, of Virginia..........................Sept. 5,1774
Henry Middleton, of South Carolina....................Oct. 22, 1774
Peyton Randolph, of Virginia ....May 10, 1775
John Hancock, of Massachusetts.......................May 24, 1775
Henry Laurens, of South Carolina.......................Nov. 1, 1777
John Jay, of New York...... ....Dec. 10, 1778
Samuel Huntington, of Connecticut....................Sept. 28, 1779
Thomas McKean, of Delaware...........................July 10, 1781
John Hanson, of Maryland..............................Nov. 5, 1781
Elias Boudinot, of New Jersey.... ....Nov. 4, 1782
Thomas Mifflin, of Pennsylvania.......................Nov. 3, 1783
Richard Henry Lee, of Virginia........................Nov. 30, 1784
John Hancock, Massachusetts..... ....Jan. 11, 1785
Nathaniel Gorham, of Massachusetts.... ....June 6, 1786
Arthur St. Clair, of Pennsylvania.....................Feb. 21, 1787
Cyrus Griffin, of Virginia............................Jan. 22, 1788

Where the Continental Congresses Met

The seat of government was established first at Philadelphia, Penn., commencing Sept. 5, 1774 and May 10, 1775; at Baltimore, Md., commencing Dec. 20, 1776; at Philadelphia, Penn., commencing March 4, 1777; at Lancaster, Penn., commencing Sept. 27, 1777; at York, Penn., commencing Sept. 30, 1777; at Philadelphia, Penn., commencing July 2, 1778; at Princeton, N. J., commencing June 30, 1783; at Annapolis, Md., commencing Nov. 26, 1783; at Trenton, N. J., commencing Nov. 1, 1784; and at New York, N. Y., commencing Jan. 11, 1785.

FORMATION OF THE UNION (UNITED STATES)

On Monday, September 5, 1774, a number of men were assembled at Carpenter's Hall, in Philadelphia, who had been chosen by the several Colonies, in what now constitutes the United States, to hold a Congress for the purpose of discussing certain grievances imputed to the mother country (England). This Congress resolved that each colony should have one vote only. On Tuesday, July 2, 1776, the Congress resolved: "That these United Colonies are and of right ought to be Free and Independent States," etc.; and on Thursday, July 4, 1776, the whole Declaration of Independence having been agreed upon, was publicly read to the people.

On September 9, 1776, it was resolved that the words "United Colonies" should no longer be used and that "United States" should thenceforward be the style of the Union.

On Saturday, November 15, 1777, "Articles of Confederation and Perpetual Union of the United States of America" were agreed to by the State Delegates, subject to the ratification of the several State Legislatures. Eight of the States ratified these articles, July 9, 1778; one July 21, 1778; one July 24, 1778; one November 26, 1778; one February 22, 1779; and the last March 1, 1781.

BATTLES OF THE REVOLUTIONARY WAR

The following comprises all the battles for freedom of the American Colonies, that took place from April 19, 1775, to the closing, October 19, 1781, just 6 years and 6 months. The British sent over 134,000 soldiers and sailors (and paid Indians to do bloody work on the field and to families at home) to the war. The Colonies met them with 230,000 Colonists and 50,000 militia (and near the close the French helped a little).

The leading and notable battles of the war were as follows: Concord and Lexington, Bunker Hill, Long Island, White Plains, Trenton, Princeton, Bennington, Monmouth, King's Mountain, Cowpens, Eutaw Springs, and Yorktown.

Name of Battle	Won by Whom	When Fought
Lexington and Concord, Mass.	First skirmish	April 19, 1775
Ticonderoga, N. Y	American	May 10, 1775
Bunker Hill, Mass	American	June 17, 1775
Montreal, Canada	British	Sept. 25, 1775
St. John, Canada	American	Nov. 3, 1775
Great Bridge, Va	British	Dec. 9, 1775

Name of Battle	Won by Whom	When Fought
Quebec, Canada....................	British............	Dec. 31, 1775
Moores Creek Bridge, N. C......	American............	Feb. 27, 1776
Boston, Mass....................	British fled..........	Mar. 17, 1776
Fort Moultrie, S. C............	American............	June 28, 1776
Long Island, N. Y.............	British............	Aug. 26, 1776
Harlem Plains, N. Y...........	American............	Sept. 16, 1776
White Plains, N. Y...........	British............	Oct. 28, 1776
Fort Washington, N. Y........	British............	Nov. 16, 1776
Trenton, N. J................	American............	Dec. 27, 1776
Princeton, N. J.............	American............	Jan. 3, 1777
Hubbardtown, Vt.............	British............	July 7, 1777
Bennington, Vt.............	American............	Aug. 16, 1777
Brandywine, Penn...........	British............	Sept. 11, 1777
First Battle of Saratoga, N. Y...American............		Sept. 19, 1777
Paoli, Penn...............	British............	Sept. 20, 1777
Germantown, Penn...........	British............	Oct. 4, 1777
Fts Clinton and Montgomery, N Y.British............		Oct. 6, 1777
Second Battle of Saratoga, N. Y..American............		Oct. 7, 1777
Surrender of Burgoyne, N. Y....American............		Oct. 13, 1777
Fort Mercer, N. J.........	American............	Oct. 22, 1777
Fort Mifflin, Penn...........	British............	Nov. 1777
Monmouth, N. J..............	American............	June 28, 1778
Wyoming Massacre, N. Y........		July 3, 1778
Quaker Hill, R. I.............	American............	Aug. 28, 1778
Savannah, Ga.................	British............	Dec. 29, 1778
Kettle Creek, Ga.............	American............	Feb. 14, 1779
Briar Creek, Ga.............	British............	Mar. 3, 1779
Stone Ferry, S. C............	British............	June 20, 1779
Stony Point, N. Y...........	American............	July 16, 1779
Savannah, Ga.................	American............	Aug. 9, 1779
Paulus Hook, N. J..........	American............	Aug. 13, 1779
Chemung (Indians), N. Y........	American............	Aug. 27, 1779
Charleston, S. C............	(Sur. to the British)...	May 12, 1780
Springfield, N. J..........	American............	June 28, 1780
Rocky Mount, S. C..........	British............	July 30, 1780
Hanging Rock, S. C..........	American............	Aug. 6, 1780
Sanders' Creek, nr. Camden, N. C.British............		Aug. 16, 1780
King's Mountain, S. C.........	British............	Oct. 7, 1780
Fish Dam Ford, Broad River, S. C American............		Nov. 18, 1780
Blackstocks, S. C............	American............	Nov. 20, 1780
Cowpens, N. C...............	American............	Jan. 17, 1781
Guilford, S. C..............	British............	Mar. 15, 1781
Hookirk's Hill, S. C.........	British............	Apr. 25, 1781
Ninety-six (besieged), Ga........	American........	May and June 1781
Augusta (besieged), Ga...........	British..........	May and June 1781
Eutaw Springs, S. C..........	American............	Sept. 8, 1781
Yorktown, Va. (Cornwallis sur.).American............		Oct. 19, 1781
Peace declared................	Treaty signed at Paris.	Sept. 3, 1783

Government of the United States

The executive power is vested in the President, who holds office for four years, and receives $50,000 annually.

The President and Vice-President are elected by electors chosen by the people. The number of electors from each State is equal to the whole number of Senators and Representatives to which the State may be entitled.

The electors vote by ballot. These votes are sent sealed to the President of the Senate, who opens them in the presence of Congress. If there are two parties who have received an equal number of votes, the House of Representatives choose by ballot one of them for President.

The various Cabinet Officers are appointed by the President.

They are six in number and receive $8,000 annually.

The legislative power is vested in Congress, of which there are two branches; the Senate, which is composed of two members from each State, who hold office for six years, at an annual salary of $5,000; and the House of Representatives, who are elected by the vote of each State, to hold office two years, and receive a salary of $5,000 annually.

As President of the Senate, the Vice-President performs his entire duty, except in case of removal or death of the President, in which event he assumes the executive powers. He is elected for the same term of Office as the President, and receives $8,000 annually.

The President of the United States is Commander-in-Chief of the Army and Navy; but the direct supervision of them belongs to the Secretaries of War and of the Navy.

The Judiciary of the United States consists of a Supreme Court which sits at Washington, D. C., and which is composed of a Chief Justice, who receives $10,500 annually, and eight Associate Justices who receive $10,000 annually. They are appointed by the President and hold office during good behavior.

The United States is divided into nine Judicial Circuits, each of which has a Circuit Judge, whose salary is $6,000 annually. There are fifty-eight District Courts from which an appeal lies to the Circuit Court.

Each State and Territory has its own local government, not unlike the general government in its essential features. The executive authority is vested in the Governor.

The revenue of the Government is chiefly derived from custom-house duties on imports, proceeds of sales of public lands, and internal revenue taxes. Since the year 1865–6 the revenue has each year largely exceeded the expenditure, and there has been gradual reduction of taxes. In conformity with several enactments of Congress, the surplus revenue is devoted to the gradual redemption of the public debt.

FACTS FOR CALIFORNIANS

Legal Holidays.—January 1st; February 22d; May 30th; July 4th; General Election day; Thanksgiving Day; December 25th.

Interest.—Seven per cent is the legal rate, though any rate can be made by contract.

Statue of Limitation.—Open accounts, two years; Notes, four years; Judgments, five years.

Garnishments.—One month's wages is exempt from garnishment to the head of a family.

Justices' Court.—Jurisdiction is limited to $200.99.

Chattel Mortgage.—Is not valid on stock of merchandise, unless mortgagee takes immediate possession.

Qualification of Voters.—Must be a citizen of the United States either by birth, naturalization or treaty of Queretaro; have resided one year in the State, ninety days in the County, and thirty days in the Precinct.

Area of California.—There are 157,801 square miles or 100,992,640 acres in the State, being over 100 acres for every man, woman and child.

Land Offices.—There are nine United States land offices in the State located as follows: At Humboldt, Los Angeles, Marysville, Sacramento, Redding, Stockton, San Francisco, Susanville and Visalia.

Filing Claims.—Against estate of deceased person within four months, unless the estate exceeds $10,000, when ten months is allowed. With Assignee, no special time, but should be within three months.

Exemptions under Homestead Law.—Home worth $5,000 to head of family, together with numerous and specific articles, including household goods, implements, tools, horses and wagons, provisions, library of professionals, stock, etc., irrespective of value, besides mining tools to the value of $500; cabin, $500; and mining claim actually being worked, $500. A single man has personal property exemptions from $500 to $1,000.

Marriage Law.—Prohibited degrees are, ancestors, descendants, brothers, sisters, nephews and nieces; void marriages: the above, and also white with negro blood. Voidable: under age of consent, if no cohabitation since attaining such age; insane or idiot; physical incapacity. License is required. Male attains age at twenty-one and female at eighteen.

Divorce Law.—Six months previous residence required. Cause: violation of marriage vow; willful desertion one year; habitual drunkenness; conviction of felony; cruel and abusive treatment; failure by the husband to provide for one year.

GAME LAWS OF CALIFORNIA

When game may be killed or caught.

Male Deer or Buck.......................July 1st to December 15th.
Quail............................September 10th to February 28th.
Rail.................................   "   "   "   "
Grouse...........................   "   "   "   "
Partridge.........................   "   "   "   "
Doves...............................June 1st to December 31st.
Female Deer or Doe.................Must not be killed at any time.
Antelope.............................   "   "   "   "   "
Elk...................................   "   "   "   "   "
Mountain Sheep......................   "   "   "   "   "
Spotted Fawn........................   "   "   "   "   "
Speckled Trout...........................April 1st to October 31st.
Brook Trout.............................   "   "   "   "
Salmon Trout............................   "   "   "   "
Salmon.....................October 1st to August 1st of next year.

The eggs of Quail, Partridge or Grouse must never be taken, gathered or destroyed.

In Marin County Quail shooting begins October 1st, and Doves August 1st. Deer season ends September 15th.

Napa County, Quail shooting on August 1st.

The killing, taking or injuring of mocking birds is expressly prohibited.

In Nevada County, Elk, Deer or Antelope must not be killed between the first of February and the first of August.

Phosphorus must not be used for killing animals in Santa Clara, Contra Costa, San Joaquin, Santa Cruz or San Mateo Counties between the first of March and the first of November.

To net, pound, wear, cage or trap any quail, partridge or grouse is illegal at any time or to have in possession any that have been killed or taken that way.

Trout must not be taken except by hook and line.

The taking of any kind of fish by explosives is prohibited.

Salmon and shad must not be caught with net or seine between the sunrise of Saturday and the sunset of Sunday.

Seines or nets for catching shad or salmon must have the meshes seven and one-half inches in length.

Fishing is prohibited in the creeks or streams of Alameda County between the first day of October and the first day of April.

Traps, set-nets, wears, etc., for catching fish is illegal, while seines or nets must not extend more than one-third across any stream or water-way.

SALARIES OF CALIFORNIA STATE OFFICERS

Rank	Per Annum
Governor	$6,000
Lieutenant-Governor	$10 per day during Session
Legislators, both houses.	$8 " " " "
Secretary of State	3,000
Controller	3,000
Attorney-General	3,000
Clerk of Supreme Court	3,000
Surveyor-General	3,000
Adjutant-General	3,000
Superintendent of State Printing	2,400
State Librarian	3,000
Treasurer	3,000
Superintendent of Public Instruction	3,000

MECHANICS' LIEN LAW OF CALIFORNIA

Condensed from "Statutes and Code of California." Edition of 1886 with amendments of 1887.

Mechanics, material men, contractors, sub-contractors, artisans, architects, machinists, builders, laborers, etc., performing labor upon or furnishing materials to be used in the construction or alteration of any building or other structure, shall have a lien upon such property for the value of labor done or materials furnished. Said lien shall extend to the entire contract price and shall operate in favor of all persons, except the contractor; after all other liens are satisfied then as a lien for balance due the contractor. All contracts over $1,000 shall be in writing, duly signed, shall describe the property and character of work to be done and the amount to be paid, as also when such payments shall be due. Before beginning, this shall be filed with the County Recorder, otherwise it will be void. In such case the owner of the building or structure is responsible for all liens for labor or material.

No part of the contract work shall be paid in advance; but it may be made payable in installments after the commencement, provided that at least 25 per cent is made payable at least 35 days after completion.

No payments paid in advance, under the contract, shall be valid for the purpose of defeating a lien, except that of the contractor, even though the contractor may afterwards abandon the work or become indebted to the owner. No alterations of contract will affect any lien acquired. If contracts or alterations do not conform to the statutes, the owner will be responsible for all liens except those of the contractor. Any of the parties mentioned above except the contractor, may at any time notify the owner, in writing, that they have performed labor or furnished materials to the contractor or others acting for him; they should name the parties, state the kind of labor or material furnished, the value of same and of the whole agreed to be done or furnished. Care should be taken that the owner, his architects, or authorized agents receive such notice. Upon receipt of such notice the owner or his agents shall withhold from the contractor or his agents sufficient money to answer such claim, or any lien that may be filed therefor for record, including counsel fees, not to exceed §100 and costs.

If the land built upon belongs to the party building, said land is also subject to the lien.

Liens here mentioned are preferred to any lien, mortgage or incumbrance, attached subsequent to the commencement of the building or improvements; also of any lien, mortgage or incumbrance unrecorded at the time of such commencement.

A contractor must, within sixty days after completion of contract, and other parties within thirty days of such completion, file for record with the County Recorder, a claim under oath, containing a statement of his demand, giving all the facts in the case.

When one claim is filed against two or more buildings or structures, such claim must state the amount due on each of said buildings, or structures; otherwise the lien of such claim is postponed to other liens.

A lien does does not extend beyond the amount designated, as against other liens. A lien expires after ninety days unless proceedings be commenced in a proper court within that time. If credit be given, then ninety days after such credit is due; and no agreement of credit can extend it beyond two years.

A lien can be laid against a city lot that has been improved at the request of the owner.

An owner of land is responsible for all buildings erected or alterations made on his property unless he shall, within three days after acquiring such knowledge, give notice in writing, that he will not be responsible for the same.

A contractor can only recover amount due him according to contract, and he is also responsible for all liens filed for labor and material.

Where different liens are laid against property, those for manual labor come first; for furnishing materials, second; sub-contractors, third; original contractors, last.

Any number of persons claiming liens may join in the same action.

Material furnished for the construction or alteration of a building or structure are not subject to attachment, etc., except on a debt due for purchase money of same.

An owner or contractor cannot waive or impair the liens of other persons, except by their written consent.

Any person who shall give a false notice of his claim to the owner, or who includes work or materials not done or furnished, will forfeit his lien. If the owner or contractor shall conspire or agree that the written contract filed shall appear to show the contract price to be less than it really is, and it shall so show, such contract will be void, and the owner will be responsible for all liens except those of the contractor.

Liens for Salary and Wages

Where an assignment is made, the wages of the employees not exceeding $100 each, and for services rendered within sixty days previously and preferred claims, must be paid before other creditors.

In case of the death of an employer, wages for services rendered within sixty days next preceding the death, not exceeding $100, rank in priority next after the funeral expenses, expenses of the last sickness, the charges and expenses of administering upon the estate, and the allowance to the widow and infant children.

In case of execution, attachment, etc., employees having a claim for labor done, may give notice, with amounts, and sworn to, to the creditors and officers executing such writs, any time before the sale. Unless disputed, the officer will pay to such person, out of the proceeds of the sale, the amount the person is entitled to for services rendered within sixty days preceding the levy, not exceeding $100. If the claim is disputed the party claiming must begin action within ten days or be forever barred.

In case of dispute, the debtor or creditor shall, within ten days, serve upon the claimant and officer executing the writ, a sworn statement, in writing, denying such claim is justly due for services rendered within the sixty days next preceding the levy. If claimant brings suit which is disputed in part only, and fail to recover a sum exceeding that which was admitted to be due, he shall not recover costs.

DISTANCE FROM SAN FRANCISCO TO VARIOUS PLACES

To	Miles	To	Miles
Baltimore	3,222	National Park	1,713
Boston	3,387	New Orleans	2,449
Big Trees	168	New York	3,302
Carson	324	North Platte	1,576
Charleston	3,254	Ogden	835
Chicago	2,359	Omaha	1,867
Cheyenne	1,351	Oregon City	683
Cincinnati	2,558	Philadelphia	3,242
Colorado Springs	1,530	Pittsburgh	2,888
Columbus	2,547	Portland	782
Corinne	858	Prescott	933
Council Bluffs	1,869	Rawlins	1,206
Deming	1,198	Reno	294
Denver	1,457	Sacramento	139
Duluth	2,671	Salt Lake City	870
Geysers	95	San Jose	48
Grand Island	1,713	Santa Barbara	438
Hot Springs	1,406	Santa Cruz	80
Hanging Rock	932	Santa Fé	1,515
Indianapolis	2,530	St. Louis	2,340
Junction	17	St. Paul	2,694
Kansas City	2,096	Sydney	1,453
Laramie	1,294	Stockton	91
Lathrop	82	Tucson	978
Los Angeles	482	Virginia City	346
Merced	138	Washington	3,263
Milwaukee	2,347	Yosemite Valley	199
Monterey	125	Yuma	731

HOW IRON WEARS OUT

When a worn car-wheel tread is examined under the microscope it is perceived that the surface of the metal comes off in thin flakes or scales.

Examined under high powers the scales are found to resemble portions of a brick wall, the fractures not being in the particles of iron, but in the materials which unite the particles in a manner similar to which mortar unites the bricks of a wall. Continuous jarring breaks the cement or uniting material, thus allowing iron so treated to fall in pieces.

DISTANCE FROM NEW YORK CITY TO VARIOUS PLACES

To	Miles	To	Miles
Albany, N. Y	144	Lansing, Mich	778
Altoona, Pa	314	Leavenworth, Kan	1,393
Antwerp, Belgium	3,272	Lisbon, Portugal	2,940
Augusta, Ga	830	Little Rock, Ark	1,384
Augusta, Me	402	Liverpool, England	3,017
Baltimore, Md	186	London, England	3,143
Bangor, Me	477	Louisville, Ky	852
Bellows Falls, Vt	222	Macon, Ga	1,471
Boston, Mass	236	Melbourne, Australia	12,720
Bremen, Germany	3,800	Memphis, Tenn	1,229
Bridgeport, Conn	59	Milwaukee, Wis	1,000
Buffalo, N. Y	423	Mobile, Ala	1,628
Burlington, Vt	296	Montgomery, Ala	1,236
Cadiz, Spain	3,120	Montreal, Can	396
Cairo, Ill	1,143	Naples, Italy	4,200
Calcutta, India	12,500	Nashville, Tenn	1 037
Canton, China	14,000	New Bedford, Mass	238
Cape Horn, S. A	7,000	New London, Conn	126
Cape Race, N. F	1,000	New Orleans, La	1,483
Cape Town, Africa	6,800	Newport, R. I	162
Charleston, S. C	829	Niagara Falls, N. Y	444
Chicago, Ill	898	Ogdensburgh, N. Y	396
Chillicothe, O	674	Omaha, Neb	1,385
Cincinnati, O	744	Panama, U. S. of Col	2,066
Cleveland, O	581	Philadelphia, Penn	88
Columbus, O	624	Pittsburg, Penn	444
Concord, N. H	270	Portland, Me	349
Council Bluffs, Iowa	1,411	Providence, R. I	188
Davenport, Iowa	1,082	Quebec, Canada	567
Dayton, O	624	Quincy, Ill	1,169
Decatur, Ill	1,095	Richmond, Va	356
Denver City	2,012	Rio Janeiro, Brazil	4,733
Detroit, Mich	664	Rochester, N. Y	373
Dover, N. H	292	Rock Island, Ill	1,095
Dubuque, Iowa	1,086	Sacramento, Cal	3,082
Dunkirk, N. Y	561	Salt Lake City, Utah	2,462
Elmira, N. Y	274	San Francisco, Cal	3,302
Fernandina, Fla	841	Santa Fé, New Mexico	2,037

Distances from New York—*Continued*

To	Miles	To	Miles
Fon-du-lac, Wis	1,090	Saratoga, N. Y.	182
Fort Benton, Mont	2,870	Scranton, Penn	149
Fort Kearney, Neb	1,581	Sioux City, Iowa	1,411
Fort Laramie, Wyo	1,953	St. Joseph, Mo	1,352
Fort Wayne, Ind	765	St. Louis, Mo	1,087
Galveston, Texas	1,857	St. Paul, Minn	1,347
Geneva, Switzerland	4,065	St. Petersburg, Russia	4,679
Greenland	1,780	Shanghai, China	14,500
Halifax, N. S	557	Springfield, Ill	1,033
Harrisburg, Penn	183	Stockholm, Sweden	4,272
Hartford, Conn	112	Sydney, Australia	12,910
Havana, Cuba	1,170	Syracuse, N. Y.	292
Havre, France	3,090	Toledo, O.	693
Hong Kong, China	14,015	Toronto, Canada	528
Honolulu, S. I	13,530	Valparaiso, Chili	8,720
Hudson, N. Y	116	Venice, Italy	4,950
Indianapolis, Ind	812	Vera Cruz, Mexico	1,965
Ithaca, N. Y	262	Vicksburg, Miss	1,352
Jackson, Miss	1,307	Washington, D. C	226
Joliet, Ill	950	Wheeling, W. Va	496
Key West, Iowa	1,107	White Mountains, N. H	323
La Crosse, Wis	1,214	Worcester, Mass	192

New Standard of Railroad Time

With the enormous increase of railway traveling the necessity arose for inventing some method of counting time which should avoid the complications arising from the use of local mean time, which varies with every mile of east or west travel.

This was brought about in 1884, and the railroads of the United States, of the Dominion of Canada, and many cities and towns in these countries now use the standard time:

Name	Central Meridian	Nearest Places
Pacific	120°=8h. w. from Greenwich	1½° east of Sacramento
Mountain	105°=7h. w. from Greenwich	Denver, Colorado
Central	90°=6h. w. from Greenwich	St. Louis and New Orleans
Eastern	75°=5h. w. from Greenwich	Between N. Y. and Phila.
Intercolonial	60°=4h. w. from Greenwich	About 3½° east of Halifax

The *standard meridians* are 15 degrees of longitude or just one hour in time apart.

The Number of Days it takes to Travel to the Principal Cities of the World from San Francisco

Name of City	Days	Name of City	Days
Acapulco, Mexico	9	Halifax, Nova Scotia	8
Adelaide, Australia	28	Havana, Cuba	9
Aden, Arabia	26	Havre, France	14
Albany, West Australia	39	Hobart, Tasmania	29
Alexandria, Egypt	21	Honduras, Central America	18
Algiers, Africa	19	Hong-Kong, China	28
Amsterdam, Holland	16	Honolulu, Hawaii	7
Antigua, Leeward Is	15	Kingston, Jamaica	14
Apia, Samoa	17	La Libertad, Cen. America	14
Arica, Peru	33	La Union, Cen. America	14
Aspinwall, U. S. of Colombia	14	Launceston, Tasmania	29
Athens, Greece	20	Levuka, Fiji Islands	31
Auckland, New Zealand	20	Lima, Peru	30
Bahia, Brazil	27	Lisbon, Portugal	18
Balize, Br. Honduras	12	Liverpool, England	14
Bankok, Siam	37	London, England	14
Barbadoes, Windward Is	14	Madeira Islands	20
Barcelona, Spain	18	Madras, Hindostan	35
Batavia, Java	41	Madrid, Spain	17
Berlin, Germany	16	Magdalena Bay	4
Bermuda Islands	9	Malta Islands	19
Berne, Switzerland	16	Mazatlan, Mexico	6
Beyrout, Syria	24	Mauritius Islands	44
Bombay, Hindostan	33	Melbourne, Australia	26
Brindisi, Italy	17	Mexico City, Mexico	5
Brisbane, Australia	28	Montevideo, Uruguay	34
Brussels, Belgium	16	Moravia, Russia	18
Buenos Ayres, Arg. Republic	35	Munich, Bavaria	16
Cairo, Egypt	21	Panama, U. S. of Colombia	17
Calcutta, Hindostan	36	Paris, France	14
Callao, Peru	30	Perth, West Australia	43
Cape St. Lucas, Lower Cal	5	Quebec, Canada	8
Cape Town, South Africa	36	Rio de Janeiro, Brazil	31
Christiana, Norway	18	Rome, Italy	17
Colombo, Ceylon	35	Saigon, Cochin China	35
Constantinople, Turkey	20	St. Petersburg, Russia	18
Copenhagen, Denmark	17	Salvador, Cen. America	14
Corinto, Nicaragua	22	Samoan Islands	17
Ensenada, Lower Cal	2	San Jose de Guatemala, C. A.	13
Falkland Island	44	Santiago, Chili	44
Farao Islands	20	Shanghai, China	28
Fiji Islands	31	Sitka, Alaska	8
Genoa, Italy	16	Stockholm, Sweden	18
Gibraltar, Spain	19	Sydney, Australia	25
Glasgow, Scotland	16	Valparaiso, Chili	43
Guatemala, Cen. Am	13	Vera Cruz, Mex	13
Guayaquil, Ecuador	21	Vienna, Austria	18
Guaymas, Mexico	9	Yokohama, Japan	17

DIFFERENCE OF TIME BETWEEN WASHINGTON AND OTHER CITIES OF THE WORLD

12:00 o'clock (noon) at Washington, D. C.

12:12 P. M. at	....	New York City, N. Y.
12:24 " "	....	Boston, Mass.
12:27 " "	....	Portland, Maine
1:37 " "	....	St. John's, N. F.
3:19 " "	....	Angra, Azores
4:31 " "	....	Lisbon, Portugal
4:43 " "	....	Dublin, Ireland
4:55 " "	....	Edinburgh, Scotland
5:07 " "	....	London, England
5:17 " "	....	Paris, France
5:58 " "	....	Rome, Italy
6:02 " "	....	Berlin, Germany
6:14 " "	....	Vienna, Austria
6:22 " "	....	Cape Town, Africa
7:04 " "	....	Constantinople, Turkey
11:01 " "	....	Calcutta, India
12:54 A. M. at	....	Pekin, China
2:48 " "	....	Melbourne, Australia
4:51 " "	....	Auckland, New Zealand
8:58 " "	....	San Francisco, Cal.
9:40 " "	....	Salt Lake City, Utah Territory
11:08 " "	....	New Orleans, La.
11:18 " "	....	Chicago, Ill.
11:52 " "	....	Buffalo, N. Y.
12:00 Noon "	....	Lima, Peru

THE EXPANSION AND CONTRACTION OF RAILWAY TRACK BY THE DIFFERENT TEMPERATURES

In climates having a difference of 70 degrees of temperature between the hot and cold seasons, a railway track of 400 miles is 338 yards longer in Summer than in Winter. Of course, the length of the road remains the same, but expansion forces the lengths of metal closer together, making an aggregate closing up of space between the rails of nearly a yard in each mile.

A steel rail lasts upon the average about eighteen years.

How to Tell How Fast One is Traveling by Railroad

The number of miles per hour at which a train is running will be the same as the number of rails passed over in twenty seconds, which can be ascertained by the "click" produced by the wheels at each joint.

Value of a Bar of Iron Worked into Various Forms

A bar of iron worth five dollars, worked into horseshoes, is worth ten dollars and fifty cents; made into needles, it is worth three hundred and fifty-five dollars; made into penknife blades it is worth three thousand two hundred and eighty-five dollars; made into balance springs of watches, it is worth two hundred and fifty thousand dollars.

How to Mix Paints and Printing Ink for Tints

Mixing red and black makes.......................................brown
" lake and white makes.....................................rose
" white and brown makes............................chestnut
" white, blue and lake makes.........................purple
" blue and lead color makes..........................pearl
" white and carmine makes..............................pink
" indigo and lampblack makes.....................silver gray
" white and lampblack makes.....................lead color
" black and venetian red makes....................chocolate
" white and green makes. ....bright green
" light green and black makes.....................dark green
" white and green makes............................pea green
" white and emerald green makes..............brilliant green
" purple and white makes.......................French white
" red and yellow makes...............................orange
" white and yellow makes.........................straw color
" white, blue and black makes.....................pearl gray
" white, lake and vermilion makes.................flesh color
" umber, white and venetian red makes.................drab
" white, yellow and venetian red makes.................cream
" red, blue, black and red makes.......................olive
" yellow, white and a little venetian red makes...........buff

How to Remove Rust from Steel

Brush the rusted steel with a paste composed of half an ounce of cyanide potassium, half an ounce of castile soap, one ounce of whiting and enough water to make a paste. Then wash the steel in a solution of half an ounce of cyanide potassium in two ounces of water.

How to Write on Glass

An ink that will write on glass can be made from ammonium fluoride dissolved in water and mixed with three times its weight of barium sulphate.

How to Remove Paint from Painted Surfaces

Take, 4 pounds of Irish moss, 3 pounds of methylated spirit, and 3 pounds of Fuller's earth are mixed with 30 pounds of water, the whole boiled, and a solution of 16 pounds of caustic soda and 16 pounds of caustic potash dissolved in 28 pounds of water added, after which the product is let stand until it is cold and has solidified to a brownish gelatinous mass. The proportions of the ingredients may be varied. The compound is used by applying it to the painted surface with a brush, allowing it to remain thus from 20 minutes to one hour and then washing it off together with the paint that has been disintegrated by its action.

How to Kill Grease Spots before Painting

Wash over the smoky or greasy parts with saltpetre, or very thin lime whitewash. If soapsuds are used, they must be washed off thoroughly, as they prevent the paint from drying hard.

Number of Believers in Different Creeds

The estimated number of Christians in the world is over 408,000,000; of Buddhists, 420,000,000; of the followers of Brahma, 180,000,000; of Mohammedans, 150,000,000; of Jews, 8,000,000; of atheists, deists, and infidels, 85,000,000; of pagans, 50,000,000; and of the eleven hundred other creeds, 123,000,000

THE NAME OF GOD IN DIFFERENT LANGUAGES

Language	Name of God	Language	Name of God
Æolian	Ilos	Madagascar	Zannar
Arabic	Allah	Malay	Alla
Armorian	Teuti	Norwegian	Gud
Assyrian	Eleah	Latin	Deus
Celtic	Diu	Low Latin	Diex
Chaldaic	Eilah	Low Breton	Done
Cretan	Thios	Lapp	Jubinal
Chinese	Prussa	Olalu Tongue	Deu
Coromandel	Brama	Old Saxon	God
Danish	Gut	Peruvian	Puchecammae
Dutch	Godt	Persian	Sire
Egyptian (old)	Teut	Pannonian	Istu
Egyptian (modern)	Teun	Polish	Bog
English	God	Pollacca	Bung
Finch	Jumala	Portuguese	Deos
Flemish	Goed	Provencal	Diou
French	Dieu	Runic	As
German	Gott	Russian	Bojh
German (old)	Diet	Spanish	Dios
Greek	Theos	Swedish	Gut
Gallic	Diu	Slav	Buch
Hebrew	Elohim, Eloha	Swiss	Gott
Hindoostanee	Rain	Syriac	Allah
Japanese	Goezur	Tartar	Magatal
Irish	Dia	Turkish	Allah
Italian	Dio	Zemblain	Fetizo

CHRONOLOGICAL LIST OF NOTED EVENTS
SINCE THE CREATION OF THE WORLD

Event	Date B. C.
Creation	4004
Menes, first King of Egypt began to reign	2717
The Flood	2349
Chinese Empire founded	2637
Uranus settles in Greece	2042
Jewish history opened, birth of Abraham	1996
Abraham settles in Canaan	1921
First gold mine opened in Thrace by Cadmus	1550

Noted Events—*Continued*

Event	Date, B. C.
Areopagus founded in Greece	1506
Exodus of Jews from Egypt	1491
Jews enter Canaan	1451
Greeks colonize Italy	1293
Saul elected King of Israel	1095
Solomon's Temple completed	1004
Capture of Jerusalem by Shisshank	989-959
Date of earliest existing gold coin	800
Rome founded	753
Siege and capture of Jerusalem by Nebuchadnezzar	598
Cyrus conquers Babylon	538
Darius orders the rebuilding of Jewish Temple	520
First treaty between Rome and Carthage	508
Battle of Marathon, the Athenians defeated the Persians	490
Battle of Thermopylæ	480
Beginning of Athenian Supremacy	477
First Decemvirate at Rome	451
Battle of Syracuse	413
Expedition of Cyrus the younger	401
Prosecution and death of Socrates	399
Birth of Alexander the Great	356
Battle of Arbela, Alexander defeated Darius	331
Death of Alexander (at Babylon)	323
Alexandrian Library founded	284
Silver money first coined at Rome	269
Rome completes conquest of all Italy	265
First Roman fleet launched	260
The gate of Janus shut	235
Hannibal crosses into Italy	218
First Macedonian War	211-205
Battle of Metaurus	207
Scipio carries the war into Africa	204
Hannibal defeated at Lama	202
End of second Punic War	201
Flaminius declares the Independence of the Greeks	198
Third Punic War began	149
Birth of Pompey and Cicero	103
Birth of C. Julius Cæsar	100
Pompey, Cæsar, and Crassus form the first Triumvirate	60
Cæsar invades Britain	55-54

Noted Events—*Continued*

Event	Date, B. C.
Cæsar assassinated	44
Battle of Philippi	42
Herod appointed King of the Jews	40
Spain conquered by Augustus Cæsar	38
Battle of Actium	31
Gates of Janus shut a second time	25
Temple of Jerusalem rebuilt by Herod	17–7
Birth of Jesus Christ, according to Ussher's system	4 B. C.

Event	Date A. D.
Death of Augustus Cæsar	14
Romans invade Germany	14–16
Crucifixion of Christ	33
London founded by A. Plautus	47
Nero became Emperor	54
Rome on fire six days	64
Jerusalem destroyed by the Romans under Titus	70
Herculaneum and Pompeii destroyed	79
Great persecutions of Christians at Rome	95
Galen born	130
Polycarp martyred	166
Birth of Origin	185
Great persecution of Christians	202
New Persian monarchy founded under Artaxerxes	226
Irruption of Franks into Gaul	253–263
The Thirty Tyrants rule in Roman Empire	268
Tacitus elected Emperor of Rome	275
Persecution of Christians by Diocletian	303
Declaration of Constantine as Emperor	306
First General Council of Church, at Nice	325
Athanasius Patriarch of Alexandria	326
Death of Arius	336
Saxons invade Gaul	370
Second General Council of Church, at Constantinople	381
Alaric proclaimed King of the Goths	382
Roman legions withdraw from Britain	418
Third General Church Council, at Ephesus	431
Fourth General Church Council, at Chalcedon	451
Battle of Chalons, the Huns defeated by the Romans	451

Noted Events—*Continued*

Event	Date, A. D.
Venice founded	452
Great fire in Constantinople	465
Earthquakes at Constantinople, lasting for forty days	480
Conquest of Italy by Theodorus	480–493
Nestorian Missions began	500
Paris made the Capital	510
Benedictine Order founded	528
Plague begins in Persia, its ravages extend for thirty years	531
The Gothic War	535–540
Invasion of Roman Empire by Slavs and Huns	550
Fifth General Council, held at Constantinople	553
Conquest of Italy by Lombards	556–571
Birth of Mohammed	570 or 571
Augustine arrives in England (died 605)	597
Supremacy of Roman Bishop acknowledged	602
Mohammed begins to preach at Mecca	610
Damascus and Jerusalem taken by the Persians	614
Flight of Mohammed from Mecca	622
Battle of Beder, first victory of Mohammed	623
Death of Mohammed	632
Caliph Omar takes Jerusalem and founded Mosque of Omar	637
Invasion of Egypt and capture of Alexandria	639–640
Theodus, Pope of Rome, the first called "Sovereign Pontiff"	642
First invasion of Africa by Saracens	647
The Colossus of Rhodes destroyed	653
Sixth General Council, at Constantinople	680
Doge of Venice first elected for life	697
Carthage conquered and burned by Saracens	698
Saracens invade Spain	710
Invasion of France by Saracens	721
Conquest of Sardinia by Saracens	723
Victory over Saracens by Martel at Tours	732
Death of the Venerable Bede	735
Great Earthquake at Constantinople	740
The Plague at Constantinople	747
Merovingian line of French kings ended	752
Carlovingian line begins, Pepin crowned king	752
Council at Constantinople condemns worship with pictures, images and crucifix	754
Charlemagne begins to reign in France	772

Noted Events—*Continued*

Events   Date A. D.

Lombard Kingdom overthrown by Charlemagne................ 774
Seventh general Council at Nice re-established image worship.... 787
Charlemagne crowned Emperor of the West, at Rome........... 800
Charlemagne imposes Athanasian Creed on Church.............. 802
Death of Charlemagne............. 814
Kingdom of Navarre founded...................... 857
Russian Monarchy founded by Ruric, a Verandian chief......... 862
Eighth general Council at Constantinople...................869–970
Norwegian settlement in Iceland............................. 874
Arnuph, King of Germany, besieged Rome and is crowned Emperor 894
Tang dynasty in China ends.................................. 907
Sung dynasty in China founded.............................. 960
Deposition of Pope by Otto I, Emperor of Romans.............. 963
Pope Benedict VI Strangled at Rome....................... 979
Edward, King of England martyred........................... 975
Greenland colonized from Iceland............................ 983
Hugh Capet, founder of the Capetian line, crowned King of France 987
Greek Ritual introduced into Russia.......................... 988
Earliest canonization of a saint.............................. 993
Hungary erected by Pope Sylvester II into a Kingdom for Duke
   Stephen..1000
First invasion of India by Mahmud...........................1001
Submission of all England to Sweyn, King of Denmark......... 1013
Total defeat of Danes at Clontarf. Henry II of Germany
   crowned..1014
Bulgaria made a province of Roman Empire....................1017
Navarre divided into kingdoms of Castile and Arragon..........1035
Turks conquer Persia and found the Seljukian dynasty..........1038
Pope Leo IX taken prisoner by Robert Guiscard at battle of
   Civitello...1053
The Pope and Patriarch at Constantinople excommunicate each
   other...1054
Election of Pope vested in College of Cardinals by Nicholas II...1059
Norman Conquest of England begins 1066
Battle of Hastings ; defeat of Harold by William the Conqueror..1066
Normans capture Bari and end the Byzantine rule..............1071
Conquest of Asia Minor by Turks.......................1074–1084
Turks take Jerusalem.......................................1076
Henry IV of Germany at Council of Worms deposes the Pope,
   and the Pope in Council at Rome deposes Henry and absolves
   his subjects from allegiance to him...................1076–1080

Noted Events—*Continued*

Events	Date A. D.
Emperor Henry of Germany besieges and Captures Rome	1084
English Domesday Book completed	1086
Sejukian Empire ends with death of Sultan Melsk Shaw	1092
Knights Hospitallers founded about	1092
Preaching of Peter the Hermit; first crusade proclaimed	1095
Cistercian Order founded	1098
Jerusalem captured by Crusaders under Godfrey de Bouillon, who was proclaimed king	1099
England conquers Normandy	1106
Order of Knights Templar founded	1118
Ninth General Council at Rome	1123
Civil War in England between adherents of Stephen and Maud	1138
Portugal made a kingdom	1139
Tenth General Council at Rome	1139
Frederic Barbarossa invades Italy	1154
Barbarossa is crowned Emperor at Rome by the Pope	1155
Bank of Venice instituted	1157
Munich founded by Henry the Lion	1157
Peace ratified between England and France	1161
Henry II invades Ireland and is acknowledged King	1171
Conquest of Ireland completed	1178
Eleventh General Council at Rome	1179
Jews Banished from France	1182
Second Bulgarian Kingdom founded	1186
Infidels under Saladin recapture Jerusalem from the Christians	1187
The Order of Teutonic Knights founded	1190
War between England and France	1202
Inquisition founded by Pope Innocent III	1203
Invasion of China by Jenghiz Kahn	1210
The Children's Crusade	1212
Twelfth General Council at Rome	1215
Invasion of Russia and sack of Moscow by Tartars	1236
Moorish Kingdom of Grenada founded	1239
Thirteenth General Council and Emperor Frederick deposed, at Lyons	1245
University College, Oxford, England, founded	1249
English Laws introduced into Wales	1252
Constantinople Captured by Palæologue; Latin Empire ends	1261
Fourteenth General Council; temporary re-union of Greek and Latin Churches, at Lyons	1274

Noted Events—*Continued*

Events	Date, A. D.
Conquest of China by Moguls completed	1280
Conquest of Prussia by Teutonic knights completed	1283
Jews expelled from England by Edward I	1290
Final loss of Palestine by Christians	1291
English Parliament organized	1295
Great Charter in England confirmed by Edward I	1297
Title of "Prince of Wales" first conferred on eldest son of English king. First conferred by Edward I	1301
Philip of France condemns inquisition	1302
Fifteenth General Council, at Vienna	1312
Thirteen years' truce between England and Scotland proclaimed.	1323
Necessity of Pope's consent to Imperial elections denied by Diet at Frankfort	1323
Cannon first used by Florentines	1326
Scottish Independence acknowledged by England	1328
Ottoman Empire established	1329
Scotland invaded by the English	1332
Plague of locusts in Europe for three years	1337
First passage of Turks into Europe	1341
First English gold coinage (florin)	1344
Parliament of Paris organized by Philip VI	1344
Canary Islands discovered by Genoese and Spanish seamen	1345
Servian Empire established	1345
Massacre of Jews on suspicion of poisoning the wells	1349
"The Black Death" prevails in Europe	1348–1351
Dauphiny united to France	1349
Turks established in Europe	1353
Coast of Guinea discovered by French seamen	1364
Myng dynasty founded in China	1368
Halley's Comet appeared	1378
Conquest of Asia Minor completed by the Turks	1391
Sixteenth General Council, Huss condemned to be burnt, at Constance	1414
Eighteenth General Council, at Basle	1431
The Azores taken by the Portuguese	1432
Nine years' truce between England and Scotland proclaimed	1438
Joan of Arc's Victory over the English	1429
Union of Naples and Sicily as "The Two Sicilies" proclaimed	1442
Austria erected into an archduchy	1453
Eastern Empire ends with conquest of Constantinople by Mohammed II	1453

Noted Events—*Continued*

Event	Date A. D.
"Mazarine Bible," first book ever printed	1455
Fifteen years' truce between England and Scotland proclaimed	1464
Civil war in France	1465
War between England and Scotland breaks out again	1480
Cape of Good Hope discovered by Bartolomeo Daiz	1486
Christopher Columbus discovered the New World	1492
Discovery of mainland by Columbus	1498
Earl of Warwick executed	1499
St. Peter's Church, at Rome, commenced	1506
Ponce de Leon discovered Florida	1512
Balboa, a Spaniard, discovered Pacific Ocean	1513
Diet of Worms attended by Martin Luther	1521
Conquest of Mexico by Cortez	1521
Gustavus Vasa delivers Sweden from Danish yoke	1523
Conquest of Peru by Pizarro	1533
Ferdinand de Soto discovered the Mississippi River	1541
Council of Trent held	1545
Martin Luther (born 1483) died	1546
Elizabeth ascends the throne of England	1558
First settlement in New World (St. Augustine)	1565
Massacre of St. Bartholomew	1572
Mary, Queen of Scots beheaded	1587
Presbyterianism established in Scotland	1592
Edict of Nantes	1598
Jamestown, Va., settled	1607
Kepler's laws published	1609
Mayflower sails from Delft	1620
First house erected in Boston, Mass.	1630
Roger Williams settles Rhode Island	1635
England declared a Commonwealth	1649
Great Plague in London	1665
King Philip's war	1675
Revocation of the Edict of Nantes	1685
King William's war	1689
Salem witchcraft excitement	1692
Battle of Blenheim; the French defeated by the English	1704
Battle of Pultowa; Peter the Great defeated the Swedes	1709
First postoffice in Massachusetts	1710
Rise of Methodism in England	1728
George Washington born, Feb. 11th (old style) Feb. 22d (new style)	1732

Noted Events—*Continued*

Event	Date A. D.
Queen Anne's war	1744
Earthquake at Lima, Peru	1746
Franklin proves the identity of lightning and electricity	1752
French and Indian war	1754
Lisbon destroyed by earthquake	1755
Prisoners in Black Hole of Calcutta perish	1756
"Stamp Act" passed by British Parliament	1765
"Boston Massacre"	1770
"Boston Tea Party"	1773
American Revolution commences	1775
"The Declaration of Independence," signed	July 4, 1776
France recognizes the United States	1778
Gen. Cornwallis' forces surrendered to Washington	1781
American Revolution ended	1781
Treaty of Peace between England and United States signed	1783
Penal settlement at Botany Bay	1788
George Washington inaugurated President of the United States	April 30, 1789
Bastile destroyed	1789
Battle of Valmy, Dumouriez defeated Duke of Brunswick	1792
September massacre at Paris	1797
Reign of terror at Paris	1793
Final dismemberment of Poland	1794
Napoleon declared First Consul	1799
George Washington died	1799
Great Naval Battle of Trafalgar	1805
Tecumseh War	1804
First steamboat on the Hudson River	1807
War between United States and England	1812
War between France and Prussia	1812
Battle of Waterloo, Wellington defeated Napoleon	1815
Greek Independence declared	1822
"Monroe Doctrine" proclaimed	1823
Victoria proclaimed Queen of England	1837
First telegraph line completed	1844
Texas annexed to the United States	1845
Mexican War	1846
Great Famine in Ireland	1847
Gold discovered in California	1848
First Atlantic Cable laid	1858

Noted Events—*Continued*

Event	Date A. D.
Civil War commenced in United States	1861
Emancipation Proclamation, declaring freedom to the slaves in United States, issued by President Lincoln	1863
Assassination of President A. Lincoln	April 14, 1865
War between Prussia, Austria, Bavaria and Italy	
Maximilian, Emperor of Mexico, shot	June 19, 1867
French and German War	1870-1871
Sioux Indian Massacre	1876
Centenary of American Independence	1876
Zulu War in Africa	1879
Assassination of President J. A. Garfield	July 2, 1881
Egyptian War	1882-1883

NOTABLE HISTORICAL FIRES

Year	Place	Loss
1570	Moscow, Russia	200,000 victims
1666	London, England	13,200 houses
1812	Moscow, Russia	15,500 houses
1824	Cairo, Egypt	4,000 victims
1831	Constantinople, Turkey	18,000 houses
1835	New York City, United States	$ 20,000,000
1842	Hamburg, Germany	36,000,000
1851	San Francisco, Cal., United States	2,500 blocks
1871	Chicago, Ill., United States	$165,000,000
1872	Boston, Mass., United States	75,000,000

EXPECTATION OF HUMAN LIFE

After the first year the chances of living increase up to the fourth year, and then slowly decline. The average life of the following occupations are here given:

Occupation	Years	Occupation	Years
Rural Laborers	45.52	Stone Masons	38.19
Carpenters	45.28	Plumbers	38.18
Domestics	42.03	Mill Operatives	38.09
Bakers	41.92	Blacksmiths	37.96
Shoemakers	40.87	Bricklayers	37.70
Weavers	41.92	Printers	36.66
Tailors	39.40	Clerks	34.99
Hatters	38.91	Average population	39.88

PATENT FEES OF DIFFERENT COUNTRIES

Country	Fee	Country	Fee
Austria	$250	Netherlands	$150
Bavaria	150	Portugal	250
Belgium	150	Prussia	200
Cuba	450	Russia	550
France	150	Saxony	250
Great Britain	350	Spain	400
India	400	Sweden and Norway	600
Italy	250	United States	60 to 75

SALARIES OF UNITED STATES MILITARY AND NAVAL OFFICERS

Military Officers

Rank	Salary Per Annum
General of the Army	$13,500
Lieutenant General	11,000
Major Generals	7,500
Brigadier Generals	5,500
Colonels	3,500
Lieutenant-Colonels	3,000
Majors	2,500
Captains, mounted	2,000
Captains, not mounted	1,800
First Lieutenant, mounted	1,600
First Lieutenant, not mounted	1,500
Second Lieutenant, mounted	1,500
Second Lieutenant, not mounted	1,400
Chaplains	1,500

Naval Officers

Rank	Salary Per Annum
Admirals	$13,000
Vice Admirals	9,000
Rear Admirals	6,000
Commodores	5,000
Captains	4,500
Commanders	3,500
Lieutenant Commanders	2,800
Lieutenants	2,400
Masters	1,800
Ensigns	1,200
Midshipmen	1,000

LIMIT OF JURISDICTION WITH JUSTICE OF PEACE OF THE DIFFERENT STATES

The following table shows the largest amount in the different States and Territories which the Justice of Peace, through his position, can have jurisdiction over as follows:

State	Amount	State	Amount
Alabama	$100	Missouri	$300
Arkansas	300	Nebraska	200
California	300	Nevada	300
Colorado	300	New Hampshire	100
Connecticut	100	New Jersey	100
North and South Dakota	100	New Mexico Ter	100
Delaware	100	New York	200
Florida	100	North Carolina	200
Georgia	100	Ohio	300
Idaho Ter	100	Oregon	250
Illinois	200	Pennsylvania	300
Indiana	200	Rhode Island	100
Iowa (consent of parties 300)	100	South Carolina	100
Kansas	300	Tennessee	500
Kentucky	100	Texas	200
Louisiana	100	Utah Ter	300
Maine	20	Vermont	200
Maryland	100	Virginia	50
Massachusetts	300	Washington	100
Michigan	300	West Virginia	100
Minnesota	100	Wisconsin	300
Mississippi	150	Wyoming	100

VALUE OF ANCIENT MONEY

Denominations	Weight, Grains	Gold Value
Gold Shekel	132	$5.69
Gold Maneh	13,200	569.00
Gold Talent	1,320,000	56,900,000.00
Silver Gerah	11	.02¼
Silver Beka	110	.26½
Silver Shekel	220	.53
Silver Maneh	13,200	32.00
Silver Talent	660,000	1,660.00
Copper Shekel	528	.03 14
Persian Daric or Drachm (gold)	128	5.52.
Maccabæan Shekel (silver)	220	.53
"Piece of Money" (Stater, silver)	220	.53
Penny (Denarius, silver)	59	.14
Farthing (Quadrans, copper)	42	.00¼
Farthing (assarium, copper)	84	.00½
Mite (copper)	21	.00⅛

BANKS OF EUROPE—WHEN ESTABLISHED

The first bank was established in Italy in 808. Other banks were established as follows:

Bank of	Year	Bank of	Year
Venice	1151	England	1694
Geneva	1345	Scotland	1695
Barcelona	1401	Copenhagen	1736
Genoa	1407	Berlin	1765
Amsterdam	1607	Ireland	1783
Hamburg	1619	St. Petersburg	1780
Rotterdam	1635	France	1803
Stockholm	1688	New York (U. S.)	1784

FACTS ABOUT BANKS IN THE UNITED STATES

Bank of North America, Philadelphia, incorporated by Congress 1781; by State of Pennsylvania, 1782.

Bank of the United States, incorporated 1791; went into operation 1794; capital, $10,000,000; charter limited to 20 years.

Bank of New York founded 1784.

Bank of Massachusetts founded 1784.

New United States Bank chartered 1816; capital, $35,000,000. Act re-chartering vetoed by President Jackson, 1832. United States funds withdrawn, September, 1833.

Re-chartered by Pennsylvania 1836; temporarily suspended payment of specie, 1831, and again October 9, 1837; resumed in compliance with Act of Pennsylvania Legislature, January 15, 1840; finally suspended February 4, 1840, having sunk its entire capital.

State banks nearly all suspended specie payments in 1837, resuming again the following year, again in 1857, and still again in 1861.

February 25, 1863, act creating the system of national banks in the United States was passed. No bank should be of less capital than $50,000. In cities of over 10,000 inhabitants, no bank should be of less capital than $100,000. Ninety per cent of the par value of United States bonds deposited as security allowed in circulating notes. Aggregate circulation allowed $300,000,000.

July 12, 1870, act allowing $54,000,000 additional circulation. No bank to exceed in capital $500,000.

January 14, 1875, repeal of all limitation on amount of circulation, thus making national banking practically free.

FACTS ABOUT THE BANK OF ENGLAND

February 26, 1797. Bank of England suspended payment of specie.

May 1, 1821. Resumed payment of notes in bullion at mint prices.

May 1, 1821. Resumed payment of notes in current coin of the realm.

July 19, 1844. Issue of notes limited in amount to £14,000,000. For all circulation above that sum bank must hold an equal amount of coin for its redemption.

October 25, 1847. Suspension of the limitation clause of 1844, and bank allowed to make extra issue.

November 25, 1857. Extra issue of bank notes to the amount of £2,000,000 allowed.

1866. Similar suspension of bank act.

Bank of England notes are legal tender everywhere in England save at the bank. No interest on deposits allowed. Has entire charge of the British national debt.

A FEW FACTS ABOUT GOLD

A cubic inch of gold is worth $210; a cubic foot is worth $362,380; a cubic yard is worth $9,792,762. This is valuing it at $18 an ounce. At the commencement of the Christian era there was in the world $427,000,000 in gold. This had diminished to $57,000,000 at the time America was discovered. Then it began to increase. Now the amount of gold in use is estimated to be $6,000,000,000. Yet all this welded into one mass would be contained in a cube of twenty-six feet.

The relative value of gold to silver has varied greatly at different periods. The ratio was in the days of the patriarch

Abraham.................1 to 8	A. D. 1545.............1 to 6
B. C. 1000...............1 to 12	A. D. 1551.............1 to 2
B. C. 500................1 to 13	A. D. 1600.............1 to 10
A. D. 1...............1 to 9	A. D. 1627.............1 to 13
A. D. 500..............1 to 18	A. D. 1700..... ....1 to 15½
A. D. 1100..............1 to 8	A. D. 1876.............1 to 20
A. D. 1400. ....1 to 11	A. D. 1886.............1 to 28¼

the highest point until then ever known.

Interest Laws of all the States, Canada, England, Ireland and France

Place	Penalty of Usury	Legal rate per cent.	Rate per contract per cent.
*Alabama	Forfeiture entire interest	8	8
*Arizona Ter	No penalty	10	any rate
*Arkansas	No penalty	6	10
†California	No penalty	7	any rate
†Colorado ..	...No penalty	10	any rate
†Connecticut	Forfeiture entire interest	6	6
*Dakota	Forfeiture entire interest	7 •	18
†Delaware	Forfeiture of Principal	6	6
†Dist. of Columbia	Forfeiture entire interest	6	10
†Florida	No penalty	8	any rate
†Georgia	Forfeiture interest and excess	7	8
†Idaho Ter	Forfeit 3 times the amount paid, fine $300 o. 6 months' imprisonment or both	10	
†Illinois	Forfeiture excess interest	6	8
*Indiana	Forfeiture excess interest and cost	6	8
*Iowa	Forfeiture excess interest	6	10
†Kansas	Forfeiture excess over 12 per cent	7	12
*Kentucky	Forfeiture excess interest	6	10
†Louisiana	Forfeiture entire interest	5	8
*Maine	No penalty	6	any rate
†Maryland	Forfeiture excess interest	6	6
*Massachusetts	No penalty	6	any rate
*Michigan	Forfeiture excess interest	7	10
*Minnesota	Forfeiture entire interest	7	10
*Mississippi	Forfeiture excess interest	6	10
†Missouri	Forfeiture entire interest	6	10
*Montana	No penalty	10	any rate
*Nebraska	Forfeiture entire interest	7	10
†Nevada	Forfeiture all interest	10	any rate
*New Hampshire	Forfeiture of 3 times the excess and cost	6	6
*New Jersey	Forfeiture entire interest	6	6
*New Mexico	No penalty	6	12
*New York	Forfeiture of contract	6	6
*North Carolina	Forfeiture of interest	6	8

Interest Laws—*Continued*

Place	Penalty of Usury	Legal rate per cent.	Rate per contract per cent.
†Ohio	Forfeiture of excess	6	8
*Oregon	Forfeiture of principal, interest and cost	10	12
†Pennsylvania	Forfeiture of excess	6	6
*Rhode Island	Forfeiture, unless by contract	6	any rate
*South Carolina	Forfeiture entire interest	7	any rate
*Tennessee	Forfeit of over 6 per cent and $100 fine	6	10
†Texas	No penalty	8	12
*Utah Ter	No penalty	10	any rate
†Vermont	Forfeiture of excess	6	6
†Virginia	Forfeiture of all interest	6	8
*Washington	No penalty	10	any rate
†West Virginia	Forfeiture of excess	6	6
*Wisconsin	Forfeiture of all interest	7	10
*Wyoming Ter	No penalty	12	any rate
*Canada		6	any rate
England		5	
France		5	
Ireland		6	

*Three days' grace is allowed on Sight Drafts.
†Grace not allowed on Sight Drafts.

HOW TO REMOVE TIGHT RINGS FROM THE FINGER

The removal of rings is practiced by jewelers in the following manner: The swollen finger is wrapped very tightly with a flat rubber braid, commencing at the end; the finger is then held upright for a few minutes, the braid quickly removed and again wound around it. The operation being repeated three times leaves the finger so shrunken that the ring may easily be taken off.

Area of the Most Notable Parks of the World

Name	Location	Area in Acres
Windsor Park	Windsor Castle, England	3,800
Fairmount Park	Philadelphia, U. S	2,740
Water Park	Vienna, Austria	2,300
Bois de Boulogne	Paris, France	2,100
Phœnix Park	Dublin, Ireland	1,760
Royal Park	Munich, Germany	1,300
Forest Park	St. Louis, U. S.	1,350
South Park	Chicago, Ill., U. S.	1,055
Golden Gate Park	San Francisco, Cal., U. S.	1,043
Central Park	New York City, U. S.	843
Druid Hill Park	Baltimore, Maryland, U. S.	680
Their Garten	Berlin, Germany	600
Prospect Park	Brooklyn, N. Y., U. S.	550
Regent's Park	London, England	450
Queen's Park	Edinburgh, Scotland	407
Hyde Park	London, England	400
Schloss Garten	Stuttgart, Germany	320
Grosse Garten	Dresden, Germany	300
Victoria Park	London, England	290
Eden Park	Cincinnati, U. S.	216
City Park	New Orleans, U. S.	150
Prospect Park	Buffalo, U. S.	150
Jardin des Plantes	Paris, France	77
Jardin des Tuilleries	Paris, France	50
Boston Common	Boston, U. S.	48

Number of Years Seeds Retain Their Vitality

Vegetables	Years	Vegetables	Years
Artichoke	5 to 6	Asparagus	2 to 3
Beans	2 to 3	Beets	3 to 4
Broccoli	5 to 6	Cauliflower	5 to 6
Carrots	2 to 3	Celery	2 to 3
Corn (on cob)	2 to 3	Cress	3 to 4
Cucumber	8 to 10	Egg Plant	1 to 2
Endive	5 to 6	Leek	2 to 3
Lettuce	3 to 4	Melon	8 to 10
Mustard	3 to 4	Okra	3 to 4
Onion	2 to 3	Parsley	2 to 3
Parsnip	2 to 3	Pea	5 to 6
Pepper	2 to 3	Pumpkin	8 to 10
Radish	4 to 5	Rhubarb	3 to 4
Spinach	3 to 4	Squash	8 to 10
Tomato	2 to 3	Turnip	3 to 6

Herbs

Anise	3 to 4	Caraway	2
Sage	2 to 3	Summer Savory	1 to 2
Lavender	2 to 3	Thyme	2 to 32

HARVEST DATES OF THE WORLD

January.—Harvest is ended in most districts of Australia and shipments have been made of the new crop, Chili, New Zealand, Argentine Republic.

February.—Upper Egypt, India.

March.—Egypt, India.

April.—Coast of Egypt, Syria, Cyprus, India, Persia, Asia Minor, Mexico, Cuba.

May.—Persia, Asia Minor, Algeria, Syria, Texas, Florida, Morocco, China, Japan, Central Asia.

June.—California, Oregon, Southern United States, Spain, Portugal, Italy, Hungary, Turkey, Southern Russia, Southern France, Greece, Sicily, Louisiana, Mississippi, Alabama, Georgia, North and South Carolina, Tennessee, Virginia, Kentucky, Arkansas, Kansas, Missouri, Utah, Colorado. (Fruit in California.)

July.—Oregon, Nebraska, Wisconsin, Minnesota, Iowa, Illinois, Michigan, Ohio, Indiana, New England, New York, Virginia, Upper Canada, France, Germany, Italy, Austria, Hungary, Switzerland, Poland, Russia.

August.—Great Britian, France, Germany, Belgium, Holland, British Columbia, Lower Canada, Manitoba.

September.—America, maize; England and Scotland, hops and roots; Sweden, Norway, Russia, France, beet root, buckwheat; Athabasca, wheat, barley, etc.. California vintage.

October.—Scotland and America, maize crop; France and Germany, vintage.

November.—Northern Australia, Peru, South Africa.

December.—South Australia, Chili, Argentine Republic.

THE HOUSEWIFE'S TABLE

The following is a very valuable housewife's table by which persons not having scales and weights at hand may readily measure the article wanted to form any recipe without the trouble of weighing, allowance to be made for any extraordinary dryness or moisture of the article weighed or measured:

Wheat flour, 1 pound is 1 quart.
Indian meal, 1 pound 2 ounces are 1 quart.
Butter, when soft, 1 pound is 1 quart.
Butter, when soft, the size of an egg weighs 1 ounce.
Loaf sugar, broken, 1 pound is 1 quart.
White sugar, powdered, 1 pound 1 ounce are 1 quart.
Best brown sugar, 1 pound 2 ounces are 1 quart.
Ten common sized eggs are one pound.
A common tumbler holds half a pint.
A teacup is 1 gill.
A large wineglass is 1 gill.
Forty drops are equal to 1 teaspoonful.
Four teaspoons are equal to one tablespoon.

WHAT HOUSEKEEPERS SHOULD REMEMBER

That fish may be scaled much easier by first dipping them into boiling water for a minute.

That which has changed may be sweetened or rendered fit for use again by stirring in a little soda.

That fresh meat beginning to sour will sweeten if placed out-of-doors in the cool air over night.

To keep oilcloth looking new wipe off the dust with a dry cloth, then rub with a cloth dampened with kerosene.

The cold rain water and soap will remove machine grease from washable fabrics.

To remove clinkers from stoves or fire-bricks put in about half a peck of oyster shells on top of a bright fire. This may need repeating.

That thoroughly wetting the hair once or twice with a solution of salt and water will keep it from falling out.

To restore the hair, apply equal parts of glycerine and bay rum mixed well together.

That salt fish are quickest and best freshened by soaking them in sour milk.

That salt will curdle new milk, hence in preparing porridge, gravies, etc., salt should not be added until the dish is prepared.

To clean dirty marble—sal soda one part, powdered pumice one part, whiting two parts, oxalic acid half a part. Mix. Spread the preparation on the marble, and moisten with sufficient hot water to form a paste. Rub well.

That castor oil softens boots and shoes which have been hardened by water.

That one teaspoonful of ammonia to a teacup of water applied with a rag will clean silver or gold jewelry perfectly.

That furniture may be brightened and cleaned from soiled spots by rubbing with a cloth dipped in sweet oil.

That paint stains that are dry and old may be removed from cotton or woolen goods with chloroform. It is a good plan to first cover the spot with olive oil or butter.

That when a room is to have a new paper the old ought to be removed first. A boiler of hot water set in a room, and the doors and windows closed for a while will cause the paper to loosen, so that it may be taken off without difficulty. The wood-work may then be cleaned easily, while the dirt is softened by the steam.

That charcoal is recommended as an absorber of gases in the milk-room where foul gases are present. It should be freshly powdered and kept there continually, especially in hot weather when unwholesome odors are most liable to infect the milk.

That to keep worms from fruit, a small quantity of sassafras bark placed among any kind of dried fruit will keep it free from worms for years.

For chapped hands; one ounce of glycerine, one ounce of rosewater, ten drops carbolic acid. This prevents and cures chapping of the skin, and at the same time bleaches it.

Amount of Butter and Cheese Obtainable From Milk

100 pounds of milk contains about 3 pounds pure butter.
100 " " " " 7.8 " cheese.
100 " " averages " 3.5 " common butter.
100 " " " " 11.7 " cheese.
100 " of skim milk yields 13.5 " skim milk cheese.

The time required for the full amount of cream to rise to the surface of new milk at different temperatures is as following:

10 to 12 hours if the temperature of the air is 77° Fahr.
18 to 20 " " " " " 68° "
24 " " " " " 55° "
36 " " " " " 55° "

The First United States Flag

In June, 1776, a committee was appointed by the Continental Congress to design a flag for the new government about to go in operation. Colonel George Ross was on this committee who, accompanied by George Washington, called upon an upholsterer in Philadelphia, named Mrs Ross, to instruct her how to make the new flag. Washington himself made a drawing of the flag in her parlor, and while doing this took some suggestions from her as to its design. She said that the stars should be five-cornered instead of six-cornered as Washington had made them. This ingenious lady made the first flag, and several others afterward, finishing them up in a very superior manner, entirely satisfactory to those who had the honor of first lifting them to the breeze.

ORIGIN OF ORCHARD AND GARDEN FRUITS AND
NUMBER OF VARIETIES

Name	Place of Origin	Number of Varieties
Almond	North Africa	9
Apple	Europe	1,570
Banana	Asia	
Barberry	Asia	1
Blackberry	Asia	20
Butternut	America	1
Cherry	Asia Minor	209
Chestnut	Asia Minor	4
Citron	Media	2
Cranberry	Both hemispheres	3
Cucumber	Asia	
Currant	Europe	27
Egg-plant	Africa	
Fig	Asia and Barbary	15
Filbert	Europe	8
Gooseberry	Europe and Asia	81
Grape	Persia	232
Hickory-nut	America	2
Lemon	Asia	2
Lime	Asia	1
Medlar	Europe	
Melon Musk	Persia	17
Mulberry, black	Persia	
" white	China	7
Nectarine	Northern India	32
Olive	Asia and Africa	6
Orange	Africa	10
Peach	Persia and China	239
Pear	Asia Minor	1,087
Pecan	United States	
Pineapple	Tropical America	
Plum	Asia Minor	297
Pomegranate	China	8
Pumpkin	Uncertain	
Quince	Europe	10
Raspberry	Asia Minor	88
Service	France and Italy	
Shaddock	China and Japan	
Squash	East Indies	
Tomato	America	
Walnut	Persia	5
Watermelon	Old World	15

AMOUNT OF OIL IN SEEDS

The amount of oil in a certain seed will vary according to the conditions of growth. In a scale of 100 this is considered about the average per cent.

Name	Per cent of Oil	Name	Per cent of Oil
Bitter Almond	37	Oats	6½
Hempseed	19	Sweet Almond	47
Linseed	17	Turnip seed	45
Rapeseed	55	White Mustard	37

THE FIRST STEAM-PROPELLED VESSEL THAT CROSSED THE OCEAN

The *Times* (of London, England), in the issue of May 8, 1819, thus announced the expected event:

"GREAT EXPERIMENT.—A new steam-vessel of 300 tons has been built at New York for the express purpose of carrying passengers across the Atlantic. She is to come to Liverpool direct."

This steamer, named the *Savannah*, the first that crossed the Atlantic, was built at New York by Francis Ficket. Her engines were made by Stephen Vail, of Morristown. She was launched on the 22d of August, 1818. She could carry only seventy-five tons of coal and twenty-five cords of wood. Commanded by Captain Moses Rogers, of New London, Conn., the *Savannah* sailed from Savannah, Ga., on the 25th of May, 1819, bound for St. Petersburg via Liverpool. She reached the latter port on the 20th of June, having used steam eighteen days out of the twenty-six.

UNITED STATES SQUADRON STATIONS

North Atlantic	Headquarters at Washington, D. C.
South Atlantic	" Rio Janeiro, Brazil
North Pacific	" San Francisco, Cal.
South Pacific	" Panama, U. S. of Col.
European	" London, England
Asiatic	" Hong Kong, nr. China

MOTTOES OF THE STATES AND TERRITORIES

United States.—*E pluribus unum* (Latin). One composed of many.

Alabama.—Here we rest.

Arizona.—*Ditat Deus.* God enriches.

Arkansas.—*Regnant populi* (Latin). The people rule.

California.—*Eureka* (Greek). I have found it.

Colorado.—*Nil sine numine* (Latin). Nothing without God.

Connecticut.—*Qui transtulit sustinet* (Latin). He who transplanted still sustains.

Dakota.—Liberty and Union, now and forever, one and inseparable.

Delaware.—Liberty and Independence.

District of Columbia.—*Justitia Omnibus* (Latin). Justice to all.

Florida.—In God is our trust.

Georgia.—Wisdom, justice and moderation.

Idaho.—*Salve* (Latin). In good condition.

Illinois.—State Sovereignty—National Union.

Iowa.—Our Liberties we prize, and our Rights we will maintain.

Kansas.—*Ad astra per aspera* (Latin). To the stars through difficulties.

Kentucky.—United we stand, divided we fall.

Louisiana.—Union, Justice and Confidence.

Maine.—*Dirigo* (Latin). I direct or guide.

Maryland.—*Crescite et multiplicamini* (Latin). Grow, or increase and multiply.

Massachusetts.—*Ense petit placidam sub libertate quietem* (Latin). With the sword she seeks quiet place under liberty.

Michigan.—*Si quæris peninsulam amœnam circumspice* (Latin). If thou seekest a beautiful peninsula, behold it here.

Minnesota.—*L'etoil du nord* (French). The star of the North.

Missouri.—*Salus populi suprema est lex* (Latin). The welfare of the people is the supreme law.

Montana.—*Oro y Plata* (Spanish). Gold and Silver.

Nebraska.—Equality before the law.

Nevada.—*Volens et potens* (Latin). Able and willing.

New York.—*Excelsior* (Latin). Higher, more elevated.

Oregon.—*Alis volat propriis* (Latin). She flies with her own wings.

Pennsylvania.—Virtue, Liberty, Independence.

Rhode Island.—Hope.

South Carolina.—*Animis opibusque parati—Dum, Spiro, Spero* (Latin). Prepared in mind and resources, ready to give life and property—While I breathe, I hope.

Vermont.—Freedom and Unity.
Virginia.—*Sic semper tyrannis* (Latin).   Ever so to tyrants.
Washington.—*Al-ki* (Indian).   Bye-and-bye.
West Virginia.—*Montani semper liberi* (Latin).   Mountaineers are always freemen.
Wyoming.—*Cedant arma togæ* (Latin).   Let arms yield to the gown.
Wisconsin.—Fo. ward.

EXTREME HEAT IN VARIOUS COUNTRIES

The following figures show the extreme heat in the various countries of the world.   Bengal, 150 deg. Fahrenheit; Borgu, Sahara Desert, 153 deg.; Persia, 125 degs.; Calcutta, India, 120 deg.; Central American Republic, 129 degs.; Cape of Good Hope, South Africa, 105 deg.; Greece, 109 degs.; Arabia, 111 degs.; New York, 102 degs.; Spain, Cuba, China, and Jamaica, 110 degs.; France, Denmark, Southern Russia and the Sandwich Islands, 100 degs.; England, Ireland and Portugal, 88 degs.; Australia, 80 degs.; Scotland, 75 degs.; Sweden and Norway, 65 degs.; Iceland, 42 degs.; and Nova Zembla, 32 degs.; never above the freezing po'nt.

THE OLDEST COLLEGES IN THE UNITED STATES

College Name and Location	When Founded
Harvard, Cambridge, Mass	1638
William and Henry, Williamsburg, Va	1693
Yale, New Haven, Conn	1700
College of New Jersey, Princeton, New Jersey	1746
Washington and Lee, Lexington, Va	1749
Columbia (first named Kings), New York	1754
Brown, Providence, R. I	1764
Dartmouth, Hanover, N. H.	1769
Rutgers, New Brunswick, N. J.	1770
Dickinson, Carlisle, Penn	1783
University of Pennsylvania, Philadelphia, Penn	1785
Williams, Williamstown, Mass	1793
Union Schenectady, N. Y	1795
Bowdoin, Brunswick, Me	1798
Trinity, Hartford, Conn	1823
University of Virginia, Charlottesville, Va	1825
Wesleyan, Middletown, Conn	1830

Horses Famous in History
Annual Statistican

Bavieca, the Cid's horse. He survived his master two years and a half, during which time no one was allowed to mount him, and when he died he was buried before the gate of the monastery of Valencia, Spain, and two elms were planted to mark the site.

Bevis, the horse of Lord Marmion. The name is Norse and means swift.

Black Bess was the famous mare of Dick Turpin.

Bucephalus, the celebrated horse of Alexander the Great. Alexander was the only person who could mount him, and he always knelt down to take his master. He was thirty years old at death, and Alexander built a city for his mausoleum, which he called Bucephalæ.

Celer, the horse of the Roman Emperor Verus, was fed on almonds and raisins, and was covered with royal purple and installed in the imperial palace. At death a mausoleum in the Vatican was raised to its honor.

Incitatus, the horse of the Roman Emperor Caligula, was made a priest and consul, had a manger of ivory, and drank wine from a golden pail.

Morocco, the famous trick horse of Banks. While performing in Rome, the Pope had both horse and master arrested and burned as magicians.

Phrenicos, the horse of Hiero, of Syracuse, that won the Olympic prize for single horses, in the 73d Olympiad.

Roan Barbary, the favorite horse of King Richard II.

Shebediz, the Persian Buchephalus, belonging to the Shah Kosroes Parviz.

White Surrey, the favorite horse of King Richard III.

Insects and Mammals Most Useful to Men

The silkworm, silk; the cochineal insect, cochineal; the lac insect, lac; the gall insect, gall; the bee, honey and wax; the Spanish fly, medicinal; the Greenland whale, whale oil and whalebone; the Sperm whale, oil and spermaceti; the walrus, oil and ivory; the seal, oil and skin; the porpoise, oil and leather; the elephant, ivory and food; the beaver, mink, marten, fur; muskrat, otter, seal, sable, fur; ermine, fox, gray squirrels, fur; chinchilla, fur; the peccary, kangaroo, reindeer, food and leather; elk or moose, antelope, chamois, food and leather; bison and buffalo, sheep and cattle, food and leather.

Nicknames of the Inhabitants of Different States

Alabama—Lizards
Arkansas—Toothpicks, gophers
California—Gold Hunters
Colorado—Rovers
Delaware—Blue Hens, muskrats
Florida—Fly-up-the Creeks
Georgia—Crackers, buzzards
Illinois—Suckers
Indiana—Hoosiers
Kansas—Jayhawkers
Kentucky—Corncrackers
Louisiana—Creoles, creowls
Maine—Foxes
Maryland—Crawthumpers
Michigan—Wolverine
Minnesota—Gophers
Mississippi—Tadpoles, mudcats
Missouri—Pukes
New Hampshire—Granite Boys
New Jersey—Blues, Clam-catchers
North Carolina—Tar-boilers
Ohio—Buckeyes
Oregon—Webfeet, Hard Cases
Pennsylvania—Pennites, Leather-heads
Rhode Island—Gun-flints
South Carolina—Weasels
Tennessee—Whelps, Cotton Maniacs
Texas—Beet-heads
Vermont—Green Mountain Boys
Virginia—Beadles, Beagles
Wisconsin—Badgers

FASHION OF EXECUTION IN DIFFERENT COUNTRIES

Austria, gallows, public.
Bavaria, guillotine, private.
Belgium, guillotine, public.
Brunswick, axe, private.
China, sword or cord, public.
Denmark, guillotine, public.
Ecuador, musket, public.
France, guillotine, public.
Great Britain, gallows, private
Hanover, guillotine, private.
Italy, capital punishment abolished.
Netherlands, gallows, public.
Oldenburg, musket, public.
Portugal, gallows, public.
Prussia, sword, private.
Russia, musket, gallows, or sword, public.
Saxony, guillotine, private.
Spain, garrote, public.
Switzerland, fifteen cantons, sword, public. Two cantons, guillotine,
    private. Two cantons, guillotine, public.
United States, except New York, gallows, private.

THE NINE MUSES

Clio or Klio, the muse of History.
Calliope or Kalliope, the muse of Eloquence or Epic Poetry.
Erato, the muse of Love and Marriage.
Euterpe, the muse of the Art of Music.
Melpomene, the muse of Tragedy.
Polyhymnia or Polymnia, the muse of Song and Oratory.
Terpsichore, the muse of Dancing.
Thalia, the muse of Comedy and Burlesque.
Urania, the muse of Astronomy.

NICKNAMES OF THE UNITED STATES

Uncle Sam, Brother Jonathan, Columbia, the New World, Stars and
Stripes, Yankee Land, Yankeedom, and America.

STATUE OF LIMITATION ON DEBTS, NOTES,
JUDGMENTS, SEALED INSTRUMENTS,
ETC., OF THE STATES

States and Territories	Statue of Limitation				Slander, Libel, Assaults, etc.	States and Territories	Statue of Limitation				Slander, Libel, Assaults, etc.
	Open Accounts	Notes	Judgments	Sealed Instruments			Open Accounts	Notes	Judgments	Sealed Instruments	
	yrs.	yrs.	yrs.	yrs.	yrs.		yrs.	yrs.	yrs.	yrs.	yrs.
Alabama	3	6	20	10	1	Mississippi	3	6	7	7	1
Arizona	2	4	5	4	1	Missouri	5	10	20	10	2
Arkansas	3	5	10	10	1	Montana	2	6	6	6	2
California	2	4	5	5	1	Nebraska	4	5	5	10	1
Colorado	3	3	6	6	1	Nevada	4	6	6	6	2
Connecticut	6	6	6	17	3	N.Hampshire	6	6	2	2	2
Dakota	6	6	20	20	2	New Jersey	6	6	20	6	2
Delaware	3	6	20	6	1	New Mexico	No	stat	of	lim	1
District of Columbia	3	6	12	12	1	New York	6	6	20	20	2
						N. Carolina	3	10	10	10	1
Florida	4	5	20	20	2	Ohio	6	15	20	15	1
Georgia	4	6	7	20	1-2	Oregon	6	6	10	10	2
Idaho	4	5	6	5	3	Pennsylvania	6	6	20	20	1
Illinois	5	10	20	20	1	Rhode Island	6	6	20	20	1
Indiana	6	15	20	20	2	S. Carolina	6	6	20	20	2
Iowa	5	10	20	10	2	Tennessee	6	6	10	10	1
Kansas	3	5	5	5	1	Texas	2	4	10	10	1
Kentucky	2	15	15	15	1	Utah	2	4	5	5	1
Louisiana	3	5	10	10	1	Vermont	6	6	8	8	2
Maine	6	6	20	20	2	Virginia	2	5	20	20	5
Maryland	3	3	12	12	3	Washington	3	6	6	6	2
Mass.	6	6	20	20	2	W. Virginia	3	5	10	20	5
Michigan	6	6	12	10	2	Wisconsin	6	6	20	20	2
Minnesota	6	6	10	10	2	Wyoming	4	5	21	5	1

ARMORIES AND ARSENALS OF THE
UNITED STATES

Name	Location
Springfield Armory	Springfield, Mass.
Alleghany Arsenal	Pittsburgh, Penn.
Augusta Arsenal	Augusta, Ga.
Benicia Arsenal	Benicia, Cal.
Champlain Arsenal	Vergennes, Vt.
Charleston Arsenal	Charleston, S. C.
Columbus Arsenal	Columbus, Ohio.
Detroit Arsenal	Dearbornville, Mich.
Fort Monroe Arsenal	Old Point Comfort, Va.
Fort Union Arsenal	Fort Union, New Mexico.
Frankford Arsenal	Philadelphia, Penn.
Indianapolis Arsenal	Indianapolis, Indiana
Kennebec Arsenal	Augusta, Me.
Leavenworth Arsenal	Fort Leavenworth, Kan.
Mt. Vernon Arsenal	Mt. Vernon, Ala.
New York Arsenal	New York, N. Y.
Pikesville Arsenal	Pikesville, Md.
Rock Island Arsenal	Rock Island, Ills.
Rome Arsenal	Rome, N. Y.
St. Louis Arsenal	St. Louis, Mo.
San Antonio Arsenal	San Antonio, Texas
Vancouver Arsenal	Vancouver, Wash.
Washington Arsenal	Washington, D. C.
Watertown Arsenal	Watertown, Mass.
Watervliet Arsenal	West Troy, N. Y.

LANGUAGES AND ALPHABETS

It is said that the various nations of the earth speak about eighty-eight different dialects, but these can be traced to a much smaller number of languages, which again are all referred by the philosophers to three classes: 1. The Indo-Germanic embracing the ancient classical languages as well as those of modern Europe. 2. The Sanscrit embracing all the varieties of India. 3. The Semitic including Hebrew and Arabic.

Of old languages the Hebrew is the oldest, the most poetic; the Latin the most copious and sonorous; the Greek the most impressive and sublime. These three are generally called the dead languages.

Modern Languages : The Chinese is the most difficult; the Italian the softest, the Spanish the most pompous, the French the most polite and passionate, and the most copious and energetic.

The English language contains 26 letters; German 26; French 25; Hebrew 22; Chaldee 22; Syric 22; Greek 24; Latin 25; Spanish 27; Italian 20; Arabic 28; Persian 31; Moscovite 43; Turkish 33; Georgian 36; Copic 32; Sclavonic 27; Dutch 26; Ethiopic 222; Tartarian 222; Bengal, India 21; Brachman 19; Sanscrit 28.

The French language has about 32,000 words; the Spanish 30,000; the Italian 35,000; and the German 37,000.

The English language consists of above 40,000 words and is continually increasing its stock. It is said to contain about 20,000 Saxon words, with about 9,000 of Latin or Norman origin and about 1,500 of Greek derivation, together with the German, Welsh, Danish, Arabic, Hebrew, etc.

In English the scientific words are mostly from the Greek; terms of Art from the French, Latin and Italian and names of places and rivers and most of the particles from the Saxon.

States and Territories, their Area, when Admitted into the Union, where First Settled and When

Name	Area Sq. Mi.	When admitted into the Union	When Settled	Where Settled
Alabama	52,250	Dec. 14, 1819	1711	Mobile
Alaska Ter.	531,409			
Arizona Ter.	113,020		1580	Tucson
Arkansas	53,850	June 15, 1839	1685	Arkansas Post
California	158,360	Sept. 9, 1850	1769	San Diego
Colorado	103,925	August 1, 1876	1858	Denver
Connecticut	4,990	*Jan. 9, 1788	1633	Windsor
Delaware	2,050	*Dec. 7, 1787	1638	Wilmington
Florida	58,680	March 3, 1845	1565	St. Augustine
Georgia	59,475	*Jan. 2, 1788	1733	Savannah
Idaho Ter.	110,700		1860	
Illinois	56,650	Dec. 3, 1818	1720	Kaskaskia

Admission of States, Etc.—*Continued*

Name	Area Sq. Mi.	When Admitted into the Union.	When Settled	Where Settled
Indiana	36,350	Dec. 11, 1816	1730	Vincennes
Indian Ter	64,690		1834	
Iowa	56,025	Dec. 28, 1846	1788	Burlington
Kansas	82,080	Jan. 29, 1861	1827	Fort Leavenworth
Kentucky	40,400	June 1, 1792	1775	Boonsborough
Louisiana	48,720	April 30, 1812	1699	Iberville
Maine	33,040	March 15, 1820	1625	Bristol
Maryland	12,210	*April 28, 1788	1634	St. Mary's
Massachusetts	8,315	*Feb. 6, 1788	1620	Plymouth
Michigan	58,915	Jan. 26, 1837	1670	Detroit
Minnesota	83,365	May 11, 1858	1846	St. Paul
Mississippi	46,810	Dec. 10, 1817	1716	Natchez
Missouri	69,415	August 10, 1821	1764	St. Louis
Montana	143,080	Nov. 8, 1889	1800	
Nebraska	76,855	March 1, 1867	1854	Omaha
Nevada	110,700	Oct. 31, 1864	1860	Washoe
New Hampshire	9,305	*June 21, 1788	1623	Little Harbor
New Jersey	7,815	*Dec. 18, 1787	1664	Elizabeth
N. Mexico Ter.	122,580		1582	
New York	49,170	*July 26, 1788	1614	New York City
North Dakota	74,000	Nov. 2, 1889	1812	
North Carolina	52,250	*Nov. 21, 1789	1650	Chowan River
Ohio	41,060	Nov. 29, 1802	1788	Marietta
Oregon	96,030	Feb. 14, 1859	1811	Astoria
Pennsylvania	45,215	*Dec. 12, 1787	1682	Philadelphia
Rhode Island	1,250	*May 29, 1790	1636	Providence
South Carolina	30,570	*May 23, 1788	1670	Ashley River
South Dakota	75,100	Nov. 2, 1889	1812	
Tennessee	42,050	June 1, 1796	1759	Fort Loudon
Texas	265,780	Dec. 29, 1845	1692	San Antonio
Utah Ter.	84,970		1847	
Vermont	9,565	March 4, 1791	1724	Fort Dummer
Virginia	42,450	*June 25, 1788	1607	Jamestown
Washington	69,180	Nov. 11, 1889	1845	
West Virginia	24,780	June 19, 1863	1601	Jamestown
Wisconsin	56,040	May 29, 1847	1669	Green Bay
Wyoming	97,890			
Dist. of Columbia	70			

* The original thirteen States, when they ratified the Constitution.

POSTAGE RATES

Letters within U. S.	Per oz.
Letters to any part.....	2 cts.
City drop letters	2 cts.
Postal Cards to any part..	1 ct. each
Registered letters proper postage and......................	10 cts.
Immediate delivery letters, besides regular postage, special stamp...	10 cts.

POSTAGE ON SECOND-CLASS MATTER—WHICH embraces newspapers, magazines, and periodicals published not less than four times a year—one cent, prepaid, per pound or fraction thereof, when mailed by publisher or news-agent *to regular subscribers*. Second-class matter mailed by other persons than publishers or news-agents becomes special matter, specially entitled to pass through the mails at one cent for each four ounces or fraction thereof.

POSTAGE ON THIRD-CLASS MATTER—Books, pamphlets, circulars and other matter wholly in print, such as hand-bills, posters, music, photographs, lithographs, corrected proof-sheets and manuscripts accompanying the same, seed-cuttings, bulbs, roots, etc.—*one cent*, prepaid by stamp, for *every two ounces* or fraction thereof.

Packages of transient printed matter are limited to four pounds each, unless in the case where a *single* volume of a book shall exceed that weight. The sender may write his name and address on the wrapper, preceded by the word "from," and may mark a passage of the text, or write on a fly-leaf a simple inscription or dedication. Packages must be wrapped with open sides or ends.

POSTAGE ON FOURTH-CLASS MATTER—Merchandise, blank cards, patterns, letter envelopes, letter-paper with or without printing, printed blanks, original paintings in oil or water-colors, maps mounted on cloth, printed letter-heads, models, ores, metals, and all mailable matter not embraced in the foregoing classes—*one cent*, prepaid by stamp, for *each ounce* or fraction thereof. Liquids (except poisons, explosive, inflammable or offensive articles), in packages properly secured, may be transported. The limit of weight is four pounds.

Postal Notes and Money Orders

Postal Notes under $5, payable to bearer, 3 cts.

Money Orders in U. S.—Not exceeding $5, 5 cents; $5 to $10, 8 cents; exceeding $10 to $15, 10 cents; exceeding $15 to $30, 15 cents; exceeding $30 to $40, 20 cents; exceeding $40 to $50, 25 cents; exceeding $50 to $60, 30 cents; exceeding $60 to $70, 35 cents; exceeding $70 to $80, 40 cents; exceeding $80 to $100, 45 cents.

Money Orders to Foreign Countries—Great Britain and Ireland, France, German Empire, Canada, Belgium, Italy, Switzerland, Portugal, Algeria, Jamaica, Windward Islands, Sandwich Islands, Victoria, Tasmania, Queensland, Cape Colony, Japan, Hong Kong, New Zealand, New South Wales, Leeward Islands and Sweden, not over $10, 10 cts.; not over $20, 20 cents; not over $30, 30 cents; not over $40, 40 cents; not over $50, 50 cents; Canada, not over $100, $1; Germany, not over $97, $1.

Foreign Postage

From the United States to all following countries and places, which are in the Universal Postal Union, the postage on LETTERS is FIVE (5) CENTS for each HALF OUNCE or fraction thereof (prepayment optional), TWO CENTS for each postal card, and ONE CENT for each TWO OUNCES NEWSPAPERS: Argentine Republic, Austria and Hungary, Belgium, Bolivia, Brazil, Bulgaria, Ceylon, China via Hong Kong, Chili, Cuba, Denmark and Danish colonies, Ecuador, Egypt, Falkland Islands, France and French colonies, Germany, Great Britain and British West Indies, Greece, Greenland, Guatemala, Hayti, Holland or Netherlands and Netherland colonies, Honduras, Hong Kong, India (British), Ireland, Italy, Japan, Liberia, Luxembourg, Malacca, Mauritius, Montenegro, Newfoundland, Norway, Paraguay, Patagonia, Penang, Persia, Peru, Portugal and Portuguese colonies, Roumania, Russia, St. Bartholomew, Salvador, Servia, Siam, Singapore, Spain and Spanish colonies, Straits Settlements, Sweden, Switzerland, Trinidad, Turkey, United States of Colombia, Uruguay, Venezuela.

POSTAGE TO COUNTRIES AND PLACES NOT IN POSTAL UNION.

Pre-Payment Compulsory.

COUNTRIES AND PLACES.	Letters not exceeding ½ oz.	Newspapers.
Australia via England........................	12 cts.	2 cts.
Australia, except New South Wales, Queensland, Victoria and Tasmania, via San Francisco.....	5 "	2 "
Canada and British N. A. provinces, except Newfoundland...............................	{each oz. } 2 cts.	{ec. 2 oz. } 1 ct.
Cape Good Hope and Colony.............	15 "	4 "
China via England............................	13 "	5 "
Natal.......................	15 "	4 "
New South Wales, Queensland, Victoria, Tasmania and New Zealand via San Francisco....	12 "	2 "
St. Helena....................................	15 "	4 "
Transvaal	21 "	5 "

CANADA.—Same as in United States.

MEXICO.—Same as United States. Limit of weight of single packages, 4 lbs. 6 oz., except single printed books, which may weigh more. Merchandise must be sent by parcel post.

BAHAMAS, BARBADOES, HONDURAS (British), JAMAICA, U. S of COLOMBIA, HAWAII ISLANDS, LEEWARD ISLANDS, SALVADOR AND MEX-ICO.—Merchandise may be sent by parcel post, 12 cents a pound, or fraction thereof. Limit of weight, 11 pounds.

Letters, postal cards, printed matter of all kinds, commercial documents and samples of merchandise are transmissible in Postal Union mails. The following are considered as printed matter, viz.: Newspapers and periodical works, books stitched or bound, pamphlets, sheets of music, visiting cards, address cards, proofs of printing with or without the manuscript relating thereto, engravings, photographs, drawings, plans, geographical maps, catalogues, prospectuses, announcements and notices of various kinds, whether printed, engraved, lithographed or autographed.

Address cards and all printed matter presenting the form and consistency of an unfolded card may be forwarded without band, envelope, fastening or fold. The maximum weight of printed matter is fixed at 2 kilograms (4 lbs. 6 oz.). Postage on printed matter, one cent for each 2 oz.

QUALIFICATIONS REQUIRED FOR SUFFRAGE IN DIFFERENT STATES

STATES	Voters must be males 21 years of age and	State	County	Voting Prec't
Alabama	Citizens or have declared intentions...	1 yr.	3 mo.	1 mo.
Arkansas	" "	1 "	6 "	1 "
California ...*	Actual Citizens	1 "	3 "	1 "
Colorado ...*	Citizens or have declared intentions...	6 mo.	....	....
Connecticut ...*	Actual Citizens	1 yr.	6 mo.	6 mo.
Delaware	Actual County Tax-Payers	1 "	1 "	....
Florida ...*	U. S. Citizens or have dec'd intentions	1 "	6 "	....
Georgia	Actual Citizens	1 "	6 "	....
Illinois ...*	"	1 "	3 "	1 mo.
Indiana	Citizens or have declared intentions...	6 mo.	2 "	1 "
Iowa ...*	Actual Citizens	6 "	2 "	....
Kansas ...‡	Citizens or have declared intentions...	6 "	....	1 mo.
Kentucky	Free White Male Citizens	2 yr.	1 yr.	2 "
Louisiana	Citizens or have declared intentions...	1 "	6 mo.	1 "
Maine ...*	Actual Citizens	3 mo.	....	....
Maryland ...*	"	1 yr.	6 mo.	....
Massachusetts ...*	Citizens	1 "	....	6 mo.
Michigan ...*	Citizens or have declared intentions...	3 mo.	....	10 dys
Minnesota	" "	1 "	....	10 "
Mississippi ...*	Actual Citizens	6 "	1 mo.	....
Missouri ...‡	Citizens or have declared intentions...	1 yr.	2 "	....
Montana	Actual Citizens	1 "	....	....
Nebraska ...*	Citizens or have declared intentions...	6 mo.	....	....
Nevada	" "	6 "	1 mo.	....
New Hampshire..*	Actual Citizens	....	....	Town 6 mo.
New Jersey ...†	"	1 yr.	5 mo.	....
New York ...†	"	1 "	4 "	1 mo.
North Carolina ...*	"	1 "	3 "	....
North Dakota	"	1 "	6 "	90 dys
Ohio	"	1 "		
Oregon	Citizens or have declared intentions	6 mo.	....	....
Pennsylvania ...*	Actual Citizens	1 yr.	....	2 mo.
Rhode Island ...*	Actual Tax-Paying Citizens	1 "	......	Town 6 mo.
South Carolina ...*	Actual Citizens	1 "	2 mo.	....
South Dakota	Citizens or have declared intentions...	1 "	6 "	30 dys
Tennessee	Actual Citizens	1 "	6 "	....
Texas	Citizens or have declared intentions...	1 "	6 "	6 mo.
Vermont ...*	Actual Citizens	1 "	....	....
Virginia ...*	"	1 "	......	Town 3 mo.
Washington	"	1 "	90 dys	30 dys
West Virginia	"	1 "	2 mo.	....
Wisconsin ...*	Citizens or have declared intentions...	1 "	....	....

Idiots, lunatics, paupers, persons convicted of various crimes (Chinese in California) are not allowed to vote in most of the States.

All the 42 States limit suffrage to male citizens, but in Colorado, Massachusetts and several other States, women may vote at school district elections.

In States marked * voters are required to register before they can vote.

In States marked † registration is required in cities having a population of 10,000 and over.

In States marked ‡ registration required in cities only.

In Ohio, registration is required only in the larger cities. (221)

WARS OF THE UNITED STATES
Statement of the Number of United States
Troops Engaged

WARS	From	To	Regulars	Militia and Volunteers	Total
War of the Revolution......	April 19, 1775	April 11, 1783	130,711	164,080	294,781
N'thwestern Indian Wars.	Sept. 19, 1790	Aug. 3, 1795	....	....	8,983
War with France............	July 9, 1798	Sept. 30, 1800	....	....	*4,593
War with Tripoli.	June 10, 1801	June 4, 1805	....	....	*3,330
Creek Indian War............	July 27, 1813	Aug. 9, 1814	600	13,181	13,781
War of 1812 with Great B.	June 18, 1812	Feb. 17, 1815	85,000	471,622	576,622
Seminole Indian War.......	Nov. 20, 1817	Oct. 21, 1818	1,000	6,911	7,911
Black Hawk Indian War..	April 21, 1831	Sept. 31, 1832	1,339	5,126	6,465
Cherokee Disturbance or Removal......	1836	1837	....	9,494	9,494
Creek Indian War or Disturbance	May 5, 1836	Sept. 30, 1837	935	12,483	13,418
Florida Indian War..........	Dec. 23, 1835	Aug. 14, 1843	11,169	29,953	41,172
Aroostook Disturbance.....	1838	1839	....	1,500	1,500
War with Mexico.............	April 24, 1846	July 4, 1848	30,954	73,776	112,230
Apache, Navajo and Utah War.............	1849	1855	1,500	1,061	2,561
Seminole Indian War..	1856	1858	....	3,687	3,687
Civil War †........................	1861	1865	....	....	2772,408

* Naval forces engaged.   † The number of troops on the Confederate side was about 600,000.

Revolutionary War cost the United States $135,193,703; War of 1812 cost the United States $107,159,003; Mexican War cost the United States $100,000,000; Civil War cost the United States $6,189-929,900.

In the War of 1812-15, there were 10 battles, 8 combats and assaults, 52 actions and bombardments. In the Mexican War there were 11 pitched battles and 35 actions, combats, sieges and skirmishes. In the Civil War of 1861-65, there were 107 pitched battles, 102 combats, and 362 actions, sieges and lesser affairs. Since 1812, the United States Army has had over 640 battles, fights and actions against Indians. Since 1789 there have been 912 garrisoned forts, arsenals and military posts in the United States. At the present time (1890) there are 144 garrisoned forts, arsenals and military posts.

Up to and including June, 1861, there were 1,966 graduates of the Military Academy, and of these there were living at the outbreak of the Civil War of 1861-65, 1,249. Of the 1,249, 428 were in civil life and 821 were in the military service of the United States. Of those in civil life, 292 took sides with the Union, and 99 joined the Confederacy, while 37 are unknown. Of the 821 in the army, 627 sided with the Union, 184 joined the Confederacy, and 10 took neither side. Of the 99 who joined the Confederacy from civil life, all, except one, were either born and brought up or were residents of Southern territory. On the other hand, of the 350 graduates born or appointed from Southern States, 162 remained loyal to the United States. Of the graduates who served in the Civil War, one-fifth were killed in battle, while one-half were wounded.

PRESIDENTS OF THE UNITED STATES

Name	From State of	Date in Office	Term of Office
George Washington	Virginia	1789 to 1797	8 yrs.
John Adams	Massachusetts	1797 to 1801	4 yrs.
Thomas Jefferson	Virginia	1801 to 1809	8 yrs.
James Madison	Virginia	1809 to 1817	8 yrs.
James Monroe	Virginia	1817 to 1825	8 yrs.
John Quincy Adams	Massachusetts	1825 to 1829	4 yrs.
Andrew Jackson	Tennessee	1829 to 1837	8 yrs.
Martin Van Buren	New York	1837 to 1841	4 yrs.
William H. Harrison	Ohio	1841 to 1841	1 month
*John Tyler	Virginia	1841 to 1845	3 yrs. 11 mos.
James K. Polk	Tennessee	1845 to 1849	4 yrs.
Zachary Taylor	Louisiana	1849 to 1850	1 yr. 4 mos.
*Millard Fillmore	New York	1850 to 1853	2 yrs. 8 mos.
Franklin Pierce	N. Hampshire	1853 to 1857	4 yrs.
James Buchanan	Pennsylvania	1857 to 1861	4 yrs.
Abraham Lincoln	Illinois	1861 to 1865	4 yrs. 1 mo.
*Andrew Johnson	Tennessee	1865 to 1869	3 yrs. 11 mos.
Ulysses S. Grant	Illinois	1869 to 1877	8 yrs.
Rutherford B. Hayes	Ohio	1877 to 1881	4 yrs.
James A. Garfield	Ohio	1881 to 1881	6½ mos.
*Chester A. Arthur	New York	1881 to 1885	3 yrs. 5½ mos.
Grover Cleveland	New York	1885 to 1889	4 yrs.
Benjamin Harrison	Indiana	1889	

* Vice-President became President on death of President.

VICE-PRESIDENTS OF THE UNITED STATES

Name	From State of	With what President
John Adams	Massachusetts	George Washington
Thomas Jefferson	Virginia	John Adams
Aaron Burr	New York	Thomas Jefferson
George Clinton	New York	Thomas Jefferson
*George Clinton	New York	*James Madison
†Wm. H. Crawford	Georgia	James Madison
*Elbridge Gerry	Massachusetts	James Madison
†John Gaillord	South Carolina	James Madison
Daniel D. Tompkins	New York	James Monroe
John C. Calhoun	South Carolina	John Quincy Adams
John C. Calhoun	South Carolina	Andrew Jackson

Vice-Presidents—*Continued*

Name	From State of	With what President
Martin Van Buren	New York	Andrew Jackson
Richard M. Johnson	Kentucky	Martin Van Buren
John Tyler	Virginia	William H. Harrison
†Samuel L. Southard	New Jersey	John Tyler
†Willie P. Mangum	North Carolina	John Tyler
George M. Dallas	Pennsylvania	James K. Polk
Millard Fillmore	New York	Zachary Taylor
†William R. King	Alabama	Millard Fillmore
*William R. King	Alabama	Franklin Pierce
†D. R. Atchinson	Missouri	Franklin Pierce
†J. D. Bright	Alabama	Franklin Pierce
John C. Breckenbridge	Kentucky	James Buchanan
Hannibal Hamblin	Maine	Abraham Lincoln
Andrew Johnson	Tennessee	Abraham Lincoln
†Lafayette S. Foster	Connecticut	Andrew Johnson
†Benjamin F. Wade	Ohio	Andrew Johnson
Schuyler Colfax	Indiana	Ulysses S. Grant
*Henry M. Wilson	Massachusetts	Ulysses S. Grant
†Thomas W. Ferry	Michigan	Ulysses S. Grant
William A. Wheeler	New York	Rutherford B. Hayes
Chester A. Arthur	New York	James A. Garfield
†Thomas F. Bayard	Delaware	Chester A. Arthur
†David Davis	Illinois	Chester A. Arthur
†George F. Edmunds	Vermont	Chester A. Arthur
*Thomas A. Hendricks	Indiana	Grover Cleveland
†John Sherman	Ohio	Grover Cleveland
†John J. Ingalls	Kansas	Grover Cleveland
Levi P. Morton	New York	Benjamin Harrison

* Died while in office.
† President *pro tem.* of the Senate.

SECRETARIES OF STATE OF THE UNITED STATES

The " State Department " was created by Act of Congress, 1789.

Name	From State of	In whose Cabinet	Appointed
Thomas Jefferson	Virginia	George Washington	1789
Edmund Randolph	Virginia	George Washington	1794
Timothy Pickering	Pennsylvania	George Washington	1795
Timothy Pickering	Pennsylvania	John Adams	1797
John Marshall	Virginia	John Adams	1800
James Madison	Virginia	Thomas Jefferson	1801
Robert Smith	Maryland	James Madison	1809
James Monroe	Virginia	James Madison	1811
John Q. Adams	Massachusetts	James Monroe	1817
Henry Clay	Kentucky	John Q. Adams	1825
Martin Van Buren	New York	Andrew Jackson	1829
Edward Livingston	Louisiana	Andrew Jackson	1831
Louis McLane	Delaware	Andrew Jackson	1833
John Forsyth	Georgia	Andrew Jackson	1834
John Forsyth	Georgia	Martin Van Buren	1837
Daniel Webster	Massachusetts	William H. Harrison	1841
Hugh S. Legare	South Carolina	John Tyler	1843
Abel P. Upshur	Virginia	John Tyler	1843
John Nelson (acting)	Maryland	John Tyler	1844
John C. Calhoun	South Carolina	John Tyler	1844
James Buchanan	Pennsylvania	James K. Polk	1845
James M. Clayton	Delaware	Zachary Taylor	1849
Daniel Webster	Massachusetts	Millard Fillmore	1850
Edward Everett	Massachusetts	Millard Fillmore	1852
William L. Marcy	New York	Franklin Pierce	1853
Lewis Cass	Michigan	James Buchanan	1857
Jeremiah S. Black	Pennsylvania	James Buchanan	1860
William H. Seward	New York	Abraham Lincoln	1861
E. B. Washburne	Illinois	Ulysses S. Grant	1869
Hamilton Fish	New York	Ulysses S. Grant	1869
William M. Evarts	New York	Rutherford B. Hayes	1877
James G. Blaine	Maine	James A. Garfield	1881
T. F. Frelinghuysen	New Jersey	Chester A. Arthur	1881
Thomas F. Bayard	Delaware	Grover Cleveland	1885
James G. Blaine	Maine	Benjamin Harrison	1889

Secretaries of Treasury of the United States

The "Treasury Department" was created by Act of Congress, 1789.

Name	From State of	In whose Cabinet	Appointed
Alexander Hamilton	New York	George Washington	1789
Oliver Wolcott	Connecticut	George Washington	1795
Oliver Wolcott	Connecticut	John Adams	1797
Samuel Dexter	Massachusetts	John Adams	1801
Samuel Dexter	Massachusetts	Thomas Jefferson	1801
Albert Gallatin	Pennsylvania	Thomas Jefferson	1801
Albert Gallatin	Pennsylvania	James Madison	1809
G. W. Campbell	Tennessee	James Madison	1814
Alexander J. Dallas	Pennsylvania	James Madison	1814
W. H. Crawford	Georgia	James Madison	1816
W. H. Crawford	Georgia	James Monroe	1817
Richard Rush	Pennsylvania	John Q. Adams	1825
S. D. Ingham	Pennsylvania	Andrew Jackson	1829
Louis McLane	Delaware	Andrew Jackson	1831
William J. Duane	Pennsylvania	Andrew Jackson	1833
Roger B. Taney	Maryland	Andrew Jackson	1833
Levi Woodbury	New Hampshire	Andrew Jackson	1834
Levi Woodbury	New Hampshire	Martin Van Buren	1837
Thomas Ewing	Ohio	William H. Harrison	1841
W. Forward	Pennsylvania	John Tyler	1841
John C. Spencer	New York	John Tyler	1843
George M. Bibb	Kentucky	John Tyler	1844
R. J. Walker	Mississippi	James K. Polk	1845
W. M. Meredith	Pennsylvania	Zachary Taylor	1849
Thomas Corwin	Ohio	Millard Fillmore	1850
James Guthrie	Kentucky	Franklin Pierce	1853
Howell Cobb	Georgia	James Buchanan	1857
Philip H. Thomas	Maryland	James Buchanan	1860
John A. Dix	New York	James Buchanan	1861
Salmon P. Chase	Ohio	Abraham Lincoln	1861
W. P. Fessenden	Maine	Abraham Lincoln	1864
Hugh McCulloch	Indiana	Abraham Lincoln	1865
Hugh McCulloch	Indiana	Andrew Johnson	1865
G. S. Boutwell	Massachusetts	Ulysses S. Grant	1869
William A. Richardson	Massachusetts	Ulysses S. Grant	1873
B. H. Bristow	Kentucky	Ulysses S. Grant	1874
Lot M. Morrill	Maine	Ulysses S. Grant	1876
John Sherman	Ohio	Rutherford B. Hayes	1877
William Windom	Minnesota	James A. Garfield	1881
Charles J. Folger	New York	Chester A. Arthur	1881
Hugh McCulloch	Indiana	Chester A. Arthur	1884
Daniel F. Manning	New York	Grover Cleveland	1885
Charles S. Fairchild	New York	Grover Cleveland	1887
William Windom	Minnesota	Benjamin Harrison	1889

The "War Department" was created by Act of
Congress, August 7, 1789

Name	From State of	In whose Cabinet	Appointed
Henry Knox	Massachusetts	George Washington	1789
Timothy Pickering	Pennsylvania	George Washington	1795
James McHenry	Maryland	George Washington	1795
James McHenry	Maryland	John Adams	1707
Samuel Dexter	Massachusetts	John Adams	1800
Roger Griswold	Connecticut	John Adams	1801
Henry Dearborn	Massachusetts	Thomas Jefferson	1801
William Eustis	Massachusetts	James Madison	1809
John Armstrong	New York	James Madison	1813
James Monroe	Virginia	James Madison	1814
William H. Crawford	Georgia	James Madison	1815
George Graham	Virginia	James Monroe	1817
John C. Calhoun	South Carolina	James Monroe	1817
James Barbour	Virginia	John Q. Adams	1825
P. B. Porter	New York	John Q. Adams	1828
J. H. Eaton	Tennessee	Andrew Jackson	1829
Lewis Cass	Michigan	Andrew Jackson	1831
B. F. Butler (acting)	New York	Andrew Jackson	1837
J. R. Pionsett	South Carolina	Martin Van Buren	1837
John Bell	Tennessee	William H. Harrison	1841
J. McLean (declined)	Ohio	John Tyler	1841
J. C. Spencer	New York	John Tyler	1841
James M. Porter	Pennsylvania	John Tyler	1843
William Wilkins	Pennsylvania	John Tyler	1844
William L. Marcy	New York	James K. Polk	1845
R. Johnson (acting)		Zachary Taylor	1849
G. W. Crawford	Georgia	Zachary Taylor	1849
Winfield Scott (ad int.)		Millard Fillmore	1850
C. M. Conrad	Louisiana	Millard Fillmore	1850
Jefferson Davis	Mississippi	Franklin Pierce	1853
John B. Floyd	Virginia	James Buchanan	1857
Joseph Holt	Kentucky	James Buchanan	1861
Simon Cameron	Pennsylvania	Abraham Lincoln	1861
Edwin M. Stanton	Pennsylvania	Abraham Lincoln	1862
E. Stanton (suspended)			1867
U. S. Grant (ad int.)	Illinois	Andrew Johnson	1867
L. Thomas (ad int).		Andrew Johnson	1868
J. M. Schofield	New York	Andrew Johnson	1868
J. A. Rawlins	Illinois	Ulysses S. Grant	1869
W. T. Sherman (ad int.)	Ohio	Ulysses S. Grant	1869
William W. Belknap	Iowa	Ulysses S. Grant	1869
G. M. Bobeson (acting)	New Jersey	Ulysses S. Grant	1876
Alfonzo Taft	Ohio	Ulysses S. Grant	1876
J. D Cameron	Pennsylvania	Ulysses S. Grant	1876
G. W. McCrary	Iowa	Rutherford B. Hayes	1877
Alexander Ramsey	Minnesota	Rutherford B. Hayes	1879
Robert T. Lincoln	Illinois	James A. Garfield	1881
Robert T. Lincoln	Illinois	Chester A. Arthur	1881
William E. Endicott	Massachusetts	Grover Cleveland	1885
Redfield Proctor	Vermont	Benjamin Harrison	1889

SECRETARIES OF NAVY OF THE UNITED STATES

The "Navy Department" was created by Act of Congress, April 30, 1798.

The "War Department" had charge of Naval affairs until April 30, 1798.

Name	From State of	In whose Cabinet	Appointed
G. Cabot (declined)	Massachusetts	John Adams	1798
Benjamin Stoddert	Maryland	John Adams	1798
Benjamin Stoddert	Maryland	Thomas Jefferson	1801
Robert Smith	Maryland	Thomas Jefferson	1801
J. Crowninshield	Massachusetts	Thomas Jefferson	1805
Paul Hamilton	South Carolina	James Madison	1809
William Jones	Pennsylvania	James Madison	1813
B. W. Crowninshield	Massachusetts	James Madison	1814
B. W. Crowninshield	Massachusetts	James Monroe	1817
S. Thompson	New York	James Monroe	1818
J. Rogers (acting)	Massachusetts	James Monroe	1823
S. L. Southard	New Jersey	James Monroe	1823
S. L. Southard	New Jersey	John Q. Adams	1825
John Branch	North Carolina	Andrew Jackson	1829
L. Woodbury	New Hampshire	Andrew Jackson	1831
M. Dickerson	New Jersey	Andrew Jackson	1834
M. Dickerson	New Jersey	Martin Van Buren	1837
J. K. Paulding	New York	Martin Van Buren	1838
G. E. Badger	North Carolina	William H. Harrison	1841
A. P. Upshur	Virginia	John Tyler	1841
D. Henshaw	Massachusetts	John Tyler	1843
T. W. Gilmer	Virginia	John Tyler	1844
John Y. Mason	Virginia	John Tyler	1844
George Bancroft	Massachusetts	James K. Polk	1845
John Y. Mason	Virginia	James K. Polk	1846
William B. Preston	Virginia	Zachary Taylor	1849
William A. Graham	North Carolina	Millard Fillmore	1850
J. P. Kennedy	Maryland	Millard Fillmore	1852
James C. Dobbin	North Carolina	Franklin Pierce	1853
Isaac Toucey	Connecticut	James Buchanan	1857
Gideon Welles	Connecticut	Abraham Lincoln	1861
Gideon Welles	Connecticut	Andrew Johnson	1865
Adolph E. Borie	Pennsylvania	Ulysses S. Grant	1869
G. M. Robeson	New Jersey	Ulysses S. Grant	1869
R. W. Thompson	Indiana	Rutherford B. Hayes	1877
Nathan Goff	West Virginia	Rutherford B. Hayes	1881
William H. Hunt	Louisiana	James A. Garfield	1881
William C. Chandler	New Hampshire	Chester A. Arthur	1882
William C. Whitney	New York	Grover Cleveland	1885
B. F. Tracy	New York	Benjamin Harrison	1889

POSTMASTERS-GENERAL OF THE
UNITED STATES

The " Postoffice Department " was established by the
old Congress.

Name	From State of	In whose Cabinet	Appointed
Samuel Osgood	Massachusetts	George Washington	1789
Timothy Pickering	Pennsylvania	George Washington	1791
Joseph Habersham	Georgia	George Washington	1795
Joseph Habersham	Georgia	John Adams	1797
Joseph Habersham	Georgia	Thomas Jefferson	1801
Gideon Granger	Connecticut	Thomas Jefferson	1802
Gideon Granger	Connecticut	James Madison	1809
Return J. Meigs, Jr.	Ohio	James Madison	1814
Return J. Meigs, Jr.	Ohio	James Monroe	1817
John McLean	Ohio	James Monroe	1823
John McLean	Ohio	John Q. Adams	1825
William T. Barry	Kentucky	Andrew Jackson	1829
Amos Kendall	Kentucky	Andrew Jackson	1835
Amos Kendall	Kentucky	Martin Van Buren	1837
John M. Niles	Connecticut	Martin Van Buren	1840
Francis Granger	New York	William H. Harrison	1841
Charles A. Wickliffe	Kentucky	John Tyler	1841
Cave Johnson	Tennessee	James K. Polk	1845
Jacob Collamer	Vermont	Zachary Taylor	1849
Nathan K. Hall	New York	Millard Fillmore	1850
Samuel D. Hubbard	Connecticut	Millard Fillmore	1852
James Campbell	Pennsylvania	Franklin Pierce	1853
Aaron V. Brown	Tennessee	James Buchanan	1857
Joseph Holt	Kentucky	James Buchanan	1859
Horatio King	Maine	James Buchanan	1861
Montgomery Blair	Maryland	Abraham Lincoln	1861
William Dennison	Ohio	Abraham Lincoln	1864
Alexander W. Randall	Wisconsin	Andrew Johnson	1866
John A. Cresswell	Maryland	Ulysses S. Grant	1869
Marshall Jewell	Connecticut	Ulysses S. Grant	1874
James N. Tyner	Indiana	Ulysses S. Grant	1876
David McK. Key	Tennessee	Rutherford B. Hayes	1877
Horace Maynard	Tennessee	Rutherford B. Hayes	1880
Thomas L. James	New York	James A. Garfield	1881
Timothy O. Howe	Wisconsin	Chester A. Arthur	1881
Walter Q. Gresham	Indiana	Chester A. Arthur	1883
Frank Hatton		Chester A. Arthur	1884
William F. Vilas	Wisconsin	Grover Cleveland	1885
Don M. Dickinson	Michigan	Grover Cleveland	1887
John Wanamaker	Pennsylvania	Benjamin Harrison	1889

ATTORNEYS-GENERAL OF THE UNITED STATES

The Attorney-General of the United States is chief law officer of the Government and as such is considered a member of the Cabinet. He is the constitutional legal adviser and defender of the Government.

Name	From State of	In whose Cabinet	Appointed
Edmund Randolph	Virginia	George Washington	1789
William Bradford	Pennsylvania	George Washington	1794
Charles Lee	Virginia	George Washington	1795
Charles Lee	Virginia	John Adams	1797
Theophilus Parson	Massachusetts	John Adams	1801
Levi Lincoln	Massachusetts	Thomas Jefferson	1801
Robert Smith	Maryland	Thomas Jefferson	1805
John Breckenridge	Kentucky	Thomas Jefferson	1805
Cæsar A. Rodney	Delaware	Thomas Jefferson	1807
Cæsar A. Rodney	Delaware	James Madison	1809
William Pinkney	Maryland	James Madison	1811
Richard Rush	Pennsylvania	James Madison	1814
William Wirt	Maryland	James Monroe	1817
William Wirt	Maryland	John Q. Adams	1825
John McP. Berrien	Georgia	Andrew Jackson	1829
Roger B. Taney	Maryland	Andrew Jackson	1831
B. F. Butler	New York	Andrew Jackson	1833
B. F. Butler	New York	Martin Van Buren	1837
Felix Grundy	Tennessee	Martin Van Buren	1838
Henry D. Gulpin	Pennsylvania	Martin Van Buren	1840
John J. Crittenden	Kentucky	William H. Harrison	1841
Hugh S. Legare	South Carolina	John Tyler	1841
John Nelson	Maryland	John Tyler	1843
John Y. Mason	Virginia	James K. Polk	1845
Nathan Clifford	Maine	James K. Polk	1846
Isaac Toucey	Connecticut	James K. Polk	1848
Reverdy Johnson	Maryland	Zachary Taylor	1849
John J. Crittenden	Kentucky	Millard Fillmore	1850
Caleb Cushing	Massachusetts	Franklin Pierce	1853
Jeremiah S. Black	Pennsylvania	James Buchanan	1857
Edwin M. Stanton	Pennsylvania	James Buchanan	1860
Edward Bates	Missouri	Abraham Lincoln	1861
T. J. Coffee (ad int.)		Abraham Lincoln	1863
James Speed	Kentucky	Abraham Lincoln	1864
Henry Stanbery	Kentucky	Andrew Johnson	1866
O. Browning (ad int.)	Illinois	Andrew Johnson	1868

Attorneys-General—*Continued*

Name	From State of	In whose Cabinet	Appointed
William M. Evarts	New York	Andrew Johnson	1868
Ebenezer R. Hoar	Massachusetts	Ulysses S. Grant	1869
Amos T. Akerman	Georgia	Ulysses S. Grant	1870
George H. Williams	Oregon	Ulysses S. Grant	1871
Edwards Pierrepont	New York	Ulysses S. Grant	1875
Alphonso Taft	Ohio	Ulysses S. Grant	1876
Charles Devens	Massachusetts	Rutherford B. Hayes	1877
Wayne MacVeagh	Pennsylvania	James A. Garfield	1881
B. H. Brewster	Pennsylvania	Chester A. Arthur	1881
A. H. Garland	Arkansas	Grover Cleveland	1885
W. H. H. Miller	Indiana	Benjamin Harrison	1889

SECRETARIES OF INTERIOR OF THE UNITED STATES

The "Interior Department" was created by Act of Congress, 1849.

Name	From State of	In whose Cabinet	Appointed
Thomas Ewing	Ohio	Zachary Taylor	1849
T. McKenna (declined)	Pennsylvania	Millard Fillmore	1850
Alex. H. H. Stuart	Virginia	Millard Fillmore	1850
Robert McClelland	Michigan	Franklin Pierce	1853
Jacob Thompson	Mississippi	James Buchanan	1857
Caleb B. Smith	Indiana	Abraham Lincoln	1861
John P. Usher	Indiana	Abraham Lincoln	1863
James Harlan	Iowa	Andrew Johnson	1865
O. H. Browning	Illinois	Andrew Johnson	1866
Jacob B. Cox	Ohio	Ulysses S. Grant	1869
Columbus Delano	Ohio	Ulysses S. Grant	1870
Zachariah Chandler	Michigan	Ulysses S. Grant	1875
*Carl Schurz	Missouri	Rutherford B. Hayes	1877
Samuel J. Kirkwood	Iowa	James A. Garfield	1881
Henry M. Teller	Colorado	Chester A. Arthur	1882
L. Q. C. Lamar	Mississippi	Grover Cleveland	1885
William F. Vilas	Wisconsin	Grover Cleveland	1887
John M. Noble	Missouri	Benjamin Harrison	1889

* Carl Schurz was a native of Prussia.

THE HOUSE OF REPRESENTATIVES OF THE UNITED STATES

Is composed of members elected every second year by popular vote, the amount being determined by the census taken every ten years. An Act of Congress passed February 16, 1882, based on the result of the census of 1880, provided that the House is thenceforth to be composed of 325 members, but since then four new States have been admitted into the Union, who have in all five members making 330 members apportioned as follows:

State	No. of Mem.	State	No. of Mem.
Alabama	8	Montana	1
Arkansas	5	Nebraska	3
California	6	Nevada	1
Colorado	1	New Hampshire	2
Connecticut	4	New Jersey	7
Delaware	1	New York	34
Florida	2	North Carolina	9
Georgia	10	North Dakota	1
Illinois	20	Ohio	21
Indiana	13	Oregon	1
Iowa	11	Pennsylvania	28
Kansas	7	Rhode Island	2
Kentucky	11	South Carolina	7
Louisiana	6	South Dakota	2
Maine	4	Tennessee	10
Maryland	6	Texas	11
Massachusetts	12	Vermont	2
Michigan	11	Virginia	10
Minnesota	5	Washington	1
Mississippi	7	West Virginia	4
Missouri	14	Wisconsin	9

In addition to the representatives from the States, each organized territory is entitled to one delegate, who has the right to debate on subjects in which his territory is interested, but is not entitled to a vote.

The salary of Members of Congress is $5,000 per annum, with traveling expenses (20 cents per mile both ways).

UNITED STATES LAND OFFICES

A complete list of the United States Land Offices as follows:

Aberdeen, S. Dak.
Ashland, Wis.
Bismarck, N. Dak.
Blackfoot, Id.
Bloomington, Neb.
Boise City, Id.
Boonville, Mo.
Bozeman, Mont.
Buffalo, Wy.
Burns, Ore.
Camden, Ark.
Carson City, Nev.
Central City, Colo.
Chadron, Neb.
Cheyenne, Wy.
Cœur d'Alene, Id.
Crookston, Minn.
Dardanelle, Ark.
Del Norte, Col.
Denver, Col.
Des Moines, Ia.
Devil's Lake, N. Dak.
Duluth, Minn.
Durango, Col.
Eau Claire, Wis.
Eureka, Nev.
Evanston, Wy.
Fargo, N. Dak
Folsom, N. M.
Gainesville, Fla.
Garden City, Kan.
Glenwood Springs, Col.
Grand Forks, N. Dak.
Grand Island, Neb.
Grayling, Mich.
Gunnison, Col.
Guthrie, Indian T.
Hailey, Id.

Harrison, Ark.
Helena, Mont.
Humboldt, Cal.
Hunstville, Ala.
Huron, S. Dak.
Independence, Cal.
Ironton, Mo.
Jackson, Miss.
Kingfisher, Indian T.
Kirwin, Kan.
La Grande, Or.
Lake View, Ore.
Lamar, Col.
Larned, Kan.
Las Cruces, N. M.
Leadville, Col.
Lewiston, Id.
Lincoln, Neb.
Little Rock, Ark.
Los Angeles, Cal.
Marquette, Mich.
Marysville, Cal.
Marshall, Minn.
McCook, Neb.
Menasha, Wis.
Miles City, Mont.
Mitchell, S. Dak.
Montgomery, Ala.
Montrose, Col.
Natchitoches, La.
Neligh, Neb.
New Orleans, La.
North Platte, Neb.
North Yakima, Wash.
Oberlin, Kan.
O'Neil, Neb.
Oregon City, Ore.
Prescott, Ari.

Land Officers—*Continued*

Pueblo, Col.
Rapid City, S. Dakota
Roseburg, Ore.
Roswell, N. M.
Sacramento, Cal.
Salina, Kan.
Salt Lake City, Utah
San Francisco, Cal.
Santa Fé, N. M.
Seattle, Wash.
Shasta, Cal.
Sidney, Neb.
Sitka, Alaska
Spokane Falls, Wash.
Springfield, Mo.
St. Cloud, Minn.

Stockton, Cal.
Susanville, Cal.
Taylor's Falls, Minn.
The Dallos, Ore.
Topeka, Kan.
Tucson, Ari.
Valentine, Neb.
Vancouver, Wash.
Visalia, Cal.
Wa-Keeney, Kan.
Walla Walla, Wash.
Watertown, S. Dakota
Wausau, Wis.
Yankton, S. Dakota

When the Legislatures of Different States Meet and When State Elections are Held

States	Legislature Meets	State Elections
Alabama	2d Mon. November	1st Mon. August
Arkansas	Tues. after 2d Mon. Nov	1st Mon. Sept.
California	1st Mon. Dec	Tues. after 1st Mon. Nov.
Colorado	1st Wed. Jan	Tues. after 1st Mon. Nov.
Connecticut	Wed. after 1st Mon. Jan	Tues. after 1st Mon. Nov.
Delaware	1st Tues. Jan	Tues. after 1st Mon. Nov.
Florida	Tues. after 1st Mon. Jan	Tues. after 1st Mon. Nov.
Georgia	2d Wed. Jan	1st Wed. Oct.
Illinois	Wed. after 1st Mon. Jan	Tues. after 1st Mon. Nov.
Indiana	1st Wed. Jan	Tues. after 1st Mon. Nov.
Iowa	2d Mon. Jan	2d Tues. Oct.
Kansas	2d Tues. Jan	Tues. after 1st Mon. Nov.
Kentucky	1st Mon. Dec	1st Mon. Aug.
Louisiana	1st Mon. Jan	Tues. after 1st Mon. Nov.
Maine	1st Wed. Jan	2d Mon. Sept.
Maryland	1st Wed. Jan	Tues. after 1st Mon. Nov.

When the Legislatures Meet, Etc.—*Continued*

States	Legislature Meets	State Elections
Massachusetts	1st Wed. Jan	Tues. after 1st Mon. Nov.
Michigan	1st Wed. Jan	Tues. after 1st Mon. Nov.
Minnesota	Tues. after 1st Mon. Jan	Tues. after 1st Mon. Nov.
Mississippi	1st Mon. Jan	Tues. after 1st Mon. Nov.
Missouri	Last Mon. Dec	Tues. after 1st Mon. Nov.
Montana	1st Mon. Jan	
Nebraska	Thur. after 1st Mon. Jan	Tues. after 1st Mon. Nov.
Nevada	1st Mon. Jan	Tues. after 1st Mon. Nov.
New Hampshire	1st Mon. Jan	Tues. after 1st Mon. Nov.
New Jersey	Mon. before 3d Tues. Jan	Tues. after 1st Mon. Nov.
New York	1st Tues. Jan	Tues. after 1st Mon. Nov.
North Carolina	Wed. after 1st Mon. Jan	Tues. after 1st Mon. Nov.
North Dakota	1st Mon. Jan	Tues. after 1st Mon. Nov.
Ohio	2d Mon. Jan	Tues. after 1st Mon. Nov.
Oregon	2d Mon. Sept	1st Mon. June
Pennsylvania	1st Tues. Jan	Tues. after 1st Mon. Nov.
Rhode Island	May and Jan	1st Wed. April
South Carolina	4th Tues. Nov	Tues. after 1st Mon. Nov.
South Dakota	1st Tues. Jan	Tues. after 1st Mon. Nov.
Tennessee	1st Mon. Jan	Tues. after 1st Mon. Nov.
Texas	2d Tues. Jan	Tues. after 1st Mon. Nov.
Vermont	1st Wed. Oct	1st Tues. Sept.
Virginia	1st Mon. Dec	Tues. after 1st Mon. Nov.
Washington		Tues. after 1st Mon. Nov.
West Virginia	1st Mon. Dec	Tues. after 1st Mon. Nov.
Wisconsin	1st Wed. Jan	Tues. after 1st Mon. Nov.

Biennial sessions of Legislature and elections in even years, as 1890, 1892, etc., in Alabama, Kentucky, Missouri, Oregon and Vermont. Biennial sessions in odd years, as 1891, 1893, etc., in California, Tennessee and Virginia. Biennial sessions in odd years (elections in the years immediately preceding) in Pennsylvania, Arkansas, Colorado, Delaware, Florida, Georgia, Illinois, Indiana, Kansas, Kentucky, Louisiana, Minnesota, Missouri, Nebraska, Nevada, New Hampshire, North Carolina, Tennessee, Texas and West Virginia. Triennial sessions, 1890, 1893, etc., in Michigan.

THE ELEVEN REBELLIONS OF THE UNITED STATES

Since the organization of the Federal Government eleven attempts have been made to resist its authority.

The first was in 1782, a conspiracy of some of the officers of the Federal Army to consolidate the Thirteen States into one and confer the supreme power under George Washington.

The second was in 1787, called Shay's Insurrection, in Massachusetts. The third was in 1794, called the Whiskey Insurrection of Pennsylvania.

The fourth was in 1814, by the Hartford Convention.

The fifth was in 1820, over the question of the admission of Missouri into the Union.

The sixth was a collision between the Legislature of Georgia and the Federal Government in regard to the land given to the Creek Indians.

The seventh was in 1830 with the Cherokees in Georgia.

The eighth was in 1832, the memorable nullifying ordinance of South Carolina.

The ninth was in 1842 in Rhode Island, between the Suffrage Association and the State authorities.

The tenth was in 1856 on the part of the Mormons who resisted the Federal authorities.

The eleventh, in 1861–1865, was the Civil War or the late attempt at secession of the Southern States.

LEGAL HOLIDAYS IN THE UNITED STATES

New Year's Day.—January 1st is a legal holiday in all the States and Territories, except Arkansas, Delaware, Kentucky, Maine, Massachusetts, New Hampshire, North Carolina, South Carolina, and Rhode Island.

January 8th.—Anniversary of the Battle of New Orleans, in Louisiana.

February 12th.—Lincoln's Birthday.—In Louisiana.

February 22d.—Washington's Birthday.—In all States and Territories, except Alabama, Arkansas, Florida, Illinois, Iowa, Indiana, Kansas, Maine, Missouri, North Carolina, Ohio, Oregon, Tennessee, and Texas.

March 1st.—Shrove Tuesday.—In Louisiana and cities of Mobile, Montgomery and Selma in Alabama.

March 2d.—Anniversary of Texan Independence in Texas.

March 4th. – Firemen's Anniversary.   In Louisiana.

Good Friday is a legal holiday in Louisiana, Florida, Minnesota, and Pennsylvania.

April 21st.—Battle of San Jacinto.   In Texas.

April 26th.—Memorial Day.   In Georgia.

May 30th.—Decoration Day.   In Colorado, Connecticut, Maine, Michigan, New Hampshire, New Jersey, New York, Pennsylvania, Rhode Island, Vermont and District of Columbia.

July 4th.—Independence Day.   In all States and Territories.

General Election Day.—Generally on Tuesday after first Monday in November.   In California, Maine, Missouri, New Jersey, New York, Oregon, South Carolina and Wisconsin.

Thanksgiving Day.—Usually last Thursday in November.   Public Fast Days whenever appointed by the President are legal holidays in all States and Territories.

December 25th.—Christmas Day.   In all the States and Territories.

THE UNITED STATES OF BRAZIL

On November 15, 1889, a startling report was received that Dom Pedro, Emperor of Brazil, had been deposed, and that the former empire of Brazil had been declared a republic. Later advices confirmed the report, with many particulars of the peaceful revolution which had been accomplished on the previous day.

The new republic is the largest of the South American countries, and covers an area estimated at from 3,000,000 to 3,219,000 square miles. In other words it is as large as the United States and the Territories, exclusive of Alaska. Its population in 1883 was estimated at 12,002,-978, including slaves and aborigines. It was divided into twenty provinces, now States each with a autonomous government. The largest city is Rio de Janeiro, the population of which is about 500,000. Each of the two cities of Bahia and Pernambuco contains between 100,000 and 200,000 inhabitants. The population is increasing largely by immigration, about 36,000 immigrants having landed in 1887.

Until 1815 Brazil was a province of Portugal; in that year it was made a kingdom of the empire of Portugal, Brazil and the Algarves by Dom John I, who had fled from Portugal before Napoleon. Brazil declared its independence of Portugal in 1822, and has since been an independent empire. Its ex-emperor, Dom Pedro II, has ruled the country with moderation for fifty-eight years, beloved by his people and respected by all who came in contact with him either as a ruler or as a man.

The provisional government proclaimed after the desposition of the emperor was announced as follows: President, Deodoro da Fonseca; minister of finance, Dr. Ruy Barbosa; minister of justice, Campos Selles; minister of Interior, Aristides Lobo; minister of foreign affairs, Equisetino Bocoyura; minister of war, Benjamin Constant; minister of marine, Admiral Vandenkock; minister of agriculture; Dimitrio Ribero.

DATE ON WHICH THE AMERICAN REPUBLICS DECLARED THEIR INDEPENDENCE

Country	Date
Argentine Republic	March 25, 1816
Bolivia	July 28, 1824
Brazil (Empire)	Oct. 12, 1822
Brazil (Republic)	Nov. 14, 1889
Chili	Sept. 18, 1816
Colombia, U. S. of	July 20, 1810
Central America	Sept. 15, 1821
Dominican Republic	Feb. 27, 1844
Hayti	Jan. 1, 1804
Mexico	Sept. 16, 1821
Paraguay	March 25, 1816
Peru	July 28, 1821
United States	July 4, 1776
Uruguay	March 25, 1816
Venezuela	July 5, 1811

THE GOVERNMENT OF FOREIGN COUNTRIES

REPUBLICS

Argentine Republic

The legislative authority is vested in a National Congress, consisting of a Senate and a House of Deputies; the executive power is entirely in the hands of the President, who is held responsible for the acts of the department.

Bolivia

The government of the republic is divided into a legislative department called a Congress, consisting of a Senate and a House of Representatives and an executive department, consisting of the President, Vice-President and a Ministry, the heads of four departments.

Chili

The legislative department consists of an Assembly of two houses, the Senate and Chamber of Deputies. The executive authority is held by the President with the assistance of a Council of State and a Cabinet, the heads of five departments.

Colombia

A confederative republic. It is governed in the legislative departments by a Congress of two houses, the Senate and House of Representatives. The executive power resides with the President and seven Ministers, who are held responsible to Congress.

Costa Rica

The legislative department consists of a Congress, comprising a Senate and House of Representatives; the executive of the President and a Council of Ministers, the heads of five departments.

Ecuador

The legislative department consists of a Congress of two houses, the Senate and House of Deputies; the executive of the President and a Cabinet of three Ministers, who with the President are held responsible to Congress, and who, with seven other members, form the Council of State.

France

The legislative power is controlled by an Assembly of two houses, Chamber of Deputies and Senate. The executive authority is in the hands of the chief magistrate, called the President of the Republic.

Guatemala

The legislative power is held by a National Assembly, and the executive is administered by the President, assisted by a Ministry, the heads of six departments.

Mexico

The legislative power resides in a Congress, consisting of a Senate and a House of Representatives. The executive authority is held by the President and a Council of six, the heads of departments.

Peru

The legislative power resides in a Congress, consisting of two houses, a Senate and a House of Representatives. The executive authority is intrusted to the President, assisted by the Vice-President and a Cabinet of five Ministers.

San Domingo

The legislative power is vested in a National Congress, consisting of two houses, a Consego Conservador and the Tribunador. The executive is intrusted to the President and a Ministry, the head of five departments.

Switzerland

The supreme legislative and executive authority is exercised in an Assembly of two houses; the Standrath or State Council and the Nationalrath or National Council. United they are called the Federal Assembly. The President and Vice-President of the Federal Assembly are the First Magistrates of the Republic.

Venezuela

The legislative power is vested in a Congress consisting of two houses, the Senate and House of Representatives. The executive is controlled by the President, through a Ministry of six members and a Federal Council of sixteen members.

KINGDOMS AND EMPIRES

Austria and Hungary

Each of these countries has its own Parliament, Ministers and Government. They have a common army, navy and diplomacy and a controlling body, known as the Delegations.

Belgium

The legislative power is in the king, the Chamber of Representatives and the Senate. No act of the king has effect unless signed by one of his ministers, who are thus made responsible for all acts of the government.

China

The administration is under the supreme direction of a Nei-ko or Cabinet consisting of four members, and these are assisted by two others, who are to see that nothing goes contrary to the civil or religious laws of the empire.

Denmark

The legislative authority is exercised by the king, acting in concert with the Rigsdagor Diet, consisting of an Upper House and a House of Commons. The executive power is in the hands of the king and his responsible Ministers.

German Empire

The supreme government is vested in the King of Prussia (Emperor of Germany) the Bundelsrath and the Reichstag. The former represents the individual States, the latter the German Nation.

Greece

The executive power is vested in the King and his responsible Ministers, heads of eight departments. The legislative power is given to a single chamber of representatives, called the Boule.

Great Britain

The absolute power of the British Empire is held by a Parliament, consisting of two houses, the House of Lords and the House of Commons. The sovereign is at the head of Parliament, and can alone summon Parliment.

Italy

The legislative power rests conjointly with the King and a Parliament composed of two houses, an Upper and a Lower House. The executive department is exercised exclusively by the King, assisted by the Ministers of nine departments.

Japan

The supreme executive, as well as the highest legislative authority, is vested in the Great Council, at which the Emperor presides. The Gen-Roin, or Senate, deliberates on legislative matters, but its decisions are subject to the sanction of the Great Council. The executive powers are exercised by a Ministry of ten departments.

Netherlands

The legislative authority is vested wholly in a Parliament, called the States General. The executive is with the sovereign and a council of eight Ministers, the heads of the different departments.

Ottoman Empire

The legislative and executive power is exercised under the supreme direction of the Sultan, by two high dignitaries, the Grand Vizier, the head of the temporal government, and the Sheik-ul-Islam, the head of the church.

Persia

The Shah, or King, has absolute power over all his subjects, so far as he does not oppose the doctrines of the Mohammedan religion. Through his direction the executive powers are exercised by a Ministry of seven departments. The whole revenue of the country is at his disposal.

Portugal

The legislative authority is given to the two houses, Upper and Lower of the Cortes Geræs. The executive rests with the sovereign and a Cabinet of seven responsible Ministers.

Russia

The whole legislative, executive and judicial authority is vested in the Emperor, whose will alone is law. The administration is intrusted to four great councils: the Council of the Empire, the Directing Senate, the Holy Synod and the Committee of Ministers. They all communicate directly with the sovereign.

Siam

The legislative power is exercised by the King, in conjunction with a Supreme Council of State and a Council of Ministers.

Spain

The legislative power rests with the King and Cortes Constituyentes, consisting of a Senate and a Congress. The executive is vested under the King and a Council of nine Ministers.

Sweden and Norway

The legislative authority of Sweden is vested in Diet or Parliament of the realm, in concert with the sovereign. Every new law must have the assent of the crown. The executive power is held by the King, who acts under the advice of a Council of State, consisting of the Ministers of State and ten other members. The legislative power of Norway is held entirely by the Storthing, or Great Court. The King has the right of veto over the laws passed by the Storthing, but only for a limited period. The executive power is in the hands of the King, who acts by the advice of a Council of State composed of two Ministers of State and nine Councilors.

THE PRINCIPAL COUNTRIES OF THE WORLD, THEIR FORM OF GOVERNMENT, TITLE OF RULER AND TERM OF OFFICE

Country	Form of Government	Title of Ruler	Term of Office
Abyssinia	Absolute Despotism	Sultan	Life
Afghanistan	Absolute Despotism	Amir	Life
Anam Kingdom	Absolute Despotism	King	Life
Austro-Hungary	Limited Monarchy	Emperor	Life
Argentine Republic	Republic	President	7 yrs.
Belgium	Limited Monarchy	King	Life
Bolivia	Republic	President	4 yrs.
Bokhara	Absolute Monarchy	Khan	Life
Brazil	Republic	President	
China	Absolute Despotism	Emperor	Life

Country	Form of Government	Title of Ruler	Term of Office
Chili	Republic	President	5 yrs.
Colombia, U. S. of	Republic	President	2 yrs.
Congo Free State	Free State	Sovereign	Life
Costa Rica	Republic	President	4 yrs.
Denmark	Limited Monarchy	King	Life
Dominican Republic	Republic	President	6 yrs.
Ecuador	Republic	President	4 yrs.
Egypt	Absolute Monarchy	Khedive	Life
France	Republic	President	7 yrs.
German Empire	Limited Monarchy	Emperor or Kaiser	Life
Great Britain	Limited Monarchy	Queen	Life
Greece	Limited Monarchy	King	Life
Guatemala	Republic	President	6 yrs.
Haytien Republic	Republic	President	7 yrs.
Honduras	Republic	President	4 yrs.
Italy	Limited Monarchy	King	Life
Japan	Limited Monarchy	Emperor	Life
Madagascar	Absolute Despotism	Queen	Life
Mexico	Republic	President	4 yrs.
Montenegro	Absolute Despotism	Prince	Life
Morocco	Absolute Despotism	Sultan	Life
Netherlands	Limited Monarchy	King	Life
Nicaragua	Republic	President	4 yrs.
Orange Free State	Republic	President	5 yrs.
Paraguay	Republic	President	4 yrs.
Persia	Absolute Despotism	Shah	Life
Peru	Republic	President	4 yrs.
Portugal	Limited Monarchy	King	Life
Russia	Absolute Despotism	Emperor or Czar	Life
Sandwich Islands	Limited Monarchy	King	Life
San Salvador	Republic	President	4 yrs.
Servia	Limited Monarchy	King	Life
Siam	Absolute Despotism	King	Life
Spain	Limited Monarchy	King	Life
Sweden and Norway	Limited Monarchy	King	Life
Switzerland	Republic	President	1 year
Turkey	Absolute Monarchy	Sultan	Life
Transvaal	Republic	President	
United States	Republic	President	4 yrs.
Uruguay	Republic	President	4 yrs.
Venezuela	Republic	President	2 yrs.

Principal Countries of the World, their Ruler's Name, Ruler's Salary or Civil List and Prevailing Religion

Country	Ruler's Name	Salary or Civil List	Prevailing Religion
Abyssinia	Johannes II		Coptic Christian
Afghanistan	Abdurrahman Khan		Buddic
Anam Kingdom	Tu-Duc		Pagan
Austro-Hungary	Francis Joseph I	*$3,775,800.00	Catholic
Argentine Republic	Juarez Celman	†$20,000.00	Catholic
Belgium	Leopold II	*$650,000.00	Catholic
Bolivia	Don Aniceto Arce		Catholic
Bokhara	Seid Abdul Ahad		Buddic
Brazil	Deodora da Fonseca		Catholic
China	Kuang Su		Buddic
Chili	Jose M. Balmaceda	†$18,000.00	Catholic
Colombia, U. S. of	Rafael Nunez		Catholic
Congo Free State	Leopold		Pagan
Costa Rica	Bernardo Soto		Catholic
Denmark	Christian IX	*$277,775.00	Protestant
Dominican Republic	Ulysses Heureaux		St. Catholic
Ecuador	Antonio Flores		Catholic
Egypt	Mohammed Tewfie	*$1,875,000.00	Mohammedan
France	Sadi-Carnot	†$123,800.00	Catholic
German Empire	William II	*$2,957,077.00	Protestant
Great Britain	Victoria	*$1,925,000.00	Protestant
Greece	George I	*$252,541.52	Greek Church
Guatemala	Manuel L. Barillas		Catholic
Haytien Republic	General Hippolyte	†$24,000	Catholic
Honduras	Luiz Bogran		Catholic
Italy	Humbert	*$3,146,000.00	Catholic
Japan	Mutsuhito	*$1,784,785.00	Buddic
Madagascar	Ranavalona III		Pagan
Mexico	Porfirio Diaz		Catholic
Montenegro	Nicholas	*$20,000.00	Greek Church
Morocco	Mulai Hassan	*$2,420,000.00	Mohammedan
Netherlands	William III	*$250,000.00	Protestant
Nicaragua	Evaresto Carazo		Catholic
Orange Free State	Judge Reitz		
Paraguay	General Escobar	†$9,500.00	Catholic
Persia	Nasr ed din	*$20,000,000.00	Mohammedan

Country	Ruler's Name	Salary or Civil List	Prevailing Religion
Peru	Andres A. Caceres		Catholic
Portugal	Don Carlos I	*$410,000.00	Catholic
Russia	Alexander	*$9,608,000.00	Greek Church
Sandwich Is'.nds	David Kalakaua	†$25,000	Protestan
San Salvador	Franciscus Menendez		Catholic
Servia	Milan		Catholic
Siam	Khulalonkorn I		Buddic
Spain	Alphonso XIII	*$1,400,000.00	Catholic
Sweden & Norway	Oscar	*$575,525.00	Protestant
Switzerland	Louis Ruchonmet	†$2,904.00	Protestant
Turkey	Abdul Hamid II	{*$5,000,000.00 to $10,000,000.00	Mohammedan
Transvaal	S. J. Paul Kruger		
United States	Benjamin Harrison	†$50,000.00	Protestant
Uruguay	Maximo Tajes		Catholic
Venezuela	Pable Rojas Paúl		Catholic

* Civil list per annum.

† Salary per annum.

Besides their salary or civil list they are allowed household expenses and other appropriations.

Principal Treaties of the World Ratified by Different Nations Since 1140

(People's Atlas)

1140.—Hanseatic League projected between the port-towns and cities of Germany against Danish and Swedish pirates; signed 1241.

1217, Sept. 11.—First treaty made by England was with the Dauphin Louis of France.

1272.—First treaty of commerce made by England with any foreign nation was with Flanders, time of Edward I.; the second with Portugal and Spain, 1308, Edward II.

1371.—Public Peace of Westphalia made between the Emperor Charles IV. and the States of the empire for maintaining peace of Germany.

1420.—Troyes, treaty between England, France and Burgundy to secure to Henry V. the throne of France after the death of Charles VI.

1508, Dec. 10.—League of Cambray between Pope Julius II., Maximilian, Louis XII. of France and Ferdinand of Spain against the republic of Venice.

1526, Jan. 14.—The Madrid Concord between Charles V. and Francis I.

1530, Dec. 31.—League of Schmalkald, entered by the Elector of Brandenburg and the other princes of Germany as a defense against Charles V. and in favor of Protestantism.

1555, Sept. 15.—"Peace of Religion," signed at Augsburg, between Catholics and Protestants.

1576–93.—Holy League of French Roman Catholics formed by the Duke of Guise at Peronne as a barrier to the succession of Henry IV., who was a Protestant. Dissolved in 1593 when the king became a Roman Catholic.

1620, July 3.—Treaty of Ulm, between the Emperor Ferdinand II., the dukes of Bavaria, the kings of Spain and of Poland, the elector of Saxony, the Pope and the Roman Catholic league on one hand and the allied princes of the Protestant. Union of Germany.

1630, Oct. 13.—Ratisbon, peace concluded between France and Germany.

1635, Aug. 13.—Prague peace between Austria and Prussia.

1648, Aug. 6.—First peace of Westphalia, concluded between Germany and Sweden, terminated the "Thirty Years' War."

1648, Oct. 24.—Second peace of Westphalia, concluded at Münster, between Germany, France and Sweden.

1660, May 27.—Copenhagen; peace concluded between Sweden and Denmark.

1668, Jan. 23.—Alliance between the States-General and England against France to protect the Spanish Netherlands; Sweden joined the league April 25th, thereafter known as the "Triple Alliance."

1668, Feb. 13.—Lisbon; peace between Spain and Portugal. Defensive alliance with Great Britain signed at Lisbon, May 16, 1703, and treaties of commerce, Dec. 27, 1703, and July 3, 1842.

1668, May 2.—First peace of Aix-la-Chapelle negotiated by England Sweden, the Netherlands, France and Spain.

1669, May 7.—Treaty between Portugal and Holland.

1674, Feb. 19.—Westminster, peace concluded between England and Holland.

1683, March 31.—Warsaw; alliance between Austria and Poland against Turkey.

1686, July 9.—League of Augsburg, Holland and other powers against France.

1689, May 12.—The grand alliance between Austria and States-General; England joined it Dec. 30, 1689 and the King of Spain and Duke of Savoy.

1697, Sept. 20.—Ryswick; peace concluded between England, France, Spain and Holland, and signed by Germany, Oct. 30, 1697.

1709, June 28.—Alliance of Dresden between Denmark and Saxony against Sweden.

1713, April 11.—Utrecht; peace concluded between France, Great Britain, Prussia, Portugal, Savoy and the States-General.

1714, March 17.—Radstadt; treaty between Louis XIV and Charles VI. of Germany.

1716, Nov. 28.—Second triple alliance between England, France and Holland, signed by the Dutch at The Hague, Jan. 4, 1717.

1718, Aug. 12.—Quadruple alliance, concluded by Great Britain, France and Germany. Holland acceded to it Feb., 1719, whence it obtained its name. The alliance signed at London, April 22, 1834, between England, France, Portugal and Spain, is also known as the Quadruple Alliance.

1719, Nov. 20.—Peace of Stockholm between the King of England and the Queen of Sweden.

1721, Aug. 30.—Nystadt; between Peter the Great of Russia and Sweden.

1724, March 24.—Treaty of Stockholm, between Sweden and Russia.

1725, April 3.—Alliance concluded at Vienna by Germany and Spain.

1725, Sept. 3.—Alliance between England, France and Prussia.

1731, March 16.—Between Great Britain, Germany and Holland, by which Great Britain guarantees the Pragmatic Sanction. Spain accedes to it July 22, 1731.

1731, March 16.—Second Treaty of Vienna concluded between Great Britain, Germany and Holland.

1738, Nov. 18.—Third treaty of Vienna between France and Germany.

1742, June 28.—Berlin; peace between Prussia, Poland and Hungary·

1745, Dec. 25.—Peace of Dresden, between Saxony, Prussia and Hungary.

1748, Oct. 18.—Second peace of Aix-la-Chapelle, made by Great Britain, France, Holland, Hungary and some Italian States.

— 249 —

1762, May 5.—Peace of St. Petersburg, between Russia and Prussia.

1763, Feb. 10.—Peace of Paris; Canada ceded to England.

1763, Feb. 15.—Hubertsburg, peace between Austria, Prussia and Bavaria by which the "Seven Years' War" was ended.

1768, Feb. 24.—Warsaw; treaty entered into between Russia and Poland.

1772, Aug. 5.—Treaty of St. Petersburg for the partition of Poland between Russia, Prussia and Austria.

1783, Sept. 3.—Peace of Versailles between England and France.

1783, Sept. 13.—Definitive treaty of peace between Great Britain and the United States, signed at Paris.

1790, Aug. 5.—Preliminaries of peace between Prussia and Austria signed at Reichenbach. In 1791 Congress convened here by the English ministry to form an alliance against Russian aggression. The treaty that laid the foundation of the grand alliance against Napoleon I. was signed here June 14, 1813; Austria gave her adherence to it June 27th.

1793. Alliance between Austria, Prussia and Great Britain against France.

1795, Sept. 28.—Triple alliance between Great Britain, Russia and Austria, ratified at St. Petersburg.

1795, Nov. 25.—Third treaty for the partition of Poland concluded between Russia, Austria and Prussia.

1799, June 22.—Alliance between Great Britain, Germany, Russia, Naples, Portugal and Turkey against France.

1802, March 27.—Peace of Amiens, entered into by Great Britain, France, Spain and Holland.

1805, April 11.—Alliance between Great Britain and Russia against Napoleon I.

1805, Aug. 5.—Combination between Great Britain, Russia, Austria, and Naples against France.

1806, Aug. 1.—Confederation of the Rhine League of the Germanic States, formed by Napoleon Bonaparte.

1806, Aug. 6.—Alliance between Great Britain, Russia, Prussia and Saxony against France.

1807, July 7.—Peace of Tilsit, between France and Russia.

1809, April 6.—Alliance between England and Austria against France.

1809, Oct. 14.—Vienna; peace between Napoleon I and Austria.

1813, March 17.—Alliance between Russia and Prussia.

1813, June 14 and 15.—Reichenbach; alliance between Russia, Prussia, and England against France; alliance joined by Austria, June 27, 1813.

1813, Sept. 9.—Töplitz; treaty between Austria, Russia and Prussia.

1813, Oct. 3.—Töplitz; treaty between Austria and Great Britain.

1814, Jan. 14.—Treaty of Kiel concluded between Denmark, Sweden and Great Britain.

1814, Dec. 24.—Ghent; peace between Great Britain and the United States.

1815, March 25.—Vienna; alliance concluded between Great Britain, Austria, Russia and Prussia. March 27.—France accedes to the alliance. May 31.—A treaty concluded between Holland on one side and Great Britain, Austria, Prussia and Russia on the other. June 9. The general congress treaty signed.

1815, Sept. 26.—Alliance, known as Holy Alliance, between Russia, Austria and Prussia, ratified at Paris; joined afterward by nearly all European powers.

1839, Nov. 16.—Treaty of Commerce made by Great Britain with Turkey.

1845, June 25.—Treaty of Commerce made by Great Britain with the Two Sicilies.

1846, June 12.—Washington; treaty between Great Britain and the United States, fixing boundary of British America and the United States.

1848, Feb. 2.—Treaty of Guadaloupe-Hidalgo between Mexico and the United States.

1854, Mar. 31.—Treaty between United States and Japan.

1854, May 8.—Tripartite treaty concluded between England, France and Turkey.

1854, June 7.—Washington; reciprocity between England and United States, regulating trade with Canada.

1855, Nov. 21.—Treaty between England, France and Sweden.

1856, April.—Peace concluded between France and Russia.

1858, Aug. 26.—Treaty of Jeddo between Great Britain and Japan.

1859, Nov. 10.—Zürich; peace between Austria, France and Sardinia.

1860, Jan. 23.—An important commercial treaty made between Great Britain and France.

1860, Nov. 14.—Treaty between Russia and China, giving Russia free trade territories, etc.

1864, Oct. 30.—Vienna; peace between Austria, Prussia and Denmark.

1866, Oct. 3.—Vienna; peace between Austria and Italy.

1866, Oct. 21.—Berlin; peace between Prussia and Saxony.

1871, May 8.—Washington, treaty between England and United States, settling Alabama claims.

1871, May 10.—Frankfort, peace between France and Germany.

1878, March 3.—San Stefano, peace between Russia and Turkey.

1878, July 13.—Berlin treaty, entered into by Germany, Russia, Turkey, Great Britain, Austria, France, and Italy.

1881.—Second treaty between United States and China.

1889.—Samoan Treaty, between United States, Germany and England.

Portraits on Bank Notes of the U.S.

On United States Notes.—$1, Washington; $2, Jefferson; $5, Jackson; $10, Webster; $20, Hamilton; $50, Franklin; $100, Lincoln; $500, General Mansfield; $1,000, De Witt Clinton; $5,000, Madison; $10,000, Jackson. On Silver Certificates—$10, Robert Morris; $20, Commodore Decatur; $50, Edward Everett; $100, James Monroe; $500, Charles Sumner, $1,000, W. L. Marcy. On Gold Notes—$20, Garfield; $50, Silas Wright; $100, Thomas H. Benton; $500, A. Lincoln; $1,000, Hamilton; $5,000, Madison; $10,000, Jackson.

Weights and Measures
Diamond Weight

16 parts equal 1 grain equals .8 grain Troy
4 grains   "   1 carat   "   3.2   "   "
20 parts diamond weight   "   1   "   "

Assayers' Weight

1 carat   equals 10 Pennyweight Troy
1 carat grain   "   2 pwts. 12 grs. or 60 grains Troy
24 carat   "   1 pound Troy

Troy Weight

3½ grains (gr) equals 1 carat (diamond weight) K.
24   "   "   1 pennyweight, pwt.
20 pennyweights   "   1 ounce, oz.
12 ounces   "   1 pound, lb.

Troy Weight is used for measuring gold, silver, jewels and precious metals.

California Lot Measure

A 100 vara lot equals 275 feet square
A 50 vara lot equals 137½ "
A 100 vara lot contains four 50 vara lots
A vara is 33⅓ inches
A 100 vara lot contains 1.7367 acres
A 50 vara lot contains .4342 acres

Cloth Measure

OLD WAY	NEW WAY
2¼ inches equal 1 nail	2 sixteenths equal 1 eighth
4 nails " 1 quarter	2 eighths equal 1 quarter
4 quarters " 1 yard	2 quarters equal 1 half
4 quarters equal 1 yard	
3 quarters equal 1 ell Flemish	6 quarters equal 1 ell French
5 quarters equal 1 ell English	37.2 inches equal 1 ell Scotch

This measure is used in buying and selling cloth, ribbons, etc.

Drop Liquid Measure

100 drops   -   -   equal   1 spoonful
100 spoonfuls -   -   "   1 quart
100 quarts   -   -   -   "   1 cask

Iron and Lead Weight

14 pounds   -   -   -   equal   1 stone
21½ stones   -   -   -   -   "   1 pig
8 pigs   -   -   -   -   "   1 fother

Units (Measure)

20 units   -   -   -   equal   1 score
12 units   -   -   -   "   1 dozen
12 dozen   -   -   -   "   1 gross
12 gross   -   -   -   "   1 great gross

Paper Measure

24 sheets   -   -   -   equal   1 quire
20 quires   -   -   -   "   1 ream
2 reams   -   -   -   "   1 bundle
5 bundles   -   -   -   "   1 bale

United States Money

10 mills   -   -   -   equal   1 cent
10 cents   -   -   -   "   1 dime
10 dimes   -   -   -   "   1 dollar, $
10 dollars   -   -   -   "   1 eagle

The mill is not coined.

Comparison of Measures of Capacity

1 gallon (4 qts.) Wine Measure, contains 231 cubic inches.
1 gallon (4 qts.) Dry Measure, contains 268 4-5 cubic inches.
1 gallon (4 qts.) Beer Measure, contains 282 cubic inches.
1 bushel, Dry Measure, contains 2,150⅖ cubic inches.

Foreign Weights and Measures

Denomination	Where Used	U. S. Equivalent
Almude	Portugal	4.422 gals.
Arratel or Libra	Portugal	1,011 lbs. avoir.
Arroba	Portugal and Brazil	32.38 lbs.
Arroba	Spain and Buenos Ayres	25.36 lbs.
Arroba	Spain (wine)	4.26 gals.
Baril	Argentine Republic and Mexico	20.0787 gals.
Berkovet	Russia	360 lbs. avoir.
Candy	Bombay	560 lbs. avoir.
Candy	Madras	500 lbs. avoir.
Cantar	Turkey	124.7036 lbs. avoir.
Cathy	China	1.33 lbs. avoir.
Cathy	Japan	1.31 lbs.
Cathy	Java, Siam, Malacca	1.35 lbs.
Cathy	Sumatra	2.12 lbs.
Centner	Bremen	127.5 lbs.
Centner	Darmstadt and Zollverein	110.24 lbs.
Centner	Prussia	113.44 lbs.
Centner	Sweden	93.7 lbs. avoir.
Chang	China	11.75 ft.
Cheih	China	1.175 ft.
Dansk mil	Denmark	4.68 miles
Desiatine	Russia	2.7 acres
Fanega	Mexico	1.54728 bushels
Hectolitre (liquid)	France	26.41 gals.
Hectolitre (cereals)	France	2.837 busn.
Last	Belgium and Holland (dry)	85.134 bush.
Last	England, for dry Malt	82.52 bush.
Last	Prussia	112.29 bush.
Li	China	2115 ft.
Libra	Castilian	7100 grains troy
Libra	Chili	1.014 lbs. avoir.
Livre	Guiana	1.0791 lbs. avoir.
Oka	Egypt	2.7235 lbs. avoir.
Oka	Hungary	3.0817 lbs. avoir.
Oka	Turkey	2.83418 lbs. avoir.
Picul	Borneo and Celebes	135.64 lbs.
Picul	China	133¼ lbs. avoir.
Picul	Japan	130 lbs.
Picul	Java (Batavia)	135.10 lbs.

Weights—*Continued*

Denomination	Where Used	U. S. Equivalent
Pie	Argentine Republic	0.9478 ft.
Pie	Castilian	0.91407 ft.
Pik	Turkey	27.9 in.
Pood	Russia	36 lbs. avoir.
Pund	Denmark	1.102 lbs. avoir.
Quarter	England	8.252 bush.
Quintal	Brazil	130.06 lbs. avoir.
Quintal	Buenos Ayres	101.42 lbs. avoir.
Quintal	Castile, Chili, Mexico, Peru	101.61 lbs. avoir.
Quintal Metrique	France	220.4 lbs. avoir.
Tael	Cochin-China	590.75 grains troy.
Tael (weight)	China	1½ oz. avoir.
Tchetvert	Russia	5.95 bush.
Tonde (coal)	Denmark	4.82 bush.
Tonde (corn)	Denmark	3.92 bush.
Tondeland	Denmark	1.36 acres.
Tonneau (coal)	France	2,004 lbs. avoir.
Tscan	China	1.41 inches
Tunna	Sweden	4.64 bush.
Tunnland	Sweden	1.22 acres.
Vara	Castilian	0.914117 yds.
Vara	Curaçoa, Cuba and Peru	33.375 in.
Vedro	Russia	3.24 gals.
Verste	Russia	0.663 of a mile.
Zoll centner	Austria	110 lbs. avoir.

CAPACITY (SEATING) OF NOTED PUBLIC BUILDINGS

Building	Location	Capacity
Coliseum	Rome, Italy	87,000
St. Peter's Church	Rome, Italy	58,000
Theatre of Pompey	Rome, Italy	40,000
Cathedral	Milan, Italy	40,000
St. Paul's Church	Rome, Italy	39,000
St. Paul's Church	London, England	31,000
St. Petronio's Church	Bologna, Italy	25,000
Cathedral	Florence, Italy	23,500
Cathedral	Antwerp, Belgium	23,000
St. John's Latern	Rome, Italy	23,000

Capacity of Public Buildings—*Continued*

Building	Location	Capacity
Mosque of St. Sophia	Constantinople, Turkey	23,000
Notre Dame Church	Paris, France	21,500
Theater of Marcellus	Rome, Italy	20,000
Cathedral	Pisa, Italy	13,000
St. Stephen's Church	Vienna, Austria	12,400
Gilmore's Garden	New York, N. Y	8,443
Mormon Temple	Salt Lake City, Utah	8,000
St. Mark's Church	Venice, Italy	7,500
Spurgeon's Tabernacle	London, England	6,000
Bolshoi Theater	St. Petersburg, Russia	5,000
Music Hall	Cincinnati, Ohio	4,824
La Scala	Milan, Italy	4,000
Exeter Hall	London, England	3,500
Washington Hall	Paterson, N. J	3,000
Plymouth Church	Brooklyn, N. Y	3,000
City Hall	Columbus, Ohio	3,000
Boston Theater	Boston, Mass	2,972
Academy of Music	Philadelphia, Penn	2,865
Covent Garden	London, England	2,684
Music Hall	Boston, Mass	2,585
Carlo Felice	Genoa, Italy	2,560
Academy of Music	New York, N. Y	2,526
Grand Opera House	San Francisco, Cal	2,500
Cooper Union	New York, N. Y	2,500
Alexander	St. Petersburg, Russia	2,307
Grand Opera House	Paris, France	2,300
Grand Opera House	Cincinnati, Ohio	2,250
Orpheum	San Francisco, Cal	2,200
Imperial	St. Petersburg, Russia	2,161
Academy of Music	Paris, France	2,092
Tivoli Opera House	San Francisco, Cal	1,900
National Theater	Washington, D. C	1,709
New California Theater	San Francisco, Cal	1,650
Opera House	Berlin, Germany	1,636
Baldwin Theater	San Francisco, Cal	1,600
Beethoven Hall	Boston, Mass	1,500
Howard Athenæum	Boston, Mass	1,500
Theatre Royal	Montreal, Canada	1,368
Bush St. Theater	San Francisco, Cal	1,300
Museum	Boston, Mass	1,275
Alcazar Theater	San Francisco, Cal	1,200
Bijou Theater	San Francisco, Cal	900

MARVELS OF NATURE AND ART

The Largest Fortification in the World

The largest single fortification is Fortress Monroe, at Norfolk, Virginia. It has already cost the U. S. Government over three million dollars. The water battery is considered one of the finest military works of the world.

The Largest Hanging Bell in the World

The largest hanging bell in the world is in a Buddhist monastery, near Canton, China. It is eighteen feet high and forty-five feet in circumference, and is of solid bronze. It is one of eight great bells which were cast by command of the Emperor Yung-lo about A. D. 1400, and is said to have cost the lives of eight men, who were killed during the process of casting. The whole bell, both inside and out, is covered with an inscription in embossed Chinese characters about half an inch long, covering even the handle, the total number being 84,000. The characters tell a single story—one of the Chinese classics.

Largest Cave in the World

The largest cave is Mammoth Cave in Kentucky, U. S., in it is a subterranean river which is navigable and contains blind fishes.

Largest Body of Fresh Water on the Earth

The largest body of fresh water is Lake Superior, U. S., its greatest length is 400 miles and its greatest breath is 160 miles; its mean depth is 90 fathoms, its area is 32,000 square miles, it is about 635 feet above the sea level.

Largest Island in the World

The largest island is Australia. It is 2,500 miles in length from east to west and 1,950 miles from north to south; it has an area of 2,984,287 square miles, about as large as the United States of America.

The Longest Tunnel in the World

The longest tunnel is St. Gothard, on the line of railroad between Lucerne and Milan. The summit of the tunnel is 990 feet below the surface at Andermatt, and 6,600 feet beneath the peak of Kastelhorn of the St. Gothard group. The tunnel is 26½ feet wide and 19 feet 10 inches from floor to the crown of the arched roof, it is 48,840 feet long, nearly 10 miles.

Most Extensive Park in the World

The most extensive park is Deer Park in the environs of Copenhagen, in Denmark, Europe. The inclosure contains 4,200 acres of land and a small river runs through it.

Longest Span of Telegraph Wire in the World

The longest span of telegraph wire is in India, Asia, over the river Kistnah, between Berzorah and Soctauagrun. It is more than 6,000 feet long and is stretched between two hills, each of which is 1,200 feet high.

Most Remarkable Artificial Echo on Earth

The most remarkable artificial echo known is that in the Castle of Simoncita, about two miles from Milan, in Italy. It is occasioned by the existence of two parallel walls of considerable length. It repeats the report of a pistol sixty times.

The Largest Stationary Engine in the World

The largest stationary engine in the world is at the famous zinc mines at Friedensville, Pa. It is known as the "President," and there is no pumping engine in the world that can be compared with the monster. The number of gallons of water raised every minute is 17,500. The driving wheels are thirty-five feet in diameter and weigh forty tons each. The sweep rod is forty feet long, the cylinders 110 inches in diameter, and the piston-rod eighteen inches in diameter, with a ten-foot stroke.

The Largest Flower Known

Raffiesia Schadenbergia is the largest flower known, it grows in the Philippine Islands, it is 3 feet in diameter.

The Largest Smokestacks in the World

The Townsend Works, at Glasgow, Scotland, smokestack is 488 feet in height, of which 454 feet is masonry and 34 feet on top is a copper pipe, it has a base of 32 feet, and it cost about $40,000.

Tennent & Co. of Glasgow, Scotland, smokestack is 435 feet high, it has 40 feet base and 13½ feet flue.

Dobson & Barlow's, England, smokestack is 361½ feet high, has a base of 33 feet 10 inches and 13 feet 2 inches flue.

The fourth largest in the world and the largest in the United States is at the Fall River Iron Works, Massachusetts, it is for 40 boilers to supply three triple expansion engines of 1,350 horse-power each. The smokestack is 350 feet high, its base is 30 feet and the top of the flue is 21 feet. The entire structure rests on a solid granite foundation 55x30 feet and 16 feet deep, in its construction are used about 1,700,000 bricks, 2,000 tons of stone, 2,000 barrels of mortar, 1,000 loads of sand, 1,000 barrels of cement, and it cost $40,000.

The Largest Telescopes

The largest refractor, Lick Observatory, Mt. Hamilton, Cal., 36 inches, constructed by Clark, Warner and Swasey, 1887. The largest reflector, Lord Rosse, Birr Castle, Ireland, 72 inches, constructed by Lord Rosse, 1844.

Population of the Largest Cities of the World—*Latest Census*

Cities	Census Year	Population	Cities	Census Year	Population
London* (est., 4,282,021).	1881	3,816,483	Stockholm	1887	277,964
Paris	1886	2,344,550	Bucharest	1876	221,805
Canton	est.	1,600,000	Sydney, N. S. W	1881	220,427
Berlin	1885	1,315,287	New Orleans†	1880	216,090
Vienna	1887	1,270,000	Antwerp	1888	210,584
New York†	1880	1,206,577	Alexandria	1882	208,755
Tokio, Japan	1886	1,121,883	Belfast	1881	208,122
St. Petersburg	1884	929,100	Bristol (est., 226,510)	1881	205,874
Constantinople	1885	873,565	Palermo	1881	205,712
Calcutta	1881	871,504	Smyrna	est.	200,000
Philadelphia†	1880	847,170	Teheran, Persia	est.	200,000
Bombay	1881	773,196	Benares	1881	199,700
Moscow	1884	758,469	Havana	1888	198,261
Glasgow	1881	674,095	Rotterdam	1888	193,058
Brooklyn†	1880	566,689	Penang	1881	190,597
Liverpool (est., 509,738).	1881	552,508	Lille	1886	188,272
Chicago†	1880	503,185	Nottingh'm (es. 200,921)	1881	186,575
Peking, China	est.	500,000	Montreal	1887	186,257
Buenos Ayres	1888	466,267	Bradford (est., 249,721)	1881	183,032
Naples	1881	463,172	Salford (est., 226,836)	1881	176,235
Brussels	1888	458,639	Delhi	1881	173,393
Buda-Pesth	1886	422,557	Leipzig	1886	170,340
Melbourne	1888	410,000	Riga, Russia	1881	169,329
Warsaw	1882	406,261	Kharkoff, Russia	1884	166,921
Madras	1881	405,848	Toronto	1886	166,809
Lyons	1886	401,030	Bremen	1886	165,628
Birmi'gham (est.447,912)	1881	400,774	Prague	1880	162,323
Boston†	1885	390,405	Cologne	1885	161,260
Amsterdam	1888	390,016	Hong Kong	1881	160,402
Madrid	1887	385,688	Cleveland†	1880	160,146
Marseilles	1884	376,143	Manila	est.	160,000
Cairo	1882	368,108	Patna	est.	160,000
Osaka, Japan	1886	361,694	Milwaukee†	1885	158,509
Rio de Janiero	1885	357,332	Pittsburgh†	1880	156,389
Hyderabad, India	1881	354,692	Buffalo	1880	155,134
St. Louis†	1880	350,519	Frankfort	1885	154,504
Mexico	1888	350,000	Odessa	1885	151,240
Manchester (es. 378,164).	1881	341,414	Hull (est 202,359)	1881	154,240
Baltimore†	1880	332,313	Jersey City†	1885	153,513
Leeds (est., 351,210)	1881	309,119	Newark, U. S.	1885	152,513
Hamburg	1885	305,690	Cawnpore	1881	151,444
Breslau	1885	298,893	Konigsburg	1885	151,157
Milan	1881	295,543	Damascus	est.	150,000
Copenhagen	1887	286,000	The Hague	1888	149,447
Lucknow	1881	284,779	Ghent	1888	147,012
Sheffield (est., 321,711)	1881	284,508	Toulouse	1886	147,617
Shanghai	est.	278,000	Washington†	1880	147,293
Rome	1881	273,268	Newcastle (est, 153,003).	1881	145,359
Munich	1886	261,081	Trieste	1880	144,844
Cincinnati†	1880	255,809	Valencia	1877	143,856
Kioto, Japan	1881	255,403	Allahabad	1881	143,693
Seoul, Corea	est.	250,000	Dundee	1881	140,239
Dublin	1881	249,602	Liege	1888	140,261
Dresden	1886	246,086	Bahia	1883	140,000
Lisbon	1878	246,343	Genoa	1881	138,081
Barcelona	1888	241,062	Florence	1881	134,992
Bordeaux	1886	240,582	Christiania, Norway	1888	135,015
Santiago, Chili	1885	236,412	Seville	1877	133,938
Edinburgh	1881	236,002	Detroit†	1884	133,269
San Francisco†	1880	233,959	Venice	1881	129,445
Turin	1881	230,183			

* The population of cities given in the Statesmen's Year Book for 1889 has been selected for this table. That authority gives estimated present population of English cities which is here printed in parentheses.

† Many of the American cities do not hold their proper relative rank in the table because their last censuses were taken ten years ago, while those of most European cities are more recent.

Population of Cities in the United States

Cities	Official Census 1880	†Estimated Census 1885	†Estimated Census 1890
New York City	1,206,299	1,300,000	1,800,0(0
Philadelphia, Pa	847,170	875,000	1,250,000
Brooklyn, N. Y	566,663	604,000	835,000
Chicago, Ill	503,185	550,000	1,150,000
Boston, Mass	362,839	*390,406	416,226
St. Louis, Mo	350,518	450,000	500,000
Baltimore, Md	332,313	375,000	500,000
Cincinnati, O	255,139	280,000	325,000
San Francisco, Cal	233,959	300,000	335,000
New Orleans, La	216,090	235,000	260,000
Cleveland, O	160,146	176,000	275,000
Pittsburgh, Pa	156,389	162,000	250,000
Buffalo, N. Y	155,134	165,000	265,000
Washington, D. C	147,293	*173,606	230,000
Newark, N. J	136,508	*152,988	175,000
Louisville, Ky	123,758	130,000	200,000
Jersey City, N. J	120,722	*153,513	195,000
Detroit, Mich	116,340	*133,269	235,000
Milwaukee, Wis	115,587	*158,509	210,000
Providence, R. I	104,857	*118,070	132,000
Albany, N. Y	90,758	97,000	103,000
Rochester, N. Y	89,366	95,000	120,000
Alleghany, Pa	78,682	81,000	120,000
Indianapolis, Ind	75,056	100,000	130,000
Richmond, Va	63,600	70,000	85,000
New Haven, Conn	62,882	75,000	83,000
Lowell, Mass	59,475	*64,051	80,000
Worcester, Mass	58,291	*68,383	85,000
Troy, N. Y	56,747	60,000	65,000
Kansas City, Mo	55,785	105,000	200,000
Cambridge, Mass	52,669	*59,660	72,500
Syracuse, N. Y	51,792	55,000	87,738
Columbus, O	51,647	57,000	100,000
Paterson, N. J	51,031	*63,280	85,000
Toledo, O	50,137	55,000	90,000
Charleston, S. C	49,984.	50,000	60,000
Fall River, Mass	48,961	*56 863	70,000
Minneapolis, Minn	46,887	*46,887	225,000

Population of Largest Cities—*Continued*

Cities	Official Census 1880	†Estimated Census 1885	†Estimated Census 1890
Scranton, Pa	45,850	48,000	100,000
Nashville, Tenn	43,350	49,000	95,000
Reading, Pa	43,278	45,000	63,000
Wilmington, Del	42,478	45,000	58,000
Hartford, Conn	42,015	47,000	53,000
Camden, N. J	41,659	*52,884	75,000
St. Paul, Minn	41,473	*111,397	220,000
Lawrence, Mass	39,151	*38,812	45,600
Dayton, O	38,678	42,500	60,000
Lynn, Mass	38,274	*45,861	54,000
Atlanta, Ga	37,409	41,000	90,000
Denver, Col	35,629	45,000	130,000
Oakland, Cal	34,555	42,000	46,000
Utica, N. Y	33,914	37,000	50,000
Portland, Me	33,810	35,000	42,000
Memphis, Tenn	33,592	37,500	75,000
Springfield, Mass	33,340	*37,577	43,000
Manchester, N. H	32,630	37,250	45,000
St. Joseph, Mo	32,431	45,000	70,000
Grand Rapids, Mich	32,016	*41,934	80,000
Hoboken, N. J	30,999	*37,721	50,000
Harrisburg, Pa	30,762	32,000	43,000
Wheeling, W. Va	30,737	40,000	40,500
Savannah, Ga	30,709	31,000	58,000
Omaha, Neb	30,518	*61,835	135,000
Trenton, N. J	29,910	*34,386	67,000
Covington, Ky	29,720	33,000	45,000
Evansville, Ind	29,280	40,000	55,000
Peoria, Ill	29,259	31,000	45,500
Mobile, Ala	20,132	31,750	45,000
Elizabeth, N. J	28,229	*32,149	33,000
Erie, Pa	27,737	28,500	40,000
Bridgeport, Conn	27,643	32,000	50,000
Salem, Mass	27,563	*28,084	29,000
Quincy, Ill	27,268	30,000	40,000
Fort Wayne, Ind	26,880	30,000	40,000
New Bedford, Mass	26,845	*33,393	40,000
Terra Haute, Ind	26,042	30,000	32,500

Population of Largest Cities—*Continued*

Cities	Official Census 1880	†Estimated Census 1885	†Estimated Census 1890
Lancaster, Pa...................	25,769	28,000	31,000
Somerville, Mass...............	24,933	*29,992	32,500
Davenport, Ia.............	24,831	*23,830	30,000
Wilkesbarre, Pa...............	23,339	25,000	40,000
Des Moines, Ia.................	22,408	*32,469	35,500
Dubuque, Ia....................	22,254	*26,330	36,500
Galveston, Tex.................	22,248	30,000	45,000
Norfolk, Va....	21,966	. 25,000	35,000
Auburn, N. Y..................	21,924	23,300	26,000
Holyoke, Mass.................	21,915	*27,894	35,000
Augusta, Ga...................	21,891	22,000	47,000
Chelsea, Mass..................	21,782	*25,709	30,000
Petersburg, Va.................	21,656	24,000	25,000
Sacramento, Cal.	21,420	26,000	40,000
Taunton, Mass...	21,213	*23,674	27,000
Oswego, N. Y..................	21,116	22,500	23,000
Salt Lake, Utah................	20,768	35,000	36,000
Springfield, O.................	20,730	23,000	35,000
Bay City, Mich.................	20,693	*29,415	31,240
San Antonio, Tex..............	20,550	26,000	54,700
Elmira, N. Y..................	20,541	22,000	32,500
Newport, Ky..................	20,430	23,000	20,400
Poughkeepsie, N. Y............	20,207	21,000	24,000
Springfield, Ill................	19,743	24,600	26,000
Altoona, Pa....................	19,710	21,000	26,000
Burlington, Ia.................	19,450	*23,450	35,000
Cohoes, N. Y..................	19,416	20,750	22,000
Gloucester, Mass...............	19,329	*21,713	22,000
Lewiston, Me..................	19,083	20,000	20,000
Pawtucket, R. I................	19,030	*22,906	23,250
East Saginaw, Mich............	19,016	29,100	40,000
Williamsport, Pa..............	18,934	20,000	32,000
Yonkers, N. Y.................	18,892	19,500	30,000
Haverhill, Mass................	18,472	*21,795	25,000
Kingston, N. Y................	18,344	19,500	20,000
Zanesville, O..................	18,113 .	20,000	20,500
Newburg, N. Y................	18,049	19,250	21,500
Councils Bluffs, Iowa....... .	18,063	*21,557	35,000

Population of Largest Cities—*Continued*

Cities	Official Census 1880	†Estimated Census 1885	†Estimated Census 1890
Allentown, Pa	18,063	18,750	19,000
Waterbury, Conn	17,806	21,500	35,000
Portland, Ore	17,577	30,000	60,000
Wilmington, N. C	17,350	19,800	25,000
Binghamton, N. Y	17,317	18,500	32,000
Bloomington, Ill	17,180	20,000	25,000
New Brunswick, N. J	17,166	*18,258	20,000
Long Island City, N. Y	17,129	18,250	45,000
Newton, Mass	16,995	*19,739	20,000
Bangor, Me	16,856	17,500	18,000
Montgomery, Ala	16,713	16,900	30,000
Lexington, Ky	16,650	18,000	35,000
Leavenworth, Kan	16,546	*29,268	30,000
Houston, Tex	16,513	20,000	45,000
Akron, O	16,512	18,000	20,000
New Albany, Ind	16,423	19,000	20,500
Jackson, Mich	16,105	*19,136	27,000
Woonsocket, R. I	16,059	17,000	18,000
Racine, Wis	16,031	*19,636	20,500
Lynchburg, Va	15,959	18,000	19,000
Sandusky, O	15,838	17,000	18,500
Oshkosh, Wis	15,748	*22,064	30,000
Newport, R. I	15,693	*19,566	22,000
Meriden, Conn	15,693	17,000	17,500
Topeka, Kan	15,452	*23,499	24,500
Youngstown, O	15,435	17,000	18,500
Norwich, Conn	15,112	22,000	23,000
Atchison, Kan	15,105	*15,599	18,000
Chester, Pa	14,997	15,500	17,000
La Fayette, Ind	14,860	23,000	24,000
Leadville, Col	14,820	19,000	20,000
La Crosse, Wis	14,505	*21,740	32,000
Norwalk, Conn	13,956	16,500	17,500
York, Pa	13,940	14,500	16,000
Concord, N. H	13,843	14,600	15,500
Lincoln, R. I	13,765	16,500	17,500
Alexandria, Va	13,659	14,000	15,500
Schenectady, N. Y	13,655	14,500	23,000

Population of Largest Cities—*Continued*

Cities	Official Census 1880	†Estimated Census 1885	†Estimated Census 1890
Brockton, Mass	13,608	*20,783	21,500
Newburyport, Mass	13,538	*13,716	15,000
Lockport, N. Y	13,522	17,500	18,000
Nashua, N. H	13,397	14,822	20,000
Pittsfield, Mass	13,364	*14,466	15,500
South Bend, Ind	13,280	20,500	21,000
Pottsville, Pa	13,253	14,000	15,000
Orange, N. J	13,207	*15,231	15,500
Little Rock, Ark	13,138	13,500	40,000
Rockford, Ill	13,129	20,500	20,500
Fond du Lac, Wis	13,094	*12,726	14,000
Norristown, Pa	13,063	13,500	14,500
Lincoln, Neb	13,003	*20,004	21,500
Chattanooga, Tenn	12,892	14,750	55,000
Macon, Ga	12,749	13,000	14,500
Richmond, Ind	12,742	16,000	17,500
New Brighton, N. Y	12,679	13,500	14,000
Biddeford, Me	12,651	13,000	14,000
Georgetown, D. C	12,578	*14,322	15,000
San Jose, Cal	12,567	16,000	25,000
Fitchburg, Mass	12,429	*15,375	16,000
Canton, O	12,258	13,000	13,500
Rome, N. Y	12,194	12,750	13,250
Northampton, Mass	12,172	*12,896	13,250
Warwick, R. I	12,164	*13,286	14,000
Rutland, Vt	12,149	16,000	17,500
Hamilton, O	12,122	13,500	14,000
Keokuk, Ia	12,117	*13,151	18,000
Steubenville, O	12,093	13,500	16,000
Malden, Mass	12,017	*16,407	17,000
Easton, Pa	11,924	12,500	13,000
Aurora, Ill	11,873	18,000	20,000
Vicksburg, Miss	11,814	13,000	18,500
New Britain, Conn	11,800	13,000	14,000
Waltham, Mass	11,712	*14,609	15,000
Dover, N. H	11,687	12,882	13,250
Danbury, Conn	11,666	12,500	13,000
Rock Island, Ill	11,659	13,000	13,500

Population of Largest Cities—*Continued*

Cities	Official Census 1880	†Estimated Census 1885	†Estimated Census 1890
Joliet, Ill	11,657	13,000	18,000
Derby, Conn	11,657	12,500	18,000
Golesburg, Ill	11,437	13,000	13,500
Portsmouth, Va	11,437	14,000	13,500
Burlington, Vt	11,365	15,000	15,500
Portsmouth, O	11,321	12,000	12,250
Stamford, Conn	11,297	11,500	12,000
Chicopee, Mass	11,262	*11,528	12,000
Muskegon, Mich	11,262	*17,845	18,500
Logansport, Ind	11,192	15,000	16,000
Los Angeles, Cal	11,183	35,000	80,000
Attleborough, Mass	11,111	*13,175	13,500
Hannibal, Mo	11,074	18,000	18,500
Austin, Tex	11,013	15,000	30,000
Chillicothe, O	10,938	12,500	13,000
Woburn, Mass	10,931	*11,750	12,000
Jacksonville, Ill	10,927	12,000	25,000
Virginia City, Nev	10,917	5,500	5,000
Watertown, N. Y	10,697	13,500	14,000
Cumberland, Md	10,693	13,500	14,000
Belleville, Ill	10,683	14,000	14,500
Quincy, Mass	10,570	*12,144	14,000
Weymouth, Mass	10,570	*10,740	11,000
New London, Conn	10,537	11,000	11,250
Saginaw, Mich	10,525	*13,767	14,500
Dallas, Tex	10,358	13,500	61,000
Ogdensburg, N. Y	10,341	11,500	12,000
Madison, Wis	10,324	*12,064	13,500
Stockton, Cal	10,282	15,000	16,000
Winona, Minn	10,208	*15,624	16,500
North Adams, Mass	10,191	*12,540	13,000
Shenandoah, Pa	10,147	12,500	13,000
Marlborough, Mass	10,127	*10,941	11,000
Columbus, Ga	10,123	10,500	16,500
Eau Clair, Wis	10,119	*21,668	27,000
Cedar Rapids, Ia	10,104	*15,426	20,000
Columbia, S. C	10,036	13,000	15,500
Knoxville, Tenn	9,693	11,000	35,000

* State offical census 1885.

† Estimated by State Officials.

OFFICIAL CENSUS OF THE UNITED STATES

In 1776 the population was 2,614,300 including slaves.

Date	Official Census	Date	Official Census
1790	3,929,827	1840	17,068,666
1800	5,305,940	1850	23,191,074
1810	7,239,814	1860	31,443,332
1820	9,638,190	1870	38,555,983
1830	12,866,020	1880	50,155,783

Estimated population (by State Officials) 1890 is 66,235,525.

THE CAPITOL CITY (WASHINGTON, D. C.)

The Capitol of the United States has been located at different times at the following places: At Philadelphia from Sept. 5, 1774, until December, 1776; at Baltimore from December 20, 1776, to March, 1777; at Philadelphia from March 4, 1777, to September, 1777; at Lancaster, Penn., from Sept. 27, 1777, to September 30, 1777; at York, Penn., from September 30, 1777, to July 1778; at Philadelphia from July 2, 1778, to June 30, 1783; at Princeton, N. J., June 30, 1783, to November 20, 1783; Annapolis, Md., November 26, 1783, to November 30, 1784; Trenton from November, 1784, to January, 1785; New York from January 11, 1785, to 1790; then the seat of government was removed to Philadelphia, where it remained until 1800, since which time it has been at Washington.

The cornerstone of the CAPITOL building was laid by President Washington in 1793, and the north only was completed when the Government took possession. In 1814 it was partially destroyed by fire, set by the British forces, but was immediately repaired. The entire building, as originally designed, was finally completed in 1827. The extensions subsequent were commenced in 1851 and completed in 1859. The Capitol is situated in latitude 38° 53' 20".4 north, longtitude 77° 00' 35".7 west. It fronts east, and stands on a plateau eighty-eight feet above the level of the Potomac. The entire length of the building from north to south is seven hundred and fifty-one feet four inches, and its greatest dimensions from east to west three hundred and fifty feet. The area covered is one hundred and fifty-three thousand one hundred and twelve square feet.

The dome was completed in 1865. It is of iron—crowned by a bronze statue of Freedom—and weighs 8,900,200 lbs. The statue of Freedom is nineteen feet six inches high, and weighs 14,985 pounds. The height of the dome is two hundred and eighty-seven feet five inches. Its diameter at the base is one hundred and thirty-five feet five inches. The rotunda is ninety-five feet six inches in diameter, and its height from the floor to the top of the canopy is one hundred and eighty feet three inches.

PEN NAMES OF POPULAR WRITERS

(Annual Statistican)

Pen Name

A. L. O. E. (A Lady of English).....................Mrs. C. Tucker

Artemus Ward............................. ....Charles F. Browne

Arthur Skethley......................................George Rose

Asa Trenchard.....................................Henry Watterson

Barry Cornwall.......................... Bryan Waller Procter

Betsy B..Mrs Mary Austin

Bibliophile.....................................S. A. Allibone

Bill Nye...William E. Nye

Boz...Charles Dickens

Brick Pomeroy.....................................Mark M. Pomeroy

Burleigh......................................Matthew Hale Smith

Carlton......... ....C. C. Coffin

*Clara Belle..................................Mrs. Wm. Thomson

Colly Cibber.....................................James Rees

Dick Tinto...F. B. Goodrich

Doesticks..M. Thompson

Elia...Charles Lamb

Eli Perkins.......................................M. D. Landon

Fanny Fern.....................................Mrs. James Parton

Fat Contributor........................ ....A. M. Griswold

Father Prout...........................Rev. Francis Mahoney

Frank Forrester.......................... ....Henry W. Herbert

Gail Hamilton...................................Mary M. Dodge

Gath...............................George Alfred Townsend

Geo. Eliot.............................Mrs. Lewes or Mrs Cross

Geo. Sand......................................Mme. Dudevant

Grace Greenwood.........................Mrs. S. J. C. Lippincott

Hans Breitman...............................Charles G. Leland

Harper's Easy Chair ....George W. Curtis

H. H....................................... ...Helen Hunt Jackson

Ik. Marvel...................................... Donald G. Mitchell

Irenæus.......... ....Rev. Dr. S. J. Prime

Jacob Omnium..................................M. J. Higgins

Jenny June.................................Mrs. J. C. Croly

John Phœnix..G. H. Derby'

Josh Billings ....H. W. Shaw

Joshua Coffin.............................Henry W. Longfellow

*Now name of a news syndicate.

Pen Names—*Continued*

Pen Name

J. S. of Dale ....F. J. Stimson
Junius..J. H. Brown
Knickerbocker...............................Washington Irving
Laicus.......................................Rev. Lyman Abbott
Marion Harland..............................Mrs. M. V. Terhune
Mark Twain..................................Samuel L. Clemens
Max Adler...C. H. Clark
Max O'Rell .... Paul Bluett
Miles O'Reilly................................C. G. Halpine
Miss Muloch ....Mrs. D. M. Craik
M. Quad.......................................Charles B. Lewis
Mrs. Partington................................B. P. Shillaber
Nellie Bly.......................................Mrs. Cochrane
Nym Crinkle........ ....A. C. Wheeler
Oliver Optic.................................William T. Adams
Orpheus C. Kerr...............................R. H. Newell
Ouida..................................... ....Louisa de la Rame
Our Member for Paris.............................H. Labouchere
Owen Meredith..............................Bulwer Lytton, Jr.
Perly...Ben. Perley Poore
Peter Parley..................... .... Samuel G. Goodrich
Peter Pindar....................................John Wolcott
Petroleum V. Nasby................................D. R. Locke
Philip Quilibet.................................George C. Pond
Pisistratus Brown....................William Black
Porte Crayon........................... ......D. H. Strother
Sam Slick............................Judge T. C. Haliburton
Saxcholm......................................Miss Rush Ellis
Shirley Dare....................................P. E. Dunning
Sophie Sparkle................................Jennie C. Hicks
Susan Coolidge...................................Miss Woolsey
Sylvanus Urban.............................Ed. Gent. Magazine
Sylvanus Cobb, Jr.....................................S. Cobb
Thomas Ingoldsby ....R. H. Barham
Timothy Titcomb...........................Dr. J. G. Holland
Trusta......................................Elizabeth S. Phelps
Veteran Observer.................................E. D. Mansfield
Warrington................................W. P. Robinson
Warwick...F. B. Ottarson

BRIEF HISTORY OF THE STANDARD SILVER DOLLAR

It was authorized to be coined, Act of Congress, April 2, 1792. Weight, 416 grains standard silver; fineness, 892.4; equivalent to 371¼ grains of fine silver, with 44¾ grains alloy of pure copper. Weight changed by Act of Congress January 18, 1837, to 412½ grains, and fineness changed to 900, preserving the same amount of pure silver, equivalent to 371¼ grains with $\frac{1}{10}$ alloy.

Coinage discontinued by Act of Congress, February 12, 1873.

Total amount coined from 1792 to 1873 was $8,045,838.

Coinage revived, two millions per month required to be coined, and issue made legal tender for all debts, public and private, Act of Congress February 28, 1878. Total amount coined from February 28, 1878 to November 1, 1885, was $213,257,594.

IMPORTANT EPOCHS AND ERAS

Epochs and Eras	Period of Commencement
Grecian Year of the World	September 1, B. C. 5598
Julian Period	January 1, B. C. 4713
Jewish Mundane Era	Vernal Equinox, B. C. 3761
Destruction of Troy	June, B. C. 1184
Building of Solomon's Temple	May, B. C. 1015
Era of Olympiads	New Moon, Summer Solstice, B. C. 776
Roman Era	April 24, B. C. 753
Era of Nebonasser	February 26, B. C. 747
Metonic Cycle	July 15, B. C. 432
Julian Year	January 1, B. C. 45
Augustan Era	February 14, B. C. 27
Indiction of Constantinople	September 1, B. C. 3
Christian Era	January 1, A. D. 1; A. M. 4004
Destruction of Jerusalem	September 21, A. D. 69
Era of Diocletian	September 17, A. D. 284
Era of Hegira	July 16, A. D. 622
Persian Era	June 16, A. D. 632
Conquest of England	October 14, A. D. 1066
Declaration American Independence	July 4, A. D. 1776

GENERALS COMMANDING THE UNITED STATES ARMY

Name	From	To
George Washington	1775	1783
Henry Knox	1783	1784
Josiah Harmer	1788	1791
Arthur St. Clair	1791	1796
James Wilkinson	1796	1798
George Washington	1799	1799
James Wilkinson	1800	1812
Henry Dearborn	1812	1815
Jacob Brown	1815	1828
Alexander Macomb	1828	1841
Winfield Scott	1841	1861
George B. McClellan	1861	1862
Henry W. Halleck	1862	1864
Ulysses S. Grant	1864	1869
William T. Sherman	1869	1883
Philip H. Sheridan	1883	1888
John M. Schofield	1888	

UNITED STATES CUSTOMS DUTIES
(Abridged)

Animals for breeding purposes...	free on Consular Certificate
" otherwise	20 per cent.
Ale, porter and beer, in bottles	35 cts. per gal.
" " " in casks	20 cts. per gal.
Books, charts, new	25 per cent.
" " for colleges, libraries, or printed more than 20 years, or in use abroad more than 1 year, and not for sale..	free
Boots, shoes, articles of leather	30 per cent.
Bronze, Manufactures of	45 per cent.
Carpets, aubusson, Axminster and all woven whole for room	45 cts. per sq. yd. and 30 per cent.
" Brussels tapestry, printed on the warp or otherwise	30 cts. per sq. yd. and 30 per cent.
" Saxony, Wilton & Tournay, velvet, wrought by the Jacquard machine	45 cts. per sq. yd. and 30 per cent.

United States Customs—*Continued*

Carpets, treble ingrain, three-ply and worsted China Venetian..............................	12 cts. per sq. yd. and 30 per cent.
" velvet, patent or tapestry, printed on the warp or otherwise......................	25 cts. per sq. yd. and 30 per cent.
Carriages....................................	35 per cent.
China—porcelain and parian ware, plain..........	55 per cent.
" gilded, ornamented or decorated..........	60 per cent.
Cigars, cheroots and cigarettes...................	$2.50 per lb. and 25 per cent.
Clocks, and parts of........................	30 per cent.
Clothing, wholly or in part of wool..............	35 cts. per lb. and 35 per cent.
" linen..................................	40 per cent.
" silk component........................	50 per cent.
" all other descriptions...................	35 per cent.
Coal, Bituminous	75 cts. per ton
Cotton, manufactures of.........................	35 per cent.
Cutlery, table, etc.............................	35 per cent.
" pen, jack, and pocket knives............	50 per cent.
Diamonds, unset...........................	10 per cent.
Engravings....................................	25 per cent.
Furniture	35 per cent.
Furs, manufactured...........................	30 per cent.
Gilt and Plated Ware, etc.......................	35 per cent.
Glass Ware....................................	45 per cent.
Gloves, kid...................................	50 per cent.
Gold and Silver Ware, etc.......................	45 per cent.
Guns, rifles, muskets..........................	25 per cent.
" sporting...............................	35 per cent.
Hats and bonnets of all kinds except wool........	30 per cent.
Iron, pig and scrap.............................	$6.72 per ton
" manufactures of...........................	45 per cent.
Jewelry, gold, silver, or imitation................	25 per cent.
Jewelry, jet, and imitations of...................	25 per cent.
Laces, silk, and silk and cotton..................	50 per cent.
" thread..............................	35 per cent.
Leather, manufactures of.......................	30 per cent.
Linen—table, toweling, etc......................	35 per cent.
Machinery, brass or Iron........................	45 per cent.
" copper or steel......................	45 per cent.
Musical Instruments............................	25 per cent.

United States Customs—*Continued*

Oils—animal and olive	25 per cent.
" castor	80 cts. per gal.
Paintings	30 per cent.
" If work of an American Artist	free
Photographs	25 per cent.
Pipes—Meerschaum wood, and of all other material except Common Clay (35 per cent.)	70 per cent.
Rubber Boots, shoes, and other articles wholly of Rubber (not fabrics)	25 per cent.
" Braces, Suspenders, Webbing, etc., unless in part silk	30 per cent.
" Silk, Cotton, Worsted or Leather	50 per cent.
Saddles and Harness	35 per cent.
Shawls—Silk	50 per cent.
" Camel's Hair or other wool	{35 cts. per lb. and 40 per ct.
Silk—dress and piece	50 per cent.
Skins, dressed	20 per cent.
Snuff	50 cts. per lb.
Soap—Castile	20 cts. per lb.
" fancy, perfumed, Toilet and Windsor	15 cts. per lb.
Statuary, marble	30 per cent.
Stereoscopic views on glass or paper	{40 and 25 per ct. respectively
Spirits—Brandy, whiskey, gin, etc.	$2 per proof gal.
Sugars, above No. 16, Dutch Standard	3 cts. per lb.
" " " 20, " "	3½ cts. per lb.
Tobacco, manufactured	40 cts. per lb.
Toys	35 per cent.
Umbrellas—Silk or alpaca	50 per cent.
Velvet—Silk	50 per cent.
" Cotton or mostly cotton	40 per cent.
Watches	25 per cent.
Wines—All *still* wines, such as Sherry, Claret or Hock in casks	50 cts per gal.
Ditto, per case of 12 bottles	$1.60 per case
All Champagnes and Sparkling Wines in cases of 1 doz. quarts or 2 doz. pints	$7 per case (and bottles extra, 3 cts. each).

Articles Free of Duty

Actors' Costumes and Effects intended for personal use.
Animals for breeding purposes.
Antiquities not for sale.
Articles and Tools of Trade.
Art Works of American Artists.
Bed Feathers.
Birds, Land and Water Fowl.
Books printed over 20 years.
Bullion, Gold and Silver.
Coal, Anthracite.
Cocoa, crude.
Coffee.
Collections of Antiquities, etc, for use in Colleges, Museums, Incorporated Societies, etc.
Diamonds, rough.
Drugs, crude, used in dyeing or tanning.
Effects of American citizens dying abroad, if accompanied by Consular certificate.
Engravings (engraved over 20 years).
Farina.
Fertilizers—Manures.
Fruits and Nuts, green, ripe, dried.
Furs, undressed.
Hides, raw.
Household effects in use abroad over one year, and not for sale.
India Rubber, crude.
Instruments, professional, in use.
Macaroni and Vermicelli.
Mineral Waters, natural.
Natural History Specimens (not for sale).
Newspapers and Periodicals.
Olives.
Plants, Trees and Shrubs.
Rags, not wool, for paper stock.
Sausages, Bologna, German, Skins.
Scientific Instruments for colleges.
Skins, raw.
Tapioca.
Tea.
Tin in bars and pigs.

U. S. Manufactures forwarded to foreign countries and returned.
Vines and Vine Cuttings.
Wax, vegetable and mineral.
Personal Effects when old and in use over one year.*

* NOTE.—Personal effects, when old and in use *over one year*, can be entered free, provided they accompany the owners, or the owners can take oath that they have arrived in the United States within *one year* prior to the date of arrival of the goods, specifying steamer and date upon which they arrived. If the owners have not arrived within the year, duty must be paid on appraisement. Household effects, books and libraries; if used abroad *not less* than one year, and not intended for any other person, nor for sale, are entitled to *free entry*, even if the owners have resided *more than one year* in the United States. Old clothing and household effects sent as presents are dutiable. Paintings, statuary, and other works are embraced in the term "household effects." Horses, carriages and saddlery are now embraced in the term "household effects." Duty must be paid on all watches but *one* brought by a single passenger. Each passenger is entitled to bring with him fifty cigars. If above that quantity, they are liable to duty or seizure, as the case may arise.

AVERAGE PERCENTAGE OF ALCOHOL IN WINES AND LIQUORS

Name	Per Cent.	Name	Per Cent.
Beer	4.0	Sherry	19.0
Porter	4.5	Vermouth	19.0
Ale	7.4	Malmsey	19.7
Cider	8.6	Marsala	20.2
Perry	8.8	Madeira	21.0
Elder	9.3	Port	23.2
Moselle	9.6	Curacoa	27.0
Tokay	10.2	Aniseed	33.0
Rhine	11.0	Maraschino	34.0
Orange	11.2	Chartreuse	43.0
Bordeaux	11.5	Gin	51.6
Hock	11.6	Brandy	53.4
Gooseberry	11.8	Rum	53.7
Champagne	12.2	Whiskey, Irish	53.9
Claret	13.3	Whiskey, Bourbon	54.0
Burgundy	13.6	Whiskey, Rye	54.0
Malaga	17.3	Whiskey, Scotch	54.3
Canary	18.8	Cognac	55.0

The per centage as above is by volume. "Proof Spirit" contains 49.24 per cent. by weight, or 57.06 per cent. by volume of absolute alcohol.

Rifles Used in the Armies of Different Nations

Hebler Rifle is used by Switzerland, calibre .30 inch, powder 65 grains, bullet 270 grains, muzzle velocity 1,750 feet per second.

Jarmann Rifle is used by Sweden and Norway, weight 10 lbs. 1½ oz., calibre .30 inch, powder 77 grains, bullet 337 grains, muzzle velocity 1,536 feet per second.

Lee Rifle is used by Great Britain, calibre .30 inch, powder 70 grains, bullet 217 grains, muzzle velocity 1,700 feet per second.

Lebel Rifle is used by France and Russia, calibre .31 inch, muzzle velocity 1,760 feet per second.

Mannlicher Rifle is used by Austria, calibre .31 inch, powder 62 grains, bullet 240 grains, muzzle velocity 1,700 feet per second.

Mauser Rifle is used by Germany, weight 10 lbs. 2 oz., calibre .43 inch, powder 77 grains, bullet 386 grains, muzzle velocity 1,410 feet per second.

Peabody-Martine Rifle is used by Turkey, weight 9 lbs. 6 oz., calibre .45 inch, powder 70 grains, bullet 370 grains, muzzle velocity 1,400 feet per second.

Remington Rifle is used by Spain and Denmark, weight 9 lbs., calibre .45 inch, powder 70 grains, bullet 386 grains, muzzle velocity 1,340 feet per second.

Springfield Rifle is used by the United States, weight 9 lbs. 4 oz., calibre .45 inch, powder 70 grains, bullet 500 grains.

Vetterli Rifle is used by Italy, weight 10 lbs. 8 oz., calibre .41 inch, powder 55 grains, bullet 312 grains, muzzle velocity 1,427 feet per second.

How to Secure a Copyright

Send by mail or otherwise prepared a *printed* copy of the title (and two copies after publication) of the book, map, chart, dramatic or musical composition, engraving, cut, print, or photograph, or a *description* of the painting, drawing, chromo, statue, statuary, or model or design for a work of the fine arts, for which copyright is desired, addressed, Librarian of Congress, Washington, D. C. The legal fee is 50 cents, and for a *copy* of this record an additional fee of 50 cents is required, making $1, which must be inclosed.

No copyright is valid unless notice is given by inserting in every copy published, on the title page or the page following, if it be a book; or, if a map, chart, musical composition, print, cut, engraving, photograph, painting, drawing, chromo, statue, statuary, or model or design intended to be perfected as a work of the fine arts, by inscribing upon some portion thereof, or on the substance on which the same is mounted, the following words, viz: *"Entered according to act of Congress, in the year*———, *by* ————, *in the office of the Librarian of Congress, at Washington."*

The original term of copyright runs for twenty-eight years. *Within six months before* the end of that time, the author or designer, or his widow or children, may secure a renewal for the further term of fourteen years, making forty-two years in all. Citizens or residents of the United States only are entitled to copyright.

How to Apply for a Patent

A patent may be obtained by any person who has invented or discovered any new and useful art, machine, manufacture, or composition of matter, or any new or useful improvement thereof, not known nor used by others in this country, and not patented nor described in any printed publication in this or any foreign country, before his invention or discovery thereof, and not in public use or on sale for more than two years prior to his application, unless the same is proved to have been abandoned.

Application must be made to the Commissioner of Patents, signed by the inventor, by his executors or administrators, A complete application comprises the first fee of $15, a petition, specification, and oath; and drawings, model, or specimen when required. The petition, specification, and oath must be in the English language, and furnished to the Patent Office at Washington, D. C.

How to Apply for a Cadetship

How Appointments are made.—The appointments (except those *at large*) are made by the Secretary of War or Navy at the request of the Representative in Congress from the District; and the person appointed must be an actual resident of the District from which the appointment is made. Appointments *at large* are conferred by the President of the United States.

Manner of Making Applications.—Applications can be made by letter to the Secretary of War or Navy to have the name of the applicant placed upon the register that it may be furnished to the proper Representative or Delegate when a vacancy occurs. The application must exhibit the full name, exact age and permanent abode of the applicant, with the number of the Congressional District in which his residence is situated. Appointments are made one year in advance of the date of admission.

Qualifications.—The age for admission of cadets to the Academy vacancies at West Point and Annapolis is between seventeen and twenty-two years. Candidates must be unmarried, at least 5 feet in height, free from any infection or immoral disorder and from any deformity, disease or infirmity which might render them unfit for military or naval service. They must be well versed in reading, writing, orthography, arithmetic, English grammar, descriptive geography (particularly of our own country), and of the history of the United States. Upon receiving his appointment the cadet is ordered to report to the Superintendent of the Academy in time to appear before the Academic Board for examination at its meeting early in June. Upon arrival, he is subjected to a rigid physical examination by a board of experienced surgeons. If he passes this successfully, he is then examined by the Academic Board. These examinations are made promptly after the candidate reports to the Superintendent.

How to Apply for a Pension

Declaration of pension claimants must be made before any court of record or before some officer thereof having custody of its seal. Printed instructions and forms (for filling in) can be had, free of expense on application by letter to the Commissioner of Pensions at Washington, D. C. In it should be set forth the company and regiment in which the applicant served, the name of the commanding officer of the company or organization and the dates of enlistment and discharge. In navy cases the vessel upon which the claimant served should be stated.

The applicant should state his office addresses accurately and his identity must be shown by the testimony of two credible witnesses, who must appear with him before the officer by whom the declaration may be taken.

The nature of the evidence required to sustain a claim for a pension will be indicated to the claimant upon the filing of the declaration, which should be forwarded to the Commissioner of Pensions, Washington, D. C.

How to Obtain a Passport

Send five dollars to the Secretary of State, Washington, D. C. A blank will be returned to you, which on filling out, certifying to it before a Notary Public or Justice of the Peace and forwarding it to the Secretary of State, a passport will be issued. Every passport must be renewed within one year of its date. The oath of allegiance is required in all cases. When husband, wife and minor children travel together a single passport will suffice. For any other person in the party, except servants, a separate passport is required. The possession of a passport is obligatory on the Franco-Spanish frontier and may be of advantage elsewhere at any time.

THE BRITISH EMPIRE
The United Kingdom

Countries	Area Sq. Miles	How Acq. by Eng.	Date	Pop. 1881
England	50,823			24,613,926
Wales	7,363	Conquest	1282	1,360,513
Scotland	29,820	Union	1603	3,735,517
Ireland	32,531	Conquest	1172	5,174,836
Islands	295			140,260

COLONIES AND DEPENDENCIES
Europe

Countries	Area Sq. Miles	How Acq. by Eng.	Date	Pop. Est. 1890
Gibraltar	2	Conquest	1704	25,000
Malta, etc.	122	Treaty Session	1814	163,000
Heligoland	¾	Treaty Cession	1814	2,000

Asia

Countries	Area Sq. Miles	How Acq. by Eng.	Date	Population
India, including Burmah	1,649,000	Conquest .... Began 1757 Trans. f'm E. In. Co 1858		272,000,000
Ceylon	25,365	Treaty cession	1801	2,850,000
Cyprus	3,584	Con. with Turkey	1878	187,000
Aden and Socotra	3,584	(Aden) Conquest	1839	40,000
Straits Settlements	1,500	Treaty cession	1785–1824	500,000
Hong Kong	30½	Treaty cession	1872	1,406,000
British North Borneo	31,000	Cession to company	1877	150,000

Africa

Countries	Area Sq. Miles	How Acq. by England	Date	Population
Cape Colony	217,895	Treaty cession	1588–1814	1,400,000
Natal	19,000	Annexation	1843	450,000
St. Helena	47	Conquest	1673	5,000
Ascension	38	Annexation	1815	200
Sierra Leone	3,000	Settlement	1787	62,000
Gold Coast, etc	29,401	Treaty cession	1872	1,406,000
Mauritius, etc.	1,063	Conquest and cession	1810–1814	372,000

America

Countries	Area Sq. Miles	How Acq. by Eng.	Date	Population
Canada proper	370,488	Conquest	1759–60	} 5,000,000
New Brunswick	27,174	Treaty cession	1763	
Nova Scotia	20,907	Conquest	1627	
Manitoba	60,520	Settlement	1813	
British Columbia, etc	341 305	Transfer to Crown	1858	
Northwest Tys.	3,257,500	Charter to Company	1670	
Prince Edward Is.	2,133	Conquest	1745	
Newfoundland	42,200	Settlement	1583	198,000
British Guiana	76,000	Conquest and cession	1803–14	260,000
British Honduras	7,562	Conquest	1798	28,000
Jamaica	4,193	Conquest	1655	581,000
Trinidad	1,754	Conquest	1797	153,000
Barbadoes	166	Settlement	1605	171,860
Bahamas	5,794	Settlement	1629	48,000
Bermuda	41	Settlement	1612	15,000
Other Islands	8,755			274,000

Australasia

Countries	Area Sq. Miles	How Acq. by Eng.	Date	Population
New South Wales	310,700	Settlement	1788	} 4,000,000
Victoria	87,884	Settlement	1832	
South Australia	903,690	Settlement	1836	
Queensland	668,497	Settlement	1824	
Western Australia	1,060,000	Settlement	1828	
Tasmania	26,215	Settlement	1803	
New Zealand	104,032	Purchase	1845	
Fiji	7,423	Cession fm the Natives	1874	
New Guinea (British)	234,768	Annexation	1884	

NATIONAL DEBT OF THE UNITED STATES

Principal of the National Debt of the United States on January 1st, of each year from 1791 to 1842 inclusive; and on July 1st of each year from 1843 to 1886 inclusive and on December 1, 1887, 1888, 1889.

Year	Date	Amount	Year	Date	Amount
1791	Jan. 1,	$ 75,463,476.52	1841	Jan. 1,	$ 13,594,480.73
1792	"	77,217,924.66	1842	"	20,601,226 28
1793	"	80,352,634.00	1843	July 1,	32,742,922.00
1794	"	78,427,404.77	1844	"	23,461,652.50
1795	"	80,747,587.39	1845	"	15,925,303.01
1796	"	83,762,172.07	1846	"	15,550,202.97
1797	"	82,064,479.33	1847	"	38,826,534.77
1798	"	79,228,529.12	1848	"	47,044,862.23
1799	"	78,408,669.77	1849	"	63,061,858.69
1800	"	82,976,294.35	1850	"	63,452,773.55
1801	"	83,038,050.80	1851	"	68,304,796.02
1802	"	86,712,632.25	1852	"	66,199,341.71
1803	"	77,054,686.30	1853	"	59,803,117.70
1804	"	86,727,120.88	1854	"	42,242,222.42
1805	"	82,312,150.50	1855	"	35,586,858.56
1806	"	75,723,270.66	1856	"	31,972,537.90
1807	"	69,218,398.64	1857	"	28,699,831.85
1808	"	65,196,317.97	1858	"	44,911,881.03
1809	"	57,023,192.09	1859	"	58,496,837.88
1810	"	53,173,217.52	1860	"	64,842,287.88
1811	"	48 005,587.76	1861	"	90,580,873,72
1812	"	45,209,737.90	1862	"	524,176,412.13
1813	"	55,962,827.57	1863	"	1,119,772,138.63
1814	"	81,487,846.24	1864	"	1,815,784,370.57
1815	"	99,833,660.15	1865	"	2,680,647,869.74
1816	"	127,334,933.74	1866	"	2,773,236,173.69
1817	"	123,491,965.16	1867	"	2,678,126,103.87
1818	"	103,466,633.83	1868	"	2,611,687,851.19
1819	"	95,529,648.28	1869	"	2,588,452,213.94
1820	"	91,015,566.15	1870	"	2,480,672,427.81
1821	"	89,987,427.66	1871	"	2,353,211,332.32
1822	"	93,546,676.98	1872	"	2,253,251,328.78
1823	"	90,875,877.28	1873	"	2,234,482,993.20
1824	"	90,269,777.77	1874	"	2,251,690,468.43
1825	"	83,788,432.71	1875	"	2,232,284,531.95
1826	"	81,054,059.99	1876	"	2,180,395,067.15
1827	"	73,987,357.20	1877	"	2,205,301,392.10
1828	"	67,475,043.87	1878	"	2,256,205,892.53
1829	"	58,421,413.67	1879	"	2,349,567,232.04
1830	"	48,565,406.50	1880	"	2,128,791,054.63
1831	"	39,123,191.68	1881	"	2,077,389,253.58
1832	"	24,322,235.18	1882	"	1,926,688,678.03
1833	"	7,001,698.83	1883	"	1,892,547,412.07
1834	"	4,760,082.08	1884	"	1,838,904,607.57
1835	"	37,513.05	1885	"	1,872,340,557.14
1836	"	336,957.83	1886	"	1,783,438,697.78
1837	"	3,308,124.07	1887	Dec. 1,	1,664,461,536.38
1838	"	10,434,221.14	1888	"	1,680,917,706.23
1839	"	3,573,343.82	1889	"	1,617,372,419.53
1840	"	5,250,875.54			

NATIONAL DEBT OF PRINCIPAL COUNTRIES
OF THE WORLD

Countries	Fiscal Year	National Debt
Argentine Republic	1888	$ 134,672,500
*Australian Colonies	1887	787,692,665
Austria-Hungary	1888	1,741,035,609
Austria	1887	442,286,301
Hungary	1887	749,120,480
Belgium	1888	422,464,275
Bolivia	1888	6,500,000
Brazil	1885	565,035,000
Chili	1888	80,568,887
China	1886	38,500,000
Colombia, U. S. of	1887	29,163,480
Denmark	1887	54,369,325
Dominion of Canada	1889	286,702,731
Ecuador	1887	13,738,490
Egypt	1888	518,623,840
France	1889	4,289,815,222
Germany	1888	191,552,000
German States	1887	1,827,977,750
Great Britain	1889	3,492,154,855
Greece	1888	91,618,340
Hawaiian Islands	1887	1,936,500
India, British	1887	928,355,780
Italy	1887	2,246,903,485
Japan	1888	249,108,517
Mexico	1887	128,300,000
Netherlands	1887	452,000,000
Norway	1887	37,596,079
Paraguay	1887	5,151,891
Persia	1886	No debt
Peru	1887	367,226,890
Portugal	1888	490,493,599
Roumania	1886	171,292,560
Russia	1887	3,669,944,394
Servia	1888	62,550,000
Spain	1886	1,266,456,840
Sweden	1887	66,412,279
Switzerland	1888	7,543,273
Turkey	1887	522,293,530
United States	1889	(See United States National Debt)
Uruguay	1887	72,205,722
Venezuela	1887	20,556,260

* Including also New Zealand and Tasmania.

Governors of California

Spanish Rule

Name	Date	Name	Date
Gasparde Portala	1767–1771	*Jose J. de Arrilaga	1792–1794
Felipe do Barri	1771–1774	Diego do Borica	1794–1800
Felipe de Nevo	1774–1782	Jose J. de Arrilaga	1800–1814
Pedro Fajes	1782–1790	*Jose Arguello	1814–1815
Jose Antonio Romea	1790–1792	Pablo Vincente de Sola,	1815–1822

Mexican Rule

Name	Date	Name	Date
Pablo Vincente de Sola,	1822–1822	*Jose Castro	1835–1836
Louis Arguello	1823–1825	Nicolas Gutierrez	1836–1836
Jose do Echeandia	1825–1831	Juan B. Alvarado	1836–1842
Manuel Victoria	1831–1832	Manuel Micheltoreno	1842–1845
*Pio Pico	1832–1833	Pio Pico	1845–1846
Jose Figueroa	1833–1835		

United States Military

Name	Date	Name	Date
Com. John D. Sloat	1846–1846	Gen. S. W. Kearney	1847–1847
Com. R. F. Stockton	1846–1847	Col. R. B. Mason	1847–1849
Col. John C. Fremont.	1847–1847	Gen. Bennet Riley	1849–1849

State

Name	Date	Name	Date
†Peter H. Bennett	1849–1851	Henry H. Haight	1867–1871
John McDougall	1851–1852	†Newton Booth	1871–1875
John Bigler	1852–1856	Romualdo Pacheco	1875–1875
J. Neely Johnson	1856–1858	William Irwin	1875–1880
John B. Weller	1858–1860	George Perkins	1880–1883
†Milton S. Latham	1860–1860	George Stoneman	1883–1887
John G. Downey	1860–1862	Washington Bartlett	1887–1887
Leland Stanford	1862–1863	R. W. Waterman	1887
Frederick F. Low	1863–1867		

* *Ad interim.*
† Resigned.

PHILOSOPHICAL FACTS

The greatest height at which visible clouds ever exist does not exceed ten miles.

Air is about 815 times lighter than water.

The pressure of the atmosphere upon every square foot of the earth amounts to 2,160 pounds.

An ordinary-sized man, supposing his surface to be fourteen square feet, sustains the enormous atmospheric pressure of 30,240 pounds.

The barometer falls one-tenth of an inch for every seventy-eight feet elevation.

The violence of the expansion of water when freezing is sufficient to cleave a globe of copper of such thickness as to require a force of 27,000 pounds to produce the same effect.

During the conversion of ice into water 140 degrees of heat are absorbed.

Water when converted into steam increases in bulk 1,728 times.

Power of steam, steam as compared with water, occupies 1,728 times as much space. A cubic inch of water will make 1,728 cubic inches of steam at atmospheric pressure. Now, if this steam is compressed into half the space it occupies at atmospheric pressure, it will double that pressure, or 15 pounds above the atmosphere; it will then occupy only 864 cubic inches; if reduced again to half its volume, it will occupy 432 cubic inches and will have 30 pounds pressure. Reduced again to half this volume, the steam will occupy 216 cubic inches, and will have 60 pounds pressure to the square inch. We can go on reducing in this way until we find that a cubic inch of water turned into steam and compressed into a space of 3 cubic inches will have the somewhat enormous pressure of 3,840 pounds to the square inch.

Were a cannon-ball shot towards the sun and were it to maintain full speed, it would be twenty years in reaching it ; and yet light travels through this space (91,000,000 miles) in seven or eight minutes.

In one second of time, in one beat of the pendulum of a clock, light travels 192,000 miles.

Strange as it may appear, a ball of a ton weight and another of the same material of an ounce weight, falling from any height, will reach the ground at the same time.

The heat does not increase as we rise above the earth nearer the sun, but decreases rapidly until, beyond the regions of the atmosphere, in void, it is estimated that the cold is about 70 degrees below zero. The line of perpetual frost at the equator is 15,000 feet altitude, 13,000 feet between the tropics and 9,000 to 4,000 feet between the latitudes of 40 degrees and 49 degrees.

At a depth of 45 feet under the ground the temperature of the earth is uniform throughout the year.

In summer time the season of ripening moves northward at the rate of 10 miles a day.

The human ear is so extremely sensitive that it can hear a sound that lasts only the twenty-four thousandth part of a second.

The ordinary pressure of the atmosphere on the surface of the earth is 2,160 pounds to each square foot, or 15 pounds to each square inch, equal to 30 perpendicular inches of mercury or 34½ feet of water.

Sound travels at the rate of 1,142 feet per second, about 13 miles in a minute; so that if we hear a clap of thunder half a minute after the flash, we may calculate that the discharge of electricity is six and one-half miles away.

Lightning can be seen by reflection at a distance of two hundred miles.

The explosive force of closely confined gunpowder is six and a half tons to the square inch.

STRENGTH OF MATERIALS

Showing the Strength or Force Required to Tear Asunder One Square Inch

Materials	Pounds
Iron Wire, Wrought	103,000
Swedish Bar Iron	72,000
Russian Bar Iron	59,500
Mean of English Iron	53,900
Gun Metal, Mean of Iron	37,232
Clyde, No. 1 Iron	16,125
Clyde, No. 2 Iron	23,468
Sterling, Mean of Iron	25,764
American, Mean of Iron	45,970
Low Moor, No. 2 Cast Iron	14,076
Crank Shaft Iron	44,750
American Boiler Iron	48,000
American Plates Iron	62,000
English Plates, Mean	51,000
English Plates, Lengthwise	53,860
English Plates, Crosswise	48,800
German Piano Steel Wire	268,800
Cast Steel, Maximum	142,000
Cast Steel, Mean	88,000

Strength of Materials—*Continued*

Materials	Pounds
Steel	100,000 to 130,000
Chromo Steel, Mean	170,980
Shear Steel	124,000
Blistered Steel	133,000
Blistered Steel, Soft	104,000
Razor Steel	15,000
Steel Plates, Lengthwise	96,300
Steel Plates, Crosswise	93,700
Yellow Metal	48,700
Cast Copper	19,000
American Copper	24,250
Copper Bolts	38,000
Copper Wire	60,000
Brass Wire	50,000
Brass	42,000
Gold	20,490
Gold 5 Parts, Copper 1 Part	50,000
Silver, Cast	40,997
Bronze	17,698 to 56,788
Tin, Cast, Block	5,000
Tin, Banca	2,122
Platinum Wire	5,300
Zinc	7,000
Sheet Lead	3,000
Antimony	1,060
Bismuth, Cast	3,120
Ivory	16,070
Manila Rope	9,300
Tarred Hemp Rope	15,000
Wire Rope	37,000
Whalebone	7,600
Leather Belting	333
Gutta-percha	3,500
Slate	12,000
Well-burned Brick	750
Inferior Brick	100 to 290
Portland Stone	875 to 1,000
Crown Glass	42,346
Limestone	670 to 2,800
Hydraulic Lime	140
Hydraulic Cement	234
Portland Cement	414
Plaster of Paris	72

POPULAR AND ELECTORAL VOTES FOR PRESIDENTS

YEAR	CANDIDATES	PARTY	POPULAR VOTE	ELECTORAL VOTE
1824	Andrew Jackson	Democrat	152,872	99
1824	John Q. Adams	Federal	105,321	84
1824	W. H. Crawford	Republican	44,282	41
1824	Henry Clay	Republican	46,587	37
1828	Andrew Jackson	Democrat	647,231	178
1828	John Q. Adams	Federal	509,097	83
1832	Andrew Jackson	Democrat	687,502	219
1832	Henry Clay	Nat. Republican	530,189	49
1832	John Floyd	Whig		11
1832	William Wirt	Whig		7
1836	Martin Van Buren	Democrat	761,549	170
1836	W. H. Harrison	Whig	⎫	73
1836	Hugh L. White	Whig	⎬ 736,656	23
1836	Daniel Webster	Whig		14
1836	W. P. Mangum	Whig	⎭	11
1840	W. H. Harrison	Whig	1,275,017	234
1840	Martin Van Buren	Democrat	1,128,702	60
1840	J. G. Birney	Liberty	62,300	
1844	James K. Polk	Democrat	1,337,243	170
1844	Henry Clay	Whig	1,299,068	105
1844	J. G. Birney	Liberty	62,300	
1848	Zachary Taylor	Whig	1,360,101	163
1848	Lewis Cass	Democrat	1,220,544	127
1848	Martin Van Buren	Free Soil	291,263	
1852	Franklin Pierce	Democrat	1,601,474	254
1852	Winfield Scott	Whig	1,386,578	42
1852	John P. Hale	Free Soil	156,149	
1856	James Buchanan	Democrat	1,838,169	174
1856	John C. Fremont	Republican	1,341,264	114
1856	Millard Fillmore	American	874,534	8
1860	Abraham Lincoln	Republican	1,866,352	180
1860	Stephen A. Douglas	Democrat	1,375,157	12
1860	John C. Breckinridge	Democrat	845,763	72
1860	John Bell	Union	589,581	39
1864	Abraham Lincoln	Republican	2,216,067	212
1864	Geo. B. McClellan	Democrat	1,808,725	21
1868	U. S. Grant	Republican	3,015,071	214
1868	Horatio Seymour	Democrat	2,709,613	80

Electoral Votes—*Continued*

Year	Candidates	Party	Popular Vote	Electorial Vote
1872	U. S. Grant	Republican	3,597,070	286
1872	Horace Greeley	Liberal and Democrat	2,834,079	63
1872	Charles O'Connor	Democrat	29,408	
1872	James Black	Temperance	5,608	
1876	R. B. Hayes	Republican	4,033,950	185
1876	Samuel J. Tilden	Democrat	4,284,757	184
1876	Peter Cooper	Greenback	81,740	
1876	G. C. Smith	Prohibition	9,522	
1876	Scattering		2,636	
1880	James A. Garfield	Republican	4,439,745	214
1880	Winfield S. Hancock	Democrat	4,435,911	155
1880	James B. Weaver	Greenback	306,219	
1884	Grover Cleveland	Democrat	4,845,253	219
1884	James G. Blaine	Republican	4,818,671	182
1884	Benj. F. Butler	Greenback	270,359	
1884	John P. St. John	Prohibition	150,767	
1888	Benjamin Harrison	Republican	5,439,877	233
1888	Grover Cleveland	Democrat	5,538,421	168
1888	Clinton B. Fisk	Prohibition	251,147	
1888	A. J. Streeter	Labor Vote	145,961	

How the States have Voted Presidential Elections from 1824 to 1888

	1824	1828	1832	1836	1840	1844	1848	1852	1856
Alabama	D.	D.	D.	D.	D.	D.	D.	D.	D.
Arkansas				D.	D.	D.	D.	D.	D.
California								D.	D.
Colorado									
Connecticut	R.	R.	N. R.	D.	W.	W.	W.	D.	R.
Delaware	W.	R.	N. R.	W.	W.	W.	W.	D.	D.
Florida							W.	D.	D.
Georgia	W.	D.	D.	W.	W.	D.	W.	D.	D.
Illinois	D.	D.	D.	D.	D.	D.	D.	D.	D.
Indiana	D.	D.	D.	W.	W.	D.	D.	D.	D.
Iowa							D.	D.	R.
Kansas									
Kentucky	W.	D.	N. R.	W.	W.	W.	W.	W.	D.
Louisiana	D.	D.	D.	D.	W.	D.	W.	D.	D.
Maine	R.	R.	D.	D.	W.	D.	D.	D.	R.
Maryland	D.	R.	N. R.	W.	W.	W.	W.	D.	A.
Massachusetts	R.	R.	N. R.	W.	W.	W.	W.	W.	R.
Michigan				D.	W.	D.	D.	D.	R.
Minnesota									
Mississippi	D.	D.	D.	D.	W.	D.	D.	D.	D.
Missouri	W.	D.	D.	D.	D.	D.	D.	D.	D.
Nebraska									
Nevada									
New Hampshire	R.	R.	D.	D.	D.	D.	D.	D.	R.
New Jersey	D.	R.	D.	W.	W.	W.	W.	D.	D.
New York	R.	D.	D.	D.	W.	D.	W.	D.	R.
North Carolina	D.	D.	D.	D.	W.	W.	W.	D.	D.
Ohio	W	D.	D.	W.	W.	W.	D.	D.	R.
Oregon									
Pennsylvania	D.	D.	D.	D.	W.	D.	W.	D.	D.
Rhode Island	R.	R.	N. R.	D.	W.	W.	W.	D.	R.
South Carolina	D.	D.	W.	W.	D.	D.	D.	D.	D.
Tennessee	D.	D.	D.	W.	W.	W.	W.	W.	D,
Texas							D.	D.	D.
Vermont	R.	R.	A. M.	W.	W.	W.	W.	W.	R.
Virginia	W.	D.	D.	D.	D.	D.	D.	D.	D.
West Virginia									
Wisconsin							D.	D.	R.

Presidential Elections—*Continued*

	1860	1864	1868	1872	1876	1880	1884	1888
Alabama	D.	....	R.	R.	D.	D.	D.	D.
Arkansas	D.	....	R.	R.	D.	D.	D.	D.
California	R.	R.	R.	R.	R.	D.	R.	R.
Colorado	....	....	....	....	....	R.	R.	R.	R.
Connecticut	R.	R.	R.	R.	D.	R.	D.	D.
Delaware	D.	D.	D.	R.	D.	D.	D.	D.
Florida	D.	....	R.	R.	R.	D.	D.	D.
Georgia	D.	....	D.	D.	D.	D.	D.	D.
Illinois	R.	R.	R.	R.	R.	R.	R.	R.
Indiana	R.	R.	R.	R.	D.	R.	D.	R.
Iowa	R.	R.	R.	R.	R.	R.	R.	R.
Kansas	....	R.	R.	R.	R.	R.	R.	R.
Kentucky	U.	.	D.	D.	D.	D.	D.	D.
Louisiana	D.	....	D.	R.	R.	D.	D.	D.
Maine	R.	R.	R.	R.	R.	R.	R.	R.
Maryland	D.	R.	D.	D.	D.	D.	D.	D.
Massachusetts	R.	R.	R.	R.	R.	R.	R.	R.
Michigan	R.	R.	R.	R.	R.	R.	R.	R.
Minnesota	R.	R.	R.	R.	R.	R.	R.	R.
Mississippi	D.	....	....	R.	D.	D.	D.	D.
Missouri	D.	R.	R.	D.	D.	D.	D.	D.
Nebraska	....	....	R.	R.	R.	R.	R.	R.
Nevada	....	R.	R.	R.	R.	D.	R.	R.
New Hampsh're	R.	R.	R.	R.	R.	R.	R.	R.
New Jersey	D.	D.	D.	R.	D.	D.	D.	D.
New York	R.	R.	D.	R.	R.	R.	D.	R.
North Carolina	D.	....	R.	R.	D.	D.	D.	D.
Ohio	R.	R.	R.	R.	R.	R.	R.	R.
Oregon	R.	R.	D.	R.	R.	R.	R.	R.
Pennsylvania	R.	R.	R.	R.	R.	R.	R.	R.
Rhode Island	R.	R.	R.	R.	R.	R.	R.	R.
South Carolina	D.	....	R.	R.	R.	D.	D.	D.
Tennessee	U.	....	R.	D.	D.	D.	D.	D.
Texas	D.	....	....	D	D.	D.	D.	D.
Vermont	R.	R.	R.	R.	R.	R.	R.	R.
Virginia	U.	....	....	R.	D.	D.	D.	D.
West Virginia	....	R.	R.	R.	D.	D.	D.	D.
Wisconsin	R.	R.	R.	R.	R.	R.	R.	R.

R—Republican. W—Whig. D—Democratic. U—Union. A—American. A. M.—Anti-Masonic. N. R.—National Republican.

BIOGRAPHIES OF THE PRESIDENTS OF THE UNITED STATES

George Washington was born February 22, 1732, near Bridges' Creek, Westmoreland County, Virginia; paternal ancestors were English; vocation in early life was surveyor, when elected planter; religious connection Episcopalian; died December 14, 1799.

John Adams was born October 19, 1735; Quincy, Norfolk County, Massachusetts; paternal ancestors were English; vocation in early life teacher, when elected lawyer; religious connection Congregationalist; died July 4, 1826.

Thomas Jefferson was born April 2, 1743; Shadwell, Albemarle County, Virginia; paternal ancestors were Welsh; vocation in early life lawyer, when elected the same; religious connection Liberal; died July 4, 1826.

James Madison was born March 16, 1751; Port Conway, King George County, Virginia; paternal ancestors were English; vocation in early life lawyer, when elected the same; religious connection Episcopalian; died June 28, 1836.

James Monroe was born April 28, 1758; head of Monroe's Creek, Westmoreland County, Virginia; paternal ancestors were Scotch; vocation in early life lawyer, when elected statesman; religious connection Episcopalian; died July 4, 1831.

John Quincy Adams was born July 11, 1767; Quincy, Norfolk County, Massachusetts; paternal ancestors were English; vocation in early life lawyer, when elected the same; religious connection Congregationalist; died February 21, 1848.

Andrew Jackson was born March 15, 1767; near Cureton's Pond, Union County, North Carolina; paternal ancestors were Scotch-Irish; vocation in early life lawyer, when elected the same; religious connection Presbyterian; died June 8, 1845.

Marti Van Buren was born December 5, 1782; Kinderhook, Columbia County, New York; paternal ancestors were Dutch; vocation in early life lawyer, when elected the same; religious connection Reformed Dutch; died July 24, 1862.

William Henry Harrison was born February 9, 1773, Berkeley, Charles City County, Virginia; paternal ancestors were English; vocation in early life soldier, when elected farmer; religious connection Episcopalian; died April 4, 1841.

John Tyler was born March 29, 1790; Greenway, Charles City County, Virginia; paternal ancestors were English; vocation in early life lawyer, when elected the same; religious connection Episcopalian; died January 18, 1862.

James Knox Polk was born November 2, 1795; near Pineville, Mecklenburgh County, North Carolina; paternal ancestors were Scotch-Irish; vocation in early life lawyer, when elected the same; religious connection Presbyterian; died June 15, 1849.

Zachary Taylor was born September 24, 1784; near Orange Court House, Orange County, Virginia; paternal ancestors were English; vocation in early life soldier, and when elected the same; religious connection Episcopalian; died July 9, 1850.

Millard Fillmore was born January 7, 1800; Summerhill, Cayuga County, New York; paternal ancestors were English; vocation in early life tailor, when elected lawyer; religious connection Episcopalian, died March 8, 1874.

Franklin Pierce was born November 23, 1804; Hillsborough, Hillsborough County, New Hampshire; paternal ancestors English; vocation in early life lawyer, when elected the same; religious connection Episcopalian; died October 8, 1869.

James Buchanan was born April 23, 1791; Cove Gap, Franklin County, Pennsylvania; paternal ancestors were Scotch-Irish; vocation in early life lawyer, when elected the same; religious connection Presbyterian; died June 1, 1868.

Abraham Lincoln was born February 12, 1809; near Hodgenville, Larue County, Kentucky; paternal ancestors were English; vocation in early life farm-hand, when elected lawyer; religious connection Methodist; died April 15, 1865.

Andrew Johnson was born December 9, 1808; Raleigh, Wake County, North Carolina; paternal ancestors English; vocation in early life tailor, when elected statesman; religious connection Methodist; died July 31, 1875.

Ulysses Simpson Grant was born April 22, 1822; Point Pleasant, Clermont County, Ohio; paternal ancestors were Scotch; vocation in early life soldier, when elected the same; religious connection Methodist; died July 23, 1885.

Rutherford Birchard Hayes was born Oct. 4, 1822; Delaware, Delaware County, Ohio; paternal ancestors Scotch; vocation in early life lawyer, when elected the same; religious connection Methodist.

James Abram Garfield was born November 19, 1831; Orange Township, Cuyahoga County, Ohio; paternal ancestors English; vocation in early life teacher, when elected lawyer; religious connection Disciples; died September 19, 1881.

Chester Alan Arthur was born October 5, 1830, Fairfield, Franklin County, Vermont; paternal ancestors Scotch-Irish; vocation in early life teacher, when elected lawyer; religious connection Episcopalian; died November 18, 1886.

Grover Cleveland was born March 18, 1837, Caldwell, Essex County, New Jersey; paternal ancestors English; vocation in early life teacher, when elected lawyer; religious connection Presbyterian.

Benjamin Harrison was born August 20, 1833, North Bend, Ohio; paternal ancestor English; vocation in early life lawyer, when elected the same; religious connection Presbyterian.

AVERAGE ANNUAL TEMPERATURE IN THE
UNITED STATES

Place of Observation	Average Temperature
Tucson, Arizona Ter.	69
Jacksonville, Florida	69
New Orleans, Louisiana	69
Austin, Texas	67
Mobile, Alabama	66
Jackson, Mississippi	64
Little Rock, Arkansas	63
Columbia, South Carolina	62
Fort Gibson, Indian Ter.	60
Raleigh, North Carolina	59
Atlanta, Georgia	58
Nashville, Tennessee	58
Richmond, Virginia	57
Louisville, Kentucky	56
San Francisco, California	55
Washington, D. C.	55
St. Louis, Missouri	55
Baltimore, Maryland	54
Harrisburg, Pennsylvania	54
Wilmington, Delaware	53
Trenton, New Jersey	53
Columbus, Ohio	53
Portland, Oregon	53
Ft. Boise, Idaho Ter.	52
Salt Lake City, Utah Ter.	52
Romney, West Virginia	52
Indianapolis, Indiana	51
Leavenworth, Kansas	51
Santa Fe, New Mexico Ter	57
Steilacoom, Washington	51
Hartford, Connecticut	50
Springfield, Illinois	50
Camp Scott, Nevada	50
Des Moines, Iowa	49
Omaha, Nebraska	49
Denver, Colorado	48
Boston, Massachusetts	48
Albany, New York	48
Providence, Rhode Island	48
Detroit, Michigan	47
Ft. Randall, Dakota	47
Sitka, Alaska Ter.	46
Concord, New Hampshire	46
Augusta, Maine	45
Madison, Wisconsin	45
Helena, Montana	43
Montpelier, Vermont	43
St. Paul, Minnesota	42

Average Annual Rainfall in the United States

Place	Inches
Neah Bay, Washington	123
Sitka, Alaska Ter.	83
Ft. Haskins, Oregon	66
Mt. Vernon, Alabama	66
Baton Rouge, Louisiana	60
Meadow Valley, California	57
Ft. Tonson, Indian Ter	57
Ft. Meyers, Florida	56
Washington, Arkansas	54
Huntsville, Alabama	54
Natchez, Mississippi	53
New Orleans, Louisiana	51
Savannah, Georgia	48
Springdale, Kentucky	48
Fortress Monroe, Virginia	47
Memphis, Tennessee	45
Newark, New Jersey	44
Boston, Massachusetts	44
Cincinnati, Ohio	44
Brunswick, Maine	44
New Haven, Connecticut	44
Philadelphia, Pennsylvania	44
Charleston, South Carolina	43
New York City, New York	43
Gaston, North Carolina	43
Richmond, Indiana	43
Marietta, Ohio	43
St. Louis, Missouri	43
Muscatine, Iowa	42
Baltimore, Maryland	41
New Bedford, Massachusetts	41
Providence, Rhode Island	41
Ft. Smith, Arkansas	40
Hanover, New Hampshire	40
Ft. Vancouver, Washington	38
Cleveland, Ohio	37
Pittsburg, Pennsylvania	37
Washington, D. C.	37

Rainfall in the United States—*Continued*

Place	Inches
White Sulphur Springs, Virginia	37
Ft. Gibson, Indian Ter	36
Key West, Florida	36
Peoria, Illinois	35
Burlington, Vermont	34
Buffalo, New York	33
Ft. Brown, Texas	33
Ft. Leavenworth, Kansas	31
Detroit, Michigan	30
Milwaukee, Wisconsin	30
Penn Yan, New York	28
Ft. Kearney, Nebraska	25
Ft. Snelling, Minnesota	25
Salt Lake City, Utah Ter	23
Mackinac, Michigan	23
San Francisco, California	21
Dalles, Oregon	21
Sacramento, California	21
Ft. Massachusetts, Colorado	17
Ft. Marcy, New Mexico Ter	16
Ft. Randall, Dakota	16
Ft. Defiance, Arizona Ter	14
Ft. Craiz, New Mexico Ter	11
San Diego, California	9
Ft. Bliss, Texas	9
Ft. Bridger, Utah Ter	6
Ft. Garland, Colorado	6

What a Horse Can Draw

On metal rails a horse can draw: One and two-thirds times as much as on asphalt pavement; three and one-third times as much as on good Belgian blocks; five times as much as on ordinary Belgian blocks; seven times as much as on good cobble-stone; thirteen times as much as on ordinary cobble-stone; twenty times as much *as on an earth road;* and forty times as much as on sand.

A modern compilation of engineering maxims states that a horse can drag, as compared with what he can carry on his back, in the following proportions: On the worst earthern road, three times more; on a good macadamized road, nine; on plank, twenty-five; on a stone trackway, thirty-three; and on a good railway, fifty-four times as much.

CANNING FRUITS, AMOUNT OF SUGAR REQUIRED AND TIME OF BOILING

A general rule for canning fruit is as follows:

Kind of Fruit	Time of Boiling	Quantity of Sugar per quart
Bartlett Pears	20 minutes	6 ounces
Blackberries	9 "	6 "
Cherries	5 "	6 "
Gooseberries	8 "	8 "
Peaches, whole	15 "	4 "
Peaches, halves	8 "	4 "
Pie-plant, sliced	10 "	10 "
Pineapples	15 "	6 "
Plums	10 "	8 "
Quinces, sliced	15 "	10 "
Raspberries	6 "	4 "
Ripe Currants	6 "	8 "
Small Pears, whole	30 "	8 "
Siberian Apples	25 "	8 "
Sour Apples	10 "	5 "
Strawberries	8 "	8 "
Tomatoes	20 "	none
Whortleberries	5 "	4 ounces
Wild Grapes	10 "	8 "

LARGEST UNIVERSITIES

University	Location, Country	Number of Professors	When Founded
Berlin	Germany	142	1810
Buda-Pesth	Hungary	141	1635
Cambridge	England	36	1231
Copenhagen	Denmark	60	1479
Edinburgh	Scotland	43	1582
Harvard	United States	184	1636
Leipsic	Germany	120	1409
Moscow	Russia	117	1755
Munich	Germany	82	1472
Naples	Italy	110	1224
Oxford	England	40	1280
Paris	France	180	1206
Rome	Italy	50	1303
Salamanca	Spain	40	1240
Upsel	Germany	101	1476
Vienna	Austria	160	1365

Relative Value and Weight of Wood

The following table shows the comparative value of firewoods for fuel in a seasoned state, or when burnt to charcoal. Shellbark Hickory being taken at 100 as the standard.

Name	Value	Weight
American Chestnut	52	2,333
American Holly	57	2,691
American Hornbeam	65	3,218
Apple	70	3,115
Barren Oak	66	3,102
Barren Scrub Oak	73	3,339
Black Birch	63	3,115
Black Walnut	65	3,044
Butternut	51	2,534
Chestnut White Oak	86	3,955
Dogwood	75	3,643
Hard Maple	60	2,878
Jersey Pine	48	2,137
Large Magnolia	56	2,704
Mountain Laurel	66	2,963
Pignut Hickory	95	4,241
Pine Oak	71	3,339
Pitch Pine	43	1,906
Post Oak	74	3,464
Persimmon	69	3,178
Red Oak	69	3,254
Red Cedar	56	2,525
Rock Chestnut Oak	61	3,030
Service-tree or shade-bush	84	3,964
Scrub Black Oak	71	3,254
Sassafras	59	2,762
Shellbark Hickory	100	4,469
Soft Maple	54	2,668
Sour-gum	67	3,142
Spanish Oak	52	2,449
Swamp Whortleberry	73	3,361
Sweet-gum	57	2,834
Sycamore	52	2,391
Western Hickory	81	3,705
White Beech	65	3,236
White Birch	48	2,369
White Elm	58	2,592
White Ash	77	3,450
White Oak	81	3,821
White Pine	42	1,868
Witch Hazel	72	3,505
Wild Cherry	55	2,668
Yellow Oak	60	2,919
Yellow Pine, soft	54	2,463
Yellow Poplar	52	2,516

THE NEW NAVY OF THE UNITED STATES

The new navy of the United States received its first start in 1881, when, under the direction of Secretary W. H. Hunt, the first Advisory Board was appointed to report upon the pressing need of appropriate vessels to replace the old wooden vessels, many of which were unfit for repair. The Advisory Board, consisting of fifteen naval officers, and with Rear-admiral John Rogers as president met early in June, and in November it made a report recommending the building of thirty-eight unarmored steel cruising vessels. Of those, two were to be of 5,873 tons displacement, six of 4,560, ten of 3,013 tons, and twenty of 793 tons. But it was not until March 3, 1883, that Congress made an appropriation to build four vessels as recommended by the Naval Advisory Board in its report, December 20, 1882. A contract was made with John Roach and Sons to build these four vessels—the *Chicago*, the *Atlanta*, the *Boston*, and the *Dolphin*. In the building of these vessels there was an impetus given to the iron and steel industries throughout the land which promises steady employment to hundreds of thousands of men. The gun trials, the speed, and all that pertains to the construction and behavior of these four modern ships proves the wisdom maintaining the Navy in a state of usefulness and dignity.

The next legislation which provided for the construction of modern steel ships was on March 3, 1885, the last day of President Arthur's Administration. Other appropriations have since been made and when the vessels provided for have been finished, the Navy will have twenty-nine new steel unarmored and armored cruising vessels. The following is a list of the new Navy, their type, displacement, armament horse-power and cost :

The *Chicago*—a cruiser of 4,500 tons displacement ; 5,084 horse-power; armament consists of four 8-inch B. L. R., eight 6-inch B. L. R., two 5-inch B. L. R., two 6-pdr. R. F., two 1-pdr. R. F., four 47-mm. R. C., two 37-mm. R. C. and two Gatlings ; speed, 16 knots per hour ; cost $889,000 ; is in commission.

The *Boston*—a cruiser of 3,189 tons displacement; 3,780 horse-power; armament consists of two 8-inch B. L. R., six 6-inch B. L. R., two 6-pdr. R. F., two 3-pdr. R. F., two 1-pdr. R. F., two 47-mm. R. C., two 37-mm. R. C. and two Gatlings ; speed, 14 knots an hour ; cost $619,-000 ; is in commission.

The *Atlanta*—a cruiser of 3,189 tons displacement; 3,356 horse-power, armament (same as *Boston*); speed, 14 knots per hour ; cost $617,000; is in commission.

The *Dolphin*—a dispatch-boat of 1,485 tons displacement; 2,240 horse-power; armament consists of one 6-inch B. L. R., four 47-mm. R. C., two 6-pdr. R. F., two Gatlings; speed, 15 knots per hour; cost $315,000; is in commission.

The *Charleston*—a cruiser of 3,730 tons displacement; 6,666 horse-power; armament consists of two 8-inch B. L. R., six 6-inch B. L. R., four 6-pdr. R. F., two 3-pdr. R. F., two 1-pdr. R. F., four 37-mm. R. C., two Gatlings; speed, 19 knots per hour; cost, $1,017,000; is in commission.

The *Baltimore*—a cruiser of 4,413 tons displacement; 10,300 horse-power; armament consists of four 8-inch B. L. R., six 6-inch B. L. R., four 6-pdr. R. F., two 3-pdr. R. F., two 1-pdr. R. F., four 37-mm. R. C. and two Gatlings; speed, 19 knots per hour; cost, $1,325,000; is in commission.

The *Yorktown*—a gunboat of 1,700 tons displacement; 3,400 horse-power; armament consists of six 6-inch B. L. R., two 6-pdr. R. F., two 3-pdr. R. F., one 1-pdr. R. F., two 37 mm. R. C. and two Gatlings; speed, 17 knots per hour; cost, $490,000; is in commission.

The *Petrel*—a gunboat of 870 tons displacement; 1,100 horse-power; armament consists of four 6-inch B. L. R., two 3-pdr. R. F., one 1-pdr. R. F., two 37 mm. R. C., and two Gatlings; speed, 14 knots per hour; cost, $247,000; is in commission.

The *Vesuvius*—a dynamite vessel of 970 tons displacement; 3,200 horse-power; armament consists of three 15-inch dynamite guns, two 3-pdr. R. F., one 1-pdr. R. F., two 37-mm. R. C., two Gatlings; speed, 21 knots per hour; cost, $350,000; is ready for service.

The *Cushing*—a torpedo vessel of 99 tons displacement; 1,600 horse-power; armament consists of eight automobile torpedoes; two 6-pdr. R. F., speed, 23 knots per hour; cost, $82,750; is ready for service.

The *Newark*—a cruiser of 4,083 tons displacement; 8,500 (estimated) horse-power; armament consists of twelve 6-inch B. L. R., four 6-pdr. R. F., four 3-pdr. R. F., two 1-pdr. R. F., three 3-mm. R. C. and four Gatlings; speed, 20 knots per hour; cost, $1,248,000; nearly completed at Philadelphia.

The *Philadelphia*—a cruiser of 4,300 tons displacement; 10,500 (estimated) horse-power; armament (same as *Newark*); speed, 20 knots per hour; cost $1,350,000; was launched at Philadelphia, September 7, 1889.

The *San Francisco*—a cruiser of 4,083 tons displacement; 9,000 (estimated) horse-power; armament (same as *Newark*); speed, 19 knots per hour; cost $1,428,000; was launched at San Francisco, October 26, 1889.

The *Concord*—a gunboat of 1,700 tons displacement; 3,400 horse-power; armament (same as *Yorktown*); speed, 20 knots per hour; cost $490,000; is nearly completed at New York.

The *Bennington*—a gunboat, same displacement, horse-power, armament as the *Concord*; speed, 20 knots per hour.

The *Maine*—a battle-ship of 6,648 tons displacement; 9,000 (estimated) horse-power; armament consists of four 10-inch B. L. R., six 6-inch B. L. R., four 6-pdr. R. F., eight 3-pdr. R. F., two 1-pdr. R. F., four 37-mm. R. C. and four Gatlings; speed, 19 knots per hour; cost $2,844,503; building at New York Navy Yard.

The *Texas*—a battle-ship of 6,300 tons displacement; 8,600 (estimated) horse-power; armament consists of two 12-inch B. L. R., other guns same as the *Maine*; speed, 19 knots per hour; cost $2,376,000; building at Norfolk Navy Yard.

The *Puritan*—a double-turret monitor of 6,060 tons displacement; 3,058 horse-power; armament consists of four 10-inch B. L. R., two 6-pdr. R. F., two 3-pdr. R. F., two 37-mm. R. C. and two Gatlings; speed, 13¼ knots per hour; completing at New York Navy Yard.

The *Miantonomah*—a double-turret monitor of 3,815 tons displacement; 3,000 horse-power; armament same as the *Puritan* except carries no 3-pdrs; speed, 10½ knots per hour; completing at the New York Navy Yard.

The *Terror*—a double-turret monitor of the same description as the *Miantonomah*; speed, 10 knots per hour; lays at New York Navy Yard.

The *Monadnock*—a double-turret monitor of the same description as the *Miantonomah*; speed, 10 knots per hour; lays at Mare Island Navy Yard.

The *Amphitrite*—a double-turret monitor of the same description as the *Miantonomah*; speed, 10 knots per hour; lays at Norfolk Navy Yard.

The *Cruiser No. 7*—of 3,183 tons displacement; 10,000 (estimated) horse-power; armament consists of one 6-inch B. L. R., ten 4-inch B. L. R., two 6-pdr. R. F., two 3-pdr. R. F., one 1-pdr. R. F., two 37-mm. R. C.; speed, 16 knots per hour; cost $1,100,000; building at New York Navy Yard.

The *Cruiser No. 8*—of 3,183 tons displacement; 10,000 (estimated) horse-power; armament same as *Cruiser No. 7*; speed, 16 knots per hour; cost $1,100,000; building at Norfolk Navy Yard.

The *Cruiser No. 9*—of 2,000 tons displacement; 5,400 (estimated) horse-power; armament consists of two 6-inch B. L. R., eight 4-inch B. L. R., two 6-pdr. R. F., two 3-pdr. R. F., two R. C., and one Gatling; speed, 17 knots per hour; cost $612,500; building at Baltimore.

The *Cruiser No. 10*—2,000 tons displacement; 5,400 (estimated) horse-power; armament (same as *Cruiser No. 9*); speed, 17 knots per hour; cost $312,500; building at Baltimore.

The *Cruiser No. 11*—2,000 tons displacement; 5,400 (estimated) horse-power; armament (same as *Cruiser No. 9*); speed, 17 knots per hour; cost $674,000; building at Boston.

The *Gunboat No. 5*—1,000 tons displacement; 1,600 (estimated) horse-power; armament consists of eight 33-pdr. R. F., two 47-mm. R. C., two 37·mm. R. C., one Gatling; cost $350,000; building not yet begun.

The *Gunboat No. 6*—1,000 tons displacement; 1,600 (estimated) horse-power; armament and cost (same as *Gunboat No. 5*); building not yet begun.

The *Pratice Vessel*—835 tons displacement; 1,300 (estimated) horse-power; armament consists of four 33-pdr. R. F., two 6-pdr. R. F., two 3-pdr. R. F., one 1-pdr. R. F. and one 37-mm. R. C.; cost $260,000; building not yet begun.

Plans being made ready for an armored cruiser of 7,500 tons displacement; an armored cruiser of 5,300 tons displacement; a cruising monitor of 3,030 tons displacement; a harbor defense ram of 2,000 tons displacement, and a coast defense vessel of 4,000 tons displacement.

B. L. R.—Breach loading rifles.

R. C.—Revolving cannon.

R. F.—Rapid firing guns.

mm.—Millimetre, 39-1,000ths of an inch.

www.ingramcontent.com/pod-product-compliance
Lightning Source LLC
Chambersburg PA
CBHW020848020726
47497CB00005B/1305